Vision and Reality
A Survey of Twentieth Century
Irish Inter-Church Relations

To Coralie

Vision and Reality

*A Survey of twentieth century
Irish inter-church relations*

I M. Ellis

The Institute of Irish Studies
The Queen's University of Belfast

First published 1992 by the Institute of Irish Studies, The Queen's University of Belfast, University Road, Belfast.

Grateful acknowledgement for financial assistance is made to the Cultural Traditions programme of the Community Relations Council which aims to encourage acceptance and understanding of cultural diversity.

ISBN 0 85389 414 0

Printed by W.G. Baird Ltd, Antrim

Contents

Introduction

Twentieth century Ireland has been a place of determined struggle and undoubted achievement, but also of considerable frustration and great tragedy. It has been a place of true godliness and much ungodliness, a place of contradictions in which any hopes for the future have always required careful nurture. In this paradoxical and changing and challenging Ireland, the Churches have been one of the foremost influences on thought and attidudes; the inter-relationship between religion, culture, national identity and political life is a complex matrix which is difficult for the Irish, let alone for anyone from outside this island, to come to terms with fully. Nowhere is this more clearly the case than in Northern Ireland where the search for an agreed political way forward has been so long drawn-out and indeed tortuous.

If the Churches have been so closely involved in the developing life of Ireland, North and South, how have they been involved, more particularly, with one another? Given the circumstances in which the Irish Churches have found themselves during this century, to what extent have they been able to be, together, the one Body of Christ? And given the ecumenical imperative to 'maintain the unity of the Spirit in the bond of peace' (Ephesians 4:3), how far have the Churches in Ireland grown together during these unsettled years? Such questions are important both historically and from a theological perspective; this book is an attempt to find some answers and to point a way forward, not for politicians primarily, but for the people of God, the members of the Irish Churches which together make up the one Church of Christ in this part of God's world. Adapted for a wider readership from doctoral research presented to the University of Dublin in 1988, these pages try to tell the story of a vision that has been faithfully pursued by many, the vision of that oneness of God's people, and the reality of the Churches' actual situation in Ireland as it has been and as it now is.

The broad sweep of this survey follows the development of Irish inter-Church relations, relating events to their historical and theological contexts and recognizing the influence of events in Church and society outside Ireland on social and ecclesial life here: the birth of the 'reunion movement' among the Protestant Churches, the pioneering ecumenists, the major pastoral and theological concerns of the Churches, the changes brought by the Second Vatican Council, the experience of the Churches in a divided Ireland and in the Northern Ireland troubles, the most recent developments in ecumenical relations, and possibilities for the future.

What follows will attempt to illustrate how the development of inter-Church relations in Ireland has been impeded by the Churches' cultural and political associations, and also clarify the extent to which that ecumenical growth which has been witnessed has been helped by the experience of world Christianity, by the work and witness of individual Irishmen and women, and in more recent years particularly by the Churches' desire to witness for reconciliation. These last three factors have provided the basic stimulus for Irish ecumenism. However, it is also evident that there has not been any groundswell of opinion in the Churches urgently in favour of ecumenical growth. Consequently, individuals have come to the fore – men and women of prayer, faith and vision who have remained undeterred by the realities of Irish life both in the Churches and in society at large. May their vision of that unity of the Spirit and of the bond of peace soon be realized among us.

The many references here to other publications will guide the reader who wishes to pursue individual topics more closely. This work, of course, could not have been done without the previous labours of others in their specific areas of interest and the writer gratefully acknowledges the invaluable assistance given so freely and so graciously to him by many people of different traditions. To their names, which are recorded in the thesis manuscript at Trinity College, Dublin, he now adds that of Dr. Brian Walker of the Institute of Irish Studies at The Queen's University of Belfast, who has given every encouragement and advice in the adaptation of this material for publication.

viii

CHAPTER 1

First Official Contacts

1. At Home and Abroad: 1904-1911

During the later years of the nineteenth century there developed on both sides of the Atlantic an awareness of the great hindrance to the Church's mission caused by disunity. Not only did the second half of the nineteenth century see the emergence of such world confessional bodies as the Lambeth Conference (1867), the World Presbyterian Alliance (1875) and the Methodist Ecumenical Conference (1881),[1] but there had also been attempts at creating Church unions. These latter had achieved success only among different groups of the same confessional family. In Ireland the Presbyterian Church was formed in 1840 by the union of the Synod of Ulster and the Secession Synod,[2] although the 1830 breach over the Arian controversy which led to the establishing of the Non-Subscribing Presbyterian Church was not healed. The breach in Irish Methodism which came with the emergence of the Primitive Wesleyan Methodists in the early nineteenth century was ended in 1878.[3] In Scotland the much fragmented Presbyterianism succeeded in achieving sufficient union to reduce the number of Presbyterian Churches to two in 1900: the United Free Church of Scotland and the Church of Scotland.[4] Inter-confessional Church union did not, however, begin to advance until the twentieth century, and then only at a very slow pace.

Following an initiative of the Irish Presbyterian General Assembly in 1904, the Presbyterian and Methodist Churches established, in the following year, a joint committee to confer from time to time on 'matters of common interest'.[5] The Church of Ireland was very much aware of this important development in Irish inter-Church relations, and when the Rev. Anthony L. Elliott, rector of Killiney in the Diocese of Dublin, successfully proposed the formation of a Home Reunion Committee at the General Synod of 1905, the Church of Ireland was expressing its commitment to a movement which had been gaining ground both at home and abroad – the Reunion Movement.[6] Furthermore, through the decennial Lambeth Conference the Church of

Ireland was in touch with the international reunion scene. Similarly, the Presbyterian and Methodist Churches in Ireland were in touch with world developments through their membership (from the foundation) of their world confessional bodies. The Presbyterian Church in Ireland can, moreover, claim considerable credit for the formation of the World Presbyterian Alliance; the Belfast Presbytery had advocated correspondence with Presbyterian Churches throughout the world with a view to bringing about an 'ecumenical' council of Churches.[7]

The bishops of the 1888 Lambeth Conference's Committee on Home Reunion reported that the subject of reunion was being widely discussed throughout the Anglican Communion, and referred to actions taken in respect of reunion in different parts of the world, the most significant of these being the initiative of the General Convention of the American Church. The significance of the American General Convention's deliberations on the subject of reunion lay in the Chicago Quadrilateral – a four-point summary of the essentials of Anglicanism adopted by the House of Bishops of the Protestant Episcopal Church of the United States at the General Convention of that Church in Chicago in 1886.

The Churches of nineteenth century America represented the divisions of their European roots, and the challenge of the Frontier led to a religious free-for-all. Yet while there were countless denominations, the nineteenth century saw many irenic efforts at establishing unity among American Christians. The author of the document which was the basis for the Chicago Quadrilateral, William Reed Huntington (1838-1918), saw the Episcopal Church as having a special role to play in the struggle for unity in the American Church. Huntington conceived of a re-structured Episcopal Church, admitting the other ecclesial groups and, through a great reconciliation, forming the Catholic Church of America. This plan did have the appearance of absorption into an adapted episcopalianism. Don Herbert Yoder has commented: 'When it was reduced to its essence, the Episcopalian plan was actually denominational. It involved consolidation by rallying around the Episcopal banner.'.[8] Nevertheless, the plan displayed a readiness for change in the search for unity. Huntington's Quadrilateral represented the 'essentials' of the Church for him. It is a tribute to his understanding of Anglicanism that his four-point summary became, with some modifications, the Chicago and later the Lambeth Quadrilateral of 1888 which to this day remains the *locus classicus* of the Anglican position in relation to organic union. It required agreement on:

(a) The Holy Scriptures of the Old and New Testaments, as 'containing all things necessary to salvation,' and as being the rule and ultimate standard of faith.
(b) The Apostles' Creed, as the baptismal symbol; and the Nicene Creed, as the sufficient statement of the Christian faith.
(c) The two sacraments ordained by Christ Himself – Baptism and the Supper of the Lord – ministered with unfailing use of Christ's words of institution, and of the elements ordained by him.
(d) The Historic Episcopate, locally adapted in the methods of its administration to the varying needs of the nations and peoples called of God into the Unity of His Church. [9]

The 1897 Lambeth Conference re-affirmed the Quadrilateral and went further by recommending that Anglican Churches should seek to originate inter-Church conferences. Lambeth therefore, under the influence of a growing ecumenical interest, both gave encouragement to initiatives for inter-Church dialogue and also set down very definite guidelines guarding the essentials of the Anglican position in Christian doctrine and the Church's life.

The Church of Ireland bishops have participated in the Lambeth Conference since its inception. Five Irish bishops were present at the first Conference in 1867; nine attended in 1878, eleven in 1888, ten in 1897 and twelve in 1908. The moral authority of Lambeth was to prove, as we shall see, increasingly influential in the Church of Ireland with regard to participation in reunion moves among the Irish Churches.

Prayer and Action at Home

In the Church of Ireland the establishment of the annual Day of Intercession for Unity in 1906, with the approval of the bishops, was one of the first steps taken by the new Home Reunion Committee. This was distinct from the Octave of Prayer for Christian Unity (inspired by the Rev. Paul James Watson, an American Episcopalian) which eventually was sanctioned by Pius X in 1909. This Octave was observed by some High Anglicans as well as in the Orthodox and Roman Catholic communions. The fact that it was intended for prayer that the Church might be united around Rome, on a papal basis, meant that most Protestants found it unsuitable. It is surprising that it was even used in Orthodox Churches. Later, when the Abbé Couturier realized the extent of the division caused by this intention, its basis was changed by including a reference to the 'mind and purpose of Christ', thus enabling the participation of Protestants. The Day of Intercession for

Unity authorized by the Church of Ireland bishops was regularly observed and remained a measure of the commitment on the part of the Church of Ireland to the Reunion cause. In 1910 the Presbyterian General Assembly appointed the same day for intercession for unity.

Prayer was followed by action. In March 1908 a conference was held between members of the General Synod's Board of Education and the General Assembly's Elementary Education Committee. By 1910 a joint standing committee had been appointed, to which was entrusted 'the carrying out of a scheme for the amalgamation of National Schools under Protestant management'.[10] The purpose of this co-operative scheme was essentially twofold: to increase efficiency and avoid unnecessary duplication of teachers, and to ease the problems of children having to travel considerable distances to and from school each day. Provision was made for the appropriate denominational religious education of Church of Ireland and Presbyterian children. The Home Reunion Committee could declare in 1910: 'To raise the efficiency of National Schools under Protestant management, and to secure all pupils the right of receiving definite religious instruction from teachers of their denomination, is an enterprise in which it is a privilege to take part . . .'.[11] By 1912 a programme of scripture instruction for Presbyterian and Church of Ireland children attending the same school was in use.

Resolution 77 of the 1908 Lambeth Conference stated: 'The members of the Anglican Communion should take pains to study the doctrines and position of those who are separated from it and to promote a cordial mutual understanding; and, as a means towards this end, the Conference suggests that private meetings of ministers and laymen of different Christian bodies for common study, discussion, and prayer should be frequently held in convenient centres.'. This found some expression in unofficial inter-Church conferences in Ireland, as reported by the Home Reunion Committee in 1910. The following resolution (no. 78) was more significant, however, declaring that 'The constituted authorities of the various Churches of the Anglican Communion should, as opportunity offers, arrange conferences with representatives of other Christian Churches, and meetings for common acknowledgement of the sins of division, and for intercession for unity.'. An official step in this direction was taken by the Church of Ireland in 1911 when the Bishop of Clogher (Maurice Day[12]) successfully proposed at the General Synod that a committee should be appointed 'to encourage the cultivation of friendly relations between, and to co-operate in philanthropic, social and religious work, as far as such co-operation may be found possible, with the

Committee recently appointed by the General Assembly of the Presbyterian Church in Ireland.'. Bishop Day's proposal echoed the voice of the Edinburgh Missionary Conference of 1910, with his recognition of 'the ever-growing conviction amongst Christian people that our present unhappy divisions are largely responsible for the weakness of the Christian effort both at home and abroad'. At the previous year's General Assembly, the Presbyterian Church had appointed a committee to co-operate with 'any committee appointed by the Synod of the Anglican Church, or by another Evangelical Church' in this whole area of inter-Church relations.

Bishop Maurice Day of Clogher, the proposer of the General Synod resolution in 1911, was familiar with the Lambeth moves on Reunion as he had been one of the Church of Ireland bishops present at the 1908 Conference. His uncle, Bishop Maurice F. Day (Bishop of Cashel, 1872-1900) had been at the 1878, 1888 and 1897 Lambeth Conferences, the latter two – as we have seen – having had special significance for the Reunion Movement. The Bishop of Clogher's proposal that there should be a co-operating committee was fully in the spirit of Resolution 78 of Lambeth 1908 quoted above.

The development of official relations between the Presbyterian Church and the Church of Ireland in these years must, to some extent at least, reflect the influence of world confessional meetings and of the great Missionary Conference in Edinburgh in 1910. Although the Church of Ireland bishops took several years to respond decisively to Resolution 78 of Lambeth 1908, they were aware that movement in this direction was indeed appropriate. Relations between the Methodist and Presbyterian Churches were already developing and the Church of Ireland would certainly have wished to enter into this new fraternal spirit. Lambeth gave the General Synod the confidence to take further steps. With a general willingness, or even a desire to co-operate with the Presbyterians (the area of education was one where great mutual advantage was to be found through co-operation) together with the encouragement of successive Lambeth Conferences (1888, 1897 and 1908), it is not surprising that Bishop Day's proposal at the 1911 General Synod was unopposed.

At home the Protestant Churches were driven together by factors from outside their own confines, not least the Roman Catholic decree *Ne Temere*. At the General Assembly in 1911 the decree was debated and a unanimous call for its withdrawal issued; the Assembly debate had surrounded a discussion of the case of a Presbyterian (Mrs Agnes Jane McCann) who had refused to be married by a Roman Catholic priest and thus comply with the requirements of the decree. With one voice all the Protestant Churches declared their total opposition to this new law in the Roman Catholic Church. *Ne Temere* reiterated the Council of Trent's *Tametsi* decree, requiring the presence of an authorized priest at every marriage, and specifically introduced this law – originally applied only in Roman Catholic states – to Ireland. The intention of the *Tametsi* decree had been to prevent clandestine marriages. However, in a lecture to the Church of Ireland Cork Young Men's Association in 1911, J.A.F. Gregg (then rector of Blackrock, Cork and later Archbishop of Armagh) gave his understanding of why the presence of a Roman Catholic priest was now deemed necessary to validate a mixed marriage in Ireland:

> But now, since 1908, the presence of a Roman Catholic priest is declared necessary. And I will tell you the reason why. Not because there is any danger of rash or hasty marriages, but because, where the parish priest is not present there may be no agreement concerning the children signed in favour of the Roman Catholic Church. Not a word of this appears in 'Ne Temere', but this is where the worst sting lies. The decree says the parish priest must be present at the marriage, but no priest dares to be present unless such agreement has been made.[13]

Professor Barkley illustrates the extent of concern in the Protestant Churches about *Ne Temere*, when commenting on the positive spirit which marked the establishment of the early co-operating committees:

> Although it cannot have been the intention of its promulgators this decree did have a positive ecumenical effect. Public meetings of protest were organized in Belfast and Dublin and attended by Presbyterians, Anglicans, Methodists, Congregationalists and Baptists. These meetings are probably the first example of united action by all the Protestant Churches in Ireland.[14]

Protestants were able to stand together – across denominational barriers – when the need arose. These were years in which also for other reasons Protestants had learnt the importance of standing together. As F.S.L. Lyons has written, 'Both (social distinctions and political differences) were to sink quickly into insignificance the moment the supposed threat from Roman Catholicism took visible shape with the development of a dynamic Home Rule movement in the 1880s.'[15]. In 1905 the northern unionists organized the Ulster

Unionist Council, which spawned a wide network of local associations later to play such an important role in the marshalling of the Volunteer Force.

Yet, despite Protestant solidarity on the political front and in protest against the *Ne Temere* decree, it would not be correct to view the enthusiasm for inter-Church co-operation and reunion amongst the Irish Protestant Churches in the early years of the twentieth century as essentially politically and pragmatically motivated. There was a genuine movement for *rapprochement* between these Churches, a movement which, as we have seen, found its manifestation in Ireland as in other parts of the world. When the co-operating committees were formed, there truly was an ecumenical spirit at work. Yet the political factor – the Home Rule debate – did doubtlessly have its influence on the course of events and was certainly one issue on which Church of Ireland, Presbyterian and Methodist people, though with exceptions, were broadly at one. The Churches were indeed influenced by political concerns and cultural bonds; nonetheless, in these years the Protestant Churches were experiencing the beginnings of a more profound stirring of the spirit of reconciliation.

2.   From 1911 to the formation of the United Council of Christian Churches and Religious Communions in Ireland (UCCCRCI) in 1922.

Bishop Charles Brent of the Philippine Islands (and later of Western New York) left the 1910 Edinburgh Missionary Conference determined to persuade his fellow churchmen in the American Protestant Episcopal Church to originate plans for a World Conference on Faith and Order, for matters of faith and order had not been on the agenda at Edinburgh; in fact they had been excluded. At the Edinburgh Conference Bishop Brent had spoken of the ultimate ideal (of Christian Unity):

> Then in addition to the things that we have been called upon by God to do, in addition to the fresh tasks which are now confronting us, there rises that ultimate ideal, an ideal the realisation of which none of us shall live to see, but which somehow we feel to be part of our responsibility.[16]

Later in 1910 the visionary Bishop Brent spoke about the Edinburgh Conference and its spirit at a large assembly on the eve of the General Convention of the Protestant Episcopal Church in Cincinnati. He

declared his view that a World Conference on Faith and Order was
now essential – a conference at which doctrinal differences could be
discussed openly and in the spirit of brotherly love so characteristic of
Edinburgh 1910. His suggestion was taken up at the Convention, and
a commission was appointed with the mandate of bringing about 'a
Conference for the consideration of questions touching Faith and
Order'. All Christian communions confessing Jesus Christ as God and
Saviour were to be invited to join with the Episcopal Church in the
preparatory work for the conference. The secretary of the commission
was the layman and committed ecumenist, Robert Gardiner, who also
had been instrumental in bringing the issue to the Convention in the
first place. A deputation visited the British Isles in 1912 and in Ireland
met the Archbishop of Armagh (Crozier) and the Bishops of Meath
and of Down, Dromore and Connor (Keene and D'Arcy). The Archbishops of Armagh and Dublin appointed a committee to consider the
proposals and to co-operate in making preparations. The Archbishops
of York and Canterbury, and the Scottish Episcopal Church, also
appointed their committees. In the following year a further deputation was sent to the British Isles, this time to enlist the support of the
other Churches. As a result co-operating commissions were formed to
represent the Churches in preparing for the eventual world conference. In the same year, 1913, an advisory committee was constituted
in New York. This committee comprised one member of each of the
commissions which had been established world-wide (by 1914 total-
ling thirty-five). All this was a most important development on the
world reunion scene. As the Faith and Order Movement had found its
origins in Anglican circles, and as the initial contacts around the world
had been with Anglicans, the Church of Ireland was the first of the
Irish Churches to become directly involved.

Immediately after the First World War, the American Episcopal
Church Commission sent a delegation to Europe and the Near East.
Throughout its mission to the Churches in these areas it met with
positive responses to the idea of a World Conference on Faith and
Order, and a willingness to participate in its deliberations. The
response from the Vatican was, however, to prove a great disappoint-
ment. While Pope Benedict XV was personally courteous to the
delegation, the text of the official reply to the invitation to the Roman
Catholic Church to participate in the planned world conference was
to be a sad conclusion to the tour:

> The Holy Father, after having thanked them for their visit, stated
> that as successor of St Peter and Vicar of Christ he had no greater

desire than that there should be one fold and one shepherd. His Holiness added that the teaching and practice of the Roman Catholic Church regarding the unity of the visible Church of Christ was well known to everybody and therefore it would not be possible for the Catholic Church to take part in such a Congress as the one proposed. His Holiness, however, by no means wishes to disapprove of the Congress in question for those who are not in union with the Chair of Peter, on the contrary, he earnestly desires and prays that, if the Congress is practicable, those who take part in it may, by the Grace of God, see the light and become reunited to the visible Head of the Church, by whom they will be received with open arms.[17]

It was hardly to be expected that any radically different reply would be forthcoming from Rome. Yet the episode is significant in that it shows clearly that the architects of Faith and Order, from the beginning, were fully open to Roman Catholic participation in their enterprise.

The Roman Catholic Experience

What were the prevailing circumstances within the Roman Catholic Church that precluded any such contact, and which influenced its relations with other Churches? Two areas provided formative influence: law and theology.

The Code of Canon Law (*Codex Iuris Canonici*) was published in 1917 and was a complete revision and codifying of the *Corpus* of canon law which had been founded on Gratian's *Decretum* (c. 1140) and which included various decretals and decrees up to 1471. The new Code was a major formalizing of canon law, but was only one way in which the Roman Catholic Church was adopting a defensive stance. The dogma of Infallibility (Vatican I, 1869-70) had pronounced that the truths of faith are guaranteed and defined by the Church, supremely through the papal office. Again, in 1879 Leo XIII imposed neoscholasticism as the theological norm (*Aeterni Patris*). This embracing of Thomism as a theological standard was an attempt to order and control ideas in the Church, and was to be instrumental in the attempt to banish what later was described as 'the sum total of heresies' – modernism. The modernist movement arose towards the end of the nineteenth century in France, as an attempt to interpret the Christian faith for the modern world. Chief amongst the modernists were Maurice Blondel and Alfred Loisy: Blondel sought to commend the Christian faith through philosophical analysis, while Loisy chose to return to sources with the assistance of historical and biblical criticism.

The Irish-born English modernist, George Tyrrell, sought to relate faith to experience.[18] It is, however, in France that the origins of modernism are to be found, for there the Church was under particular pressures. M. Schoof writes of the Church in nineteenth century France:

> The situation of the Catholic Church in France had become very confused in various spheres by the end of the nineteenth century and this had repercussions on theology. The problem that had been debated ever since the restoration of the Bourbons, namely the attitude to be taken towards the 'principles of the Revolution', had still to be satisfactorily solved. The oldest and most influential form of French ultramontanism went back to an aristocrat of the *ancien régime*, J. de Maistre who . . . had become convinced that only the papacy could provide a new foundation for order and authority and only absolute monarchy could provide the superstructure for this foundation.
>   . . . The Catholic Church in France, then, was characterised towards the end of the nineteenth century, by a confused pattern of contrasts. After 1870, the Republic was determined to banish clericalism – with which the whole Church was identified – from the State.[19]

Modernism opposed the prevailing neoscholasticism which was based on defined and unchanging concepts of faith, and truths that were related to one another forming a unified system. Even Newman's concept of the development of dogma, under the guidance of the Holy Spirit, was not particularly favoured in neoscholastic circles, for there was an antipathy to change of any kind: truth was static.[20] Those who defended the neoscholastic *status quo* were 'integralists'. G. Daly comments that such a title 'was extremely revealing of how they saw the Church and its ideology', and indicates how, with the triumph of neoscholasticism in 1907 (the Holy Office's *Lamentabili Sane Exitu* and Pius X's *Pascendi Dominici Gregis*) there were 'three main agencies of centralized government in the Church' prior to Vatican II: first, Catholic orthodoxy, stemming from the neoscholastic system; second, the 1917 Code of Canon Law; and third, the ecclesiastical bureaucracy (and episcopal appointments in particular).[21]

Neoscholasticism, however, was not entirely monolithic. It did experience a degree of what Schoof has described as 're-orientation'. This was led by the Dominican A. Gardeil and the Jesuit P. Rousselot, both of whom pursued critical reflection.[22] Nevertheless, in the early 1900s Roman Catholic orthodoxy, which had been so successfully imposed, did not admit any variation from its central theme, namely, that Christian truth is authoritatively defined in a coherent and sealed system under the Magisterium and the Pope himself whose office guaranteed that the Church could not err in matters of faith. There was no possibility of other Churches witnessing to Christian truths which Rome neglected; only through their complete and unconditional return to Rome could the unity of the Church be advanced. Similarly, the provisions of the decree *Ne Temere* were the logical practical concomitant of the Roman Catholic Church's self-understanding. The system of theological reflection was sealed, including Rome's understanding of the identity of the Church.

Co-operation among the Protestant Churches at home

The Presbyterian – Church of Ireland Joint Co-operating Committee, established following the 1910 and 1911 resolutions at General Assembly and General Synod (see above), held its first meeting on 15th October, 1911 in Dublin. Papers were read by the Bishop of Clogher (Day) ('Points in which co-operation is practicable') and by the Rev. William Park ('Ways of removing hindrances to co-operation'). Discussion followed, and an executive committee was appointed which in turn appointed four sub-committees to deal with (1) National Insurance in Relation to Benefit Societies, (2) Temperance, especially Inebriates' Homes, (3) the Marriage question in relation to the *Ne Temere* decree, and (4) Industrial Schools.[23]

The co-operating committees confined themselves mainly to social concerns, but in 1912 the General Assembly asked its co-operating committee 'to arrange, if possible, for the mutual recognition: (1) of the status of communicants passing over on marriage to the other Church; (2) of discipline; and (3) of the ecclesiastical status of members of either Church, especially on a change of ministry'.[24] Such mutual recognition proved difficult, and Professor Barkley's record indicates the thinking on the Anglican side:

> After three years of discussion the Committee presented a detailed report in four sections the last of which contained a Reply of the Archbishops and Bishops of the Church of Ireland to a communication received from a committee of the General Assembly of the Presbyterian Church in Ireland. The three principal issues raised in the course of the discussion had been episcopal confirmation, baptismal discipline and proselytising but, except with regard to the latter no real progress was made. On the question of episcopal

confirmation the Anglicans had quoted Archbishop Peckham's
rubric of 1281: 'And there shall be none admitted to the holy
communion, until such time as he be confirmed, or be ready and
desirous to be confirmed'. In regard to baptismal discipline they
had referred to the 'ancient law' by which no minister can 'refuse
or delay to christen, according to the form in the Book of Common
Prayer, any child that is brought to the church to him on Sundays
or Holy Days to be christened either of whose parents is resident
within his cure.'[25]

The attempt to have doctrinal matters discussed by the joint co-
operating committee did not prove a successful exercise. These were
early days, and ecumenical experience was limited. The Church of
Ireland adopted a defensive position with regard to the matters raised
by the Presbyterian Church, but such discussions would recur later
when doctrinal talks aimed at Church Union were established (see
below further).

The Presbyterian and Church of Ireland representatives on the co-
operating committees met, as we have noted earlier, against the
background of the continuing Home Rule debate. Less than a month
before their first joint-meeting, a massive demonstration of some
50,000 unionists had marched from Belfast to Craigavon House to be
addressed by Sir Edward Carson,[26] and in the following year sectarian
strife was witnessed in the assault by the Ancient Order of Hibernians
procession on a Sunday-school excursion at Castledawson[27] (on account of which Roman Catholics were expelled from the Belfast
shipyards by Protestant workers[28]). September 28th., 1912 – 'Ulster
Day'- was the date of the Solemn League and Covenant, a pledge to
resist Home Rule, which was signed by unionists throughout Ulster
(and by Protestant Church leaders). The Ulster Volunteer Force was
formed in January 1913 and, speaking at Newry in the following
September, Sir Edward Carson declared that a provisional Ulster
government would be formed if Home Rule were introduced in
Ireland.[29]

When a letter signed by the leaders of the four main Churches[30] was
sent to the Prime Minister (Asquith) in 1915, it was not about the
situation in Ireland, however, but concerned the subject of temperance and the World War effort. The inclusion of Cardinal Logue as a
signatory in the letter to the Prime Minister was a significant indication
of how far the Churches could co-operate on a matter of common
interest. Given the circumstances of considerable bitterness between
the Protestant Churches and the Roman Catholic Church over the

Ne Temere issue and fundamental differences in the Home Rule debate, this letter was indeed remarkable.

As we have seen, temperance was one of the concerns of the co-operating committees, and in 1913 the General Synod and the General Assembly adopted the joint committee's proposal of forming a United Protestant Temperance Council. Temperance had also been a concern of the Roman Catholic Church, for not only had Cardinal Logue signed the Church leaders' letter to Asquith in 1915, but in 1912 the Capuchin temperance crusade in Ireland was able to report over 2,000 missions and well over a million pledges since 1905, when the Irish Roman Catholic bishops had invited the Capuchin Order to conduct the crusade.[31] On this fundamental issue of common Protestant and Roman Catholic concern, however, no joint action beyond the 1915 Church leaders' letter was to emerge.

A Council of Churches Proposed; Lambeth 1920

The General Assembly of 1919, at which the Bishop of Down (D'Arcy) was a visitor, made the suggestion that a Protestant united communion service should be held on an appropriate day. Nothing was to come of this proposal – there were obvious inherent difficulties at the time – but another resolution was of greater significance:

> That the Assembly would be favourable to an arrangement by which representatives from other Evangelical Churches would meet with representatives of this Church, either on the occasion of the sederunts of the Supreme Courts of the various Churches, or in a common Council or Conference. At this Council consultations could take place upon great moral and spiritual questions, and decisions be arrived at making for more effective witness to the Kingdom of God and better guidance of the community towards the sovereignty of the Lord Jesus Christ.[32]

The movement to form a council of Churches in Ireland had in fact originated in the 1917 report of the joint co-operation committee of the Presbyterian and Methodist Churches. That report had recommended action based on the suggestions of the then Bishop D'Arcy which appeared in *The Spectator* in February 1917, calling for 'united counsel in Synod or Convocation of all the Christian Churches of the Empire'.[33] However, the Church of Ireland-Presbyterian joint co-operating committee decided to postpone further action on the 1919 General Assembly's proposal until the 1920 Lambeth Conference had met. The Anglican members of the committee had, no doubt, been able to indicate that the Lambeth Conference would be giving careful consideration to the subject of reunion, which presumably would influence the General Synod in its response to this Presbyterian initiative. This proved to be the case. The General Synod's Home Reunion Committee report on Lambeth 1920 declared: 'The reunion of Christendom was the most important of all the questions that came before the conference in 1920'. Ten Irish bishops had been present at the Conference,[34] and four of them (Armagh, Meath, Derry and Down) had been members of the 'Committee Appointed to Consider Relations to and Reunion with Other Churches – (a) Episcopal Churches; (b) non-Episcopal Churches, with Questions as to (i) Recognition of Ministers; (ii) 'Validity' of Sacraments; (iii) Suggested Transitional Steps'. This Conference of 1920 is chiefly remembered for its *Appeal to All Christian People* (Resolution 9), which opened with the following declaration:

> We acknowledge all those who believe in our Lord Jesus Christ, and have been baptized into the name of the Holy Trinity, as sharing with us membership in the universal Church of Christ which is His Body. We believe that the Holy Spirit has called us in a very solemn and special manner to associate ourselves in penitence and prayer with all those who deplore the divisions of Christian people, and are inspired by the vision and hope of a visible unity of the whole Church.[35]

The Appeal re-affirmed the four points of the Lambeth Quadrilateral as the appropriate basis for a visibly united Church and, while the bishops did not 'for a moment' call in question 'the spiritual reality of the ministries of those Communions which do not possess the Episcopate', the Appeal saw the Episcopate as the proper means of providing a universally recognized ministry. It influenced the work of the preliminary meeting of the World Conference on Faith and Order in Geneva during August, 1920. The purpose of this gathering was 'to determine when and where the World Conference shall be held, what subjects shall be discussed, what preparations shall be made for the discussions, the basis of representation of the participating commissions, the executive direction of preliminary arrangements, and any other pertinent matters.'[36] The preliminary meeting's Subjects Committee issued its first series of questions to be discussed throughout the world – on Faith and Creed; the second series would deal with Orders, and the third with the Sacraments. This programme corresponded closely to the four conditions which Lambeth 1920 had set out as essential to any reunion (and which echoed the Lambeth Quadrilateral): 'The Holy Scriptures, as the record of God's revelation, and the Nicene Creed; the divinely instituted sacraments of Baptism and Holy Communion; a ministry acknowledged by every part of the Church as possessing not only the inward call of the Spirit, but also the commission of Christ and the authority of the whole body (the Episcopate being the one means of providing such a ministry)'.

In May 1921 the General Synod welcomed the Lambeth Appeal and unanimously agreed that the House of Bishops should be asked to initiate conferences with representatives of other Churches on its proposals. The Presbyterian General Assembly, meeting in the following month, appointed a committee to engage in discussions with the Church of Ireland. The Methodist Conference of 1921 responded to the Appeal, uniting with the Lambeth bishops in their pleas 'to manifest to the world the unity of the Body of Christ for which he prayed'. The Lambeth Appeal had been the subject of serious deliberation at Synod, Assembly and Conference.

Lambeth 1920, in its resolution 13, had recommended the establishment of councils of Churches 'as centres of united effort to promote the physical, moral and social welfare of the people, and the extension of the rule of Christ among all nations . . .'. The Presbyterian and Methodist Churches in Ireland had already been thinking along the lines of the Lambeth proposals for some time. However, with the Lambeth resolutions the Church of Ireland felt better able to enter into this new phase of inter-Church relations. The first meeting of the 'United Council of Christian Churches and Religious Communions in Ireland' was held in January 1923, when the member Churches and communions were represented by a total of twenty-three delegates, with the Bishop of Derry (Peacocke) in the Chair; business during its first year principally concerned the reform of licensing laws, the Criminal Law Amendment Bill (which the Council unanimously supported), questions regarding the League of Nations, child welfare and local councils of Churches.

The birth of the United Council was a landmark in the history of Irish inter-Church relations. Yet, as can be seen from the nature of the business of the Council during its frist months of work, doctrinal matters were not on the agenda. This contrasts unfavourably with the situation in England where in June 1922 a new inter-Church report was published: *Christian Unity – being the Report of a Joint Conference held at Lambeth Palace.* This joint conference had been between representatives of episcopal and non-episcopal communions on the subject of the Lambeth Appeal, and covered the very important dogmatic areas of the nature of the Church, the ministry and the creed in a United Church. The text of the report expressed a considerable agreement between the representatives, and it was a remarkable document.

Yet, while the United Council was established in Ireland, doctrinal conversations were not being held in this island. On the other hand, no council of Churches emerged in Britain for some years, and the Church of England's conversations with the Free Churches, despite the hopeful start, were to be short-lived.

The question as to the precise ecclesiological significance of councils of Churches has often been the subject of discussion in the ecumenical movement. The difficulty in providing any comprehensive ecclesiological definition of councils of Churches must be at least partly due to the fact that they are not an end in themselves. Moreover, councils of Churches in different countries have taken different forms, and established councils have grown and developed in the scope of the work which they have undertaken and in the profile which they have attained as ecclesiastical institutions. L. Vischer has asserted that councils of Churches are an 'ecclesiological anomaly', but has rightly seen that the conciliar structure, appropriately developed, will continue to provide the basis for the growth of ecumenical relations in the future.[37]

While councils of Churches are indeed ecclesiologically anomalous, Vischer has also reminded us that the situation of division between the Churches is itself the real anomaly. This is the fundamental anomaly with which councils of Churches have been contending in their own limited ways. The councils themselves possess little ecclesiastical authority, and while they do possess the marks of unity, holiness, catholicity and apostolicity, they exist to serve the Churches rather than be a super-Church. This certainly was the form which the United Council took in Ireland. It was to be a vehicle for inter-Church co-operation and joint action; it was to provide the means for a joint witness and outreach in those areas of Irish life in which the member institutions felt that they could speak and act more effectively together than if each were to tackle the relevant issues individually.

At the time of the foundation of the United Council in Ireland there was a great concern with effectiveness. This was largely due to the experience of the First World War and was the same concern that lay behind so much of the deliberations at the Edinburgh Missionary Conference in 1910. Just as duplication in the mission field was wasteful and inefficient, so too at home the duplication of effort was seen to amount to an irresponsible squandering of resources.

Nevertheless, it remains a fact of history that the United Council was not to succeed in reducing duplication but in fact added to it, for the Churches tended increasingly to do things through the Council as well as, rather than instead of, individually. This tendency still exists among the Churches, although is one which the new Council of Churches for Britain and Ireland (see Ch. VI, section 6) deliberately sets out to avoid.

3. From the establishment of the United Council to the appointment of the Church of Ireland – Presbyterian Joint Committee for Reunion (1931).

At Christmas 1923 the Archbishop of Canterbury (Davidson) took up a suggestion which had been made to him 'on many sides', namely that he should write to the Archbishops and Metropolitans of the Anglican Communion on the subject of reunion, giving an outline of recent developments. Various factors prompted this step: the 1920 Lambeth Appeal, conferences with the Free Churches in England (and in particular the 1922 report), discussions being held between the Church of Scotland and the United Free Church of Scotland, discussions in India between the South India United Church and the Anglican Church, new contacts between the Church of England and the Swedish Church, the Orthodox Declaration on Anglican Orders[38], and the continuing Malines talks (see below). Further, plans for the Stockholm Conference on Life and Work, and the World Conference on Faith and Order were in hand (the former eventually being held in 1925 and the latter in 1927). The post-World War I period had been one during which the Churches had engaged in an examination of themselves, particularly with regard to their role in the promotion of peace among the nations. Despite the issue of war guilt, which proved to be a difficulty in post-war international ecumenical relations, the Life and Work movement was effectively founded at the 1920 Geneva preparatory conference; it was decided that a Universal Christian Conference on Life and Work should be held. The Faith and Order Preparatory Conference was held in the same month of 1920 (August), also in Geneva. Life and Work, and Faith and Order were clearly emerging as two main streams of the ecumenical movement, alongside the International Missionary Council.

In view of all of these significant and promising developments, it was indeed appropriate that a review of the current situation should be the subject of a letter from Archbishop Davidson to his brother primates.

It was intended to be both informal and informative, and his view of
the then current state of the Reunion Movement was extensive and
encouraging: 'The vision which our Lord, as we believe, has set before
us points the road to reunion. The road may not be short, but we
believe it will be sure.'.[39]

The Malines Conversations and the Church of Ireland

The unofficial Malines Conversations (Anglican-Roman Catholic)
have been mentioned. They were held during the 1920s under the
inspiration of Lord Halifax, who had been involved in Anglican-
Roman Catholic dialogue for some thirty years. There had been, in
earlier years, a growing body of opinion on the continent in favour of
reconciliation between the Roman Catholic Church and the Anglican
Communion. The French clerics, Ferdinand Etienne Portal and the
Abbé Duchesne, had published works defending the validity of Anglican orders. However, the general climate of opinion in the Church of
England was not in favour of such pioneering ecumenical dialogue,
and in the Roman Catholic Church, as we have seen, the forces of
ultramontanism and neoscholasticism were overwhelming. These
initial expressions of a desire for reconciliation were met in 1896 with
the Papal encyclical *Apostolicae Curae* of Leo XIII, declaring Anglican
orders 'null and void'. In spite of this major setback, Halifax continued
to believe that eventually Rome and Canterbury would be re-united.
It was with the 1920 Lambeth Appeal and a favourable response from
the Archbishop of Malines, Cardinal Mercier, that Lord Halifax
prepared for action. H.R.T. Brandreth writes:

> Portal took the initiative by suggesting that he and Halifax, then
> eighty-two, should visit Cardinal Mercier. Halifax, who had thought
> his life over, jumped at the opportunity. Portal's proposal was for
> informal joint conferences, and the Cardinal had received the idea
> sympathetically... Cardinal Mercier saw the two friends and agreed
> to sponsor the desired Conversations, which were arranged to take
> place from 6-8 December 1921.[40]

The Malines Conversations continued until 1926 when the fifth
meeting was held without Cardinal Mercier and Portal, both of whom
had died. The final meeting was under the presidency of Cardinal van
Roey, the new Archbishop. The encyclical of Pius XI, *Mortalium Animos*
(6th January 1928), was generally taken as implying a condemnation
of the Malines venture.[41] At no stage, however, had these been official

discussions between the two communions; rather, they were the private endeavours of visionary churchmen which nonetheless were surrounded by a certain degree of public controversy.

In its report to the 1926 General Synod, the Church of Ireland's Home Reunion Committee echoed some of the concern about the Malines Conversations which was felt in the Church at large:

> It is impossible not to believe that the leaders in these conferences were actuated by the highest and most worthy motives . . . But these conversations have not unnaturally been the cause of some uneasiness, especially among people in our own country, where there are great opportunities of estimating the influence of the Church of Rome upon life and conduct. It has been feared that a *rapprochement* between the Anglican and Roman Communions could only be brought about at the expense of increasing the already existing hindrances to an understanding between ourselves and the other Protestants of our own country.[42]

This cautious statement expressed what was felt to be the ecumenical priority in the Church of Ireland, i.e. an advance in relations with the Presbyterian and Methodist Churches and with the smaller Protestant bodies represented in the United Council. A definite inter-Church relationship had been established in 1922 with the formation of the Council. From a religious as well as a socio-political perspective it was just impossible to conceive of the Church of Ireland jeopardizing this new set of relationships in order to contemplate reunion with Rome. Theological and non-theological factors alike combined to prohibit any such development: the Ulster unionists were determined and many Protestants in the Free State felt confused and even vulnerable. Furthermore, as Patrick Corish has written, 'Nationalist Ireland in 1923 was sore and sensitive'; the civil war was over, but it had left a legacy of 'physical and spiritual destruction'.[43] Given these circumstances, together with the priorities and theological orientation within the Church of Ireland, the above statement on the Malines Conversations was the best that could be said at the time by the Home Reunion Committee.

Life and Work

The year 1924 saw the Christian Conference on Politics, Economics and Citizenship ('Copec') in Birmingham, at which the United Council was represented by the Dean of Christ Church (Kennedy) and

Dr. Denham Osborne; there were thirteen further delegates representing the Irish Churches. This Copec conference had emerged from
the special sense of social responsibility which was felt in the Churches
after World War I and which gave birth to the Life and Work
movement. Copec was chaired by one who had the deepest concern
for the Christian response to social needs – William Temple.

Preparations for Copec had been in progress for some three years
before the conference actually was held. This Birmingham gathering
has been described by Nils Karlström as 'the most considerable effort
made up to that date anywhere in the world to focus Christian thought
and action on the urgent problems of the day'.[44] One expression of the
Life and Work movement in Ireland was the formation of citizenship
councils. In its twentieth Annual report, in 1925, The Home Reunion
Committee recorded:

> The Christian citizenship councils in Dublin and Belfast have
> already enlisted the help of representative men and women from all
> the chief religious bodies in our country with the exception of the
> Church of Rome; and attempts to secure the co-operation of Roman
> Catholics were not relinquished until plain indications were re-
> ceived that the Church of Rome was unable to depart from its
> traditional policy of aloofness.[45]

This link between the citizenship councils and the international Life
and Work movement is illustrated in the fact that the Dublin Citizenship Council included in its membership the Dublin delegates to the
Copec conference.

That the Roman Catholic Church declined to be officially involved
in these Life and Work ventures on Irish soil is not suprising, given the
circumstances and atmosphere of the day. That such strenuous efforts
were made to have the Roman Catholic Church included, as the Home
Reunion Committee reported, is a token of the degree of enthusiasm
for Christian co-operation on social matters that characterized Life
and Work in its Irish expression.

The international Life and Work movement held its first Universal
Conference in Stockholm in 1925, under the joint-presidency of the
Archbishops of Uppsala (Söderblom) and Canterbury (Davidson),
the Patriarch of Constantinople and the Rev. Dr. Judson Brown of New
York. That the Life and Work movement was firmly rooted at this time
in the aspirations of at least some Irish Christians is again witnessed by
the 1926 conference entitled, 'Towards a Better Ireland' (see further
below Ch. II). Yet the Life and Work movement is only one part of the

world ecumenical story of these inter-war years; the Faith and Order movement is another, complementary part.

Faith and Order

We have already noted the significance of the 1920 Geneva Conference, when it was decided to hold a Universal Conference on Life and Work, and that the Faith and Order Preparatory Conference was held in the same month in Geneva. Following visits of a deputation from America, Faith and Order co-operating commissions had been formed in many countries to help in the preparation for the world conference. During 1922-23 the continuation committee announced that the world conference would be held in Washington, D.C., USA, in May 1925. However, in 1924 it could be reported that

> . . . the notable increase of interest and activity consequent upon the announcement (of the date May 1925), and the steadily growing recognition of the value of the conference method as shown by the great numbers of local conference groups whose reports have been received by the General Secretary and by the Subjects Committee, have made it clear that more extended and thorough preparation, through preliminary discussion is not only possible, but most desirable. Representations were also made by the Standing Committee of the Lambeth Conference that it would be desirable that the World Conference should be delayed until near the date of the Lambeth Conference.[46]

The continuation committee thus postponed the holding of the world conference for two years – until 1927. The long awaited and much prepared First World Conference on Faith and Order was held that year in Lausanne. The Church of Ireland delegation included the Archbishhops of Armagh and Dublin (D'Arcy and Gregg), and the Home Reunion Committee urged members of the General Synod, in the light of the success of the 1925 Stockholm Life and Work Conference and the great amount of preparation for Lausanne, to 'take more than a passing interest in the proceedings of the Conference'.

At Lausanne perfect agreement was reached on the nature of the Gospel; the Orthodox could only accept the Nicene Creed without the Filioque Clause, although many Churches which did not use creeds in their liturgies accepted their importance; on the doctrines of the Church, the Ministry and the Sacraments differences were openly stated and agreements reached. As a result of the success (as it was perceived) of this conference, the Church of Ireland's Home Reunion Committee suggested that 'opportunities should be sought for local conferences between members of the Church of Ireland and other communions, in which sections of the proceedings of the Lausanne Conference might be discussed frankly'.[47] In March of the following year, 1929, a conference was called by the Irish Christian Fellowship (ICF – the graduate Irish Student Christian Movement organization) in Dublin to consider the response in Ireland to this Lausanne Faith and Order Conference. Some of the recommendations of the ICF gathering were:

(1) That the authorities of the various churches should declare their agreement with the unanimous conclusion of the Lausanne Conference, that union is their aim. (2) The urgent need of enlisting the interest and support of the ordinary Church-members in these matters. (3) That working arrangements to prevent overlapping and waste should be made in districts where numbers are small. (4) That, instead of denominational competition, emphasis should everywhere be laid on mutual helpfulness in the service of the Church Universal. (5) That interchange of pulpits is to be encouraged, at least on special occasions, when the need of unity is to be put forward.[48]

When we come to consider the SCM and ICF in Chapter II, we shall see how imaginative these groups were, and the prophetic voice with which they spoke. Such a spirit as is expressed in these comments on Lausanne was to be consistently illustrated in the contributions of SCM and ICF to the debate on reunion and the role of the Church in Irish society.

Two aspects of the report on Lausanne 1927 presented at the Presbyterian General Assembly in 1929 have been highlighted by Professor John Barkley: the sections dealing with intercommunion and ministry. On the former, the report regretted 'the failure of the Conference to hold a Communion service, or to suggest anything to the Churches along that line'. Intercommunion was viewed in this Presbyterian report as a possible means to unity, and the reason for the failure to achieve any advance in intercommunion was seen as a prevailing 'doctrine of apostolical succession and sacramental grace of a kind which they (the writers of the report) do not accept nor any of its implications, such as reordination'.

The subject of the ministry was rightly seen as lying at the heart of this issue. As Barkley notes, the Presbyterian comments on this subject were significant:

> The monarchical Diocesan episcopacy which emerged soon in the history of the Church, as distinct from the Presbyterate, they (the writers of the report) cannot regard as necessary in Church life today, still less as essential to the existence of the Church as such, especially as no particular stress is laid on such matters in the New Testament. But they are quite willing to believe that it may be a useful element in the work and constitution of the Church, either past or future, and as Presbyterians, they have no objection based on principle to an administrative superintendency, such as operated in Scotland in the days of John Knox, or as operates today in the Presbyterian Church of Hungary.
>
> They believe in the continuity of a recognised ministry in the Church from the days of the Apostles to our own time, as a historical fact of great value, and that in normal circumstances only the Church acting through its appointed ministry can offer the corporate authority which a true ministry implies. And they recognise that as in each of the now separated Churches, the ministry in existence must have the authority of that Church as a whole behind it, so in the united Church at which we aim, the minister must have an authority that shall be regarded as adequate by the whole Church . . . [49]

Professor Barkley has commented that for the sake of unity the Assembly was thus willing to accept bishops as an effective administrative office, but rejected a lineal-descent doctrine of apostolic succession. The presbyteries discussed the possibility of accepting Superintendents and, although without any further response, two models were proposed in 1931. We shall see later how the question of the ministry has dominated reunion discussions between the Presbyterian Church and the Church of Ireland throughout this century.

South India, England and Ireland

The South Indian Churches' 'Proposed Scheme of Union' was published in 1929, having been produced by a joint committee of the Church of India, Burma and Ceylon (Anglican) the South India Church (Presbyterian and Congregationalist) and the South India Provincial Synod of the Wesleyan Methodist Church. The Irish Churches were particularly aware of India through their missionaries serving in that country and naturally followed Union developments with great interest; similarly, because of the involvement of Anglicans in the proposals for Union, the Lambeth Conference of 1930[50] gave specific attention to the South Indian situation.

On these South Indian proposals Lambeth 1930 commented: 'We feel that in a sense our brethren in South India are making this experiment on behalf of the whole body of Anglican Churches . . . The whole Communion will surely stand by them with earnest prayer and generous loyalty'. The inspiration of South India was such that it led to the expression of Anglican desires to enter into direct discussions with the Church of Scotland, and to re-open the conferences with the English Evangelical Free Churches.

At home in Ireland – directly influenced by this – the 1931 General Synod resolved that 'the Lord Primate be requested to nominate a Committee to meet a Committee of the General Assembly, should such a Committee be appointed by the General Assembly, to consider the question of Reunion in Ireland, together with possible lines of advance in the light of the Lambeth Resolutions of 1920 and 1930, and to report to the General Synod'. This resolution was, in fact, slightly more general in nature than the original proposer had intended (the original words 'and to suggest a scheme for Reunion in Ireland and to submit it to the General Synod' were amended). The style of this approach to the General Assembly was reminiscent of that of the Presbyteraian approach to the Church of Ireland in 1910 when the Asseembly suggested the establishing of the Joint Co-operating Committee. The Primate and the General Assembly both duly appointed their committees.

By 1932 there had been a resumption of the conferences between representatives of the Church of England and the Federal Council of the Evangelical Free Churches of England, and consultations were being planned between representatives of the Anglican Communion and the Church of Scotland (Lambeth 1930, res. 43). At home in Ireland the Church of Ireland-Presbyterian Joint Committee for Reunion met for the first time on 21st January, 1932. Irish inter-Church relations thus took on a vital new dimension in so far as doctrinal matters were now being discussed officially with a view to Church Union. Further, plans were now being made both at home and abroad for the Second World Conference on Faith and Order.

4.   Theological Perspectives and Historical Context

In considering the first steps taken towards establishing formal inter-Church relationships in Ireland at the beginning of this century, we have noted the various factors which proved to be of significant influence. First there was the Reunion Movement itself, a new spirit in the Protestant Churches at home and abroad in which the missionary movement had been of formative influence. The Church of Ireland and the Presbyterian and Methodist Churches in Ireland were constituent member Churches of their respective world communions, all of which were grappling with reunion issues. Old suspicions certainly died hard, and there was much hesitancy in the Irish Churches' relations with one another. There were, however, committed ecumenists or 'friends of reunion' at home in Ireland and, as we will see in Chapter II, the national and international student movement was deeply involved in the widening of horizons.

The Protestant Churches were open to the influences of the wider Christian experience outside Ireland and also played their part in those world conferences which have become early landmarks in the history of modern ecumenism. The great desire on the international scene for co-operation in mission, the trauma of the First World War together with the great moral and practical issues which it raised for Christians, and the experience of world confessional fellowship, all gave extra impetus to the opening up of new horizons in thinking which was taking place at home.

In addition to this broadening of ecclesial experience there was, as we have seen, the constant background of the course of political developments in Ireland, driving the Protestant Churches ever closer to one another. Given the historical situation in which the Churches found themselves – an Ireland in political turmoil and its people deeply divided in their national aspirations, divided broadly along lines of religious affiliation – it is perhaps too easy to ask now whether the Churches truly proclaimed the Kingdom, truly renewed the world in which they found themselves, truly lived out the Gospel of reconciliation. The nationalist struggle was a search for political and cultural identity and the unionist reaction was a crisis in identity: there were fundamentally conflicting interests. The Churches were deeply involved and were too closely aligned with social, cultural and political positions to make any radical challenge to the situation. Yet many in the Churches had already realized that the future would require a greater common witness and a greater and more obvious sharing in worship and life. However, *Ne Temere* only added to the growing desire among Protestants at large for solidarity and co-operation where possible. The Orange Order, as F.S.L. Lyons notes, had been rapidly revived with the rise of the Home Rule movement and proved 'a rallying point for Protestants'.[51]

Church of Ireland-Presbyterian relations today are marked by an openness which is sometimes taken for granted. However, at the turn of the century when formal structures were developing between these two Churches there was a relatively recent history of uneasiness. Professor Barkley has commented: 'Right up to the Irish Church Act, 1869 . . . relations between the Anglican Establishment and Presbyterianism were, to put it mildly, anything but cordial.'.[52]

Thus the years covered in this chapter saw a real degree of reconciliation between the Anglican and Presbyterian Churches in Ireland. Placing these developments in their ecclesiastical-historical context enables us to see them not simply as gestures of co-operation but as real steps forward from a somewhat bitter past to a happier future. The fact that the Church of Ireland-Presbyterian Committee *for Reunion* (as opposed to co-operation) could emerge in 1931 was a remarkable development.in itself. The *rapprochement* between Anglicans, Presbyterians and Methodists was, however, undoubtedly greatly encouraged by the conflicts of the time in Ireland, but may not be interpreted solely in such terms.

From a more specifically theological perspective, the inherent relationship between mission and unity certainly was understood, for this had been clearly perceived at the Edinburgh Missionary Conference of 1910; in the language of the day, mission and 'reunion' were inter-related. Yet the fact that renewal was an essential part of this inter-relationship was not so clearly recognized, or at least its implications were not fully appreciated. There was a defensiveness evident even among the Protestant Churches in their early contacts with one another, as when the Presbyterian Church tried to introduce dogmatic issues at the joint co-operation committee only to be rebuffed by the Church of Ireland's cautious response. The formation of the United Council in 1922 was a development of the principle of co-operation but was not accompanied by any movement for fundamental renewal in the Churches. Furthermore, the Protestant and Roman Catholic Churches almost inhabited different worlds: political divisions throughout the island of Ireland were to all intents and purposes co-terminous with the religious divide. Roman Catholicism in Ireland was not only nationalist in aspiration, but also, in the tradition of Archbishops Cullen and Walsh of Dublin (1852-1878 and 1885-1921 respectively), fundamentally orientated towards Rome and the papacy – although in political matters it was prepared to take its own line and was anxious that the Vatican should not be seen as politically in league with Britain.[53]

The ecclesiological picture which emerges is of the Protestant

Churches sharing in the reunion spirit of the age, but nonetheless approaching one another with a considerable degree of caution. These Churches also had their political reasons for coming together. The Roman Catholic Church characteristically remained apart from the reunion moves, and Protestants and Roman Catholics were deeply divided in their national aspirations. In this sense, the Churches were prisoners of the cultural and political polarities of Irish life, as so often still is the case, but did not sense themselves as such: they were largely content to be what they were.

CHAPTER 2

Spirits of the Time

1. The Student Christian Movement and the Irish Christian Fellowship

Theological questions were at the centre of controversy in the Student Christian Movement during the first years of this century.[1] In particular, debate surrounded the fundamental issue of the Bible, encompassing the implications of biblical criticism and the question of the 'inerrancy' of Scripture. Not only was there this tension centering on the understanding of the Bible but there was also debate about the nature of mission and the growth of the 'Social Gospel' emphasis, a movement which lay behind the later Life and Work Conferences of 1925 and 1937 (Stockholm and Oxford). Again, considerable controversy surrounded the participation of Anglo-Catholics in the 1910 Edinburgh Missionary Conference.

Scripture, mission and the Gospel, and diversity in the Church were thus the overriding theological concerns of the SCM in these early years. What gave motivation to these essential concerns and why did they arise at this particular time? How were these tensions and debates experienced in the Irish SCM in particular?

The eighteenth and nineteenth centuries saw the rise of the critical study of the Bible. Already in the eighteenth century, the German scholar J. D. Michaelis had determined to apply the principles of historical criticism to the Bible and in the following century F. C. Baur developed the work of D. F. Strauss and founded the Tübingen School which applied the same critical principles to the interpretation of the Bible as were used in treating secular texts.[2] In England such scholars as Lightfoot, Westcott and Hort engaged in the precise critical study of the New Testament texts. Bishop Stephen Neill has emphasized how the new insights and advances of the critical study of the Bible in the eighteenth and nineteenthth centuries inevitably clashed with the accepted view of the 'verbal inerrancy' of Scripture:

Traditional Christian reverence held a view of Biblical inspiration which separated it off from every other book; these were the authentic words of God himself; and though up to a point grammatical, textual and linguistic criticism might have their place, all awkward questions were supposed to be stilled by the protection of inspiration . . . (All) accorded the Bible an unqualified reverence, and all believed that, if its inerrance was successfully impugned, the whole Christian faith would collapse.[3]

In Ireland the SCM branches at Trinity and Queen's were both divided on this and the other issues already mentioned. In Trinity the split was between the so-called 'No. 40' group and the SCM, while in Queen's it was between the Bible Union and the SCM. Two students at Trinity, Patrick Dixon and James Speedy (Medicine and Engineering) had come back from fighting in the First World War and felt that the SCM was too politically motivated and not sufficiently concerned with evangelism. They lived in room number 40 and hence the name of the group which later affiliated to the Evangelical Union.[4] The No. 40 group in Trinity was for those of a more conservative evangelical outlook, but some mixed in both societies,[5] while others started out in one society and changed allegiance to the other.[6] At the centre of the rift in Trinity and Queen's was the issue of the Bible. This controversy was by no means confined to the universities, however. In the missionary world itself the Church Missionary Society experienced similar tensions to such an extent that in 1922 the Bible Churchmen's Missionary Society was formed as a breakaway organization.

Parallel to the debate about the Bible there was also conflict about the nature of the Gospel and the mission of the Church. The international SCM was closely associated with the missionary movement; J.R. Mott, the American Methodist layman and chairman of the Student Volunteer Missionary Movement from 1888-1920, founded the World Student Christian Federation in 1895, creating a world body to which national and local SCM groups could look.[7]

Both before and after the First World War two distinct approaches to mission were developing in the Irish SCM. There were those who began to see mission less in terms of evangelism and linked it more to social witness and action. Others later felt particularly keenly that the war itself was a tragic illustration of humankind's sinfulness and saw a need for a redoubling of evangelistic efforts. There was a divergence between those who took an essentially optimistic view of humanity and those who could see no good in the human being without the kind of conversion that evangelistic efforts promoted. A. A. Fulton was secretary of the Magee SCM in 1923, but was to take a leading part in the formation of the Evangelical Union there. Dr. Fulton has recalled that his dissatisfaction with the SCM lay in its 'vagueness, liberalism and apparent inability to make an impact on individuals'.[8]

Certainly the war posed a real challenge to the liberal tradition. Alasdair Heron has written of World War I that it 'did not only transform the political and military map: by the destruction which it wrought, unparalleled in human history in its scale, it hurled a black question mark against the onward and upward progress of Christian civilization which had so strongly characterised the Liberal Theology . . .'.[9]

Nonetheless, those Irish students who were committed to the Social Gospel went from strength to strength. In 1915 the Irish Christian Fellowship (ICF) was formed as the SCM's graduate organization. The SCM and ICF held a series of major conferences (upon which we will reflect more closely below) which gave expression to their concern for a Christian witness to contemporary life in Ireland. The first was held in 1913 (by the SCM) and was entitled 'Ireland's Hope'. Tom Barker (then Irish SCM secretary) had secured a visit to Ireland in the previous year by J. R. Mott, the international student leader. Barker's intention in inviting Mott was to help students 'to face Irish questions – especially Home Rule – with a definitely Christian outlook',[10] and the visit was to help overcome a 'provinciality of outlook' in Irish Protestantism.[11] In 1926 there was the conference, 'Towards a Better Ireland', and ten years later, 'Ireland's Contribution to a Christian World Order'. Similar conferences, though not on as large a scale, were organized during and after World War II.[12]

The Irish Christian Fellowship, like the SCM, was to be greatly concerned with the implications of faith for life in Ireland – with all the problems and challenges of religion, nationality and social and economic deprivation. In such circumstances, how could Christians best witness to their faith? How could they display the way of Christ in a culturally and economically divided Irish society? Evangelism alone was not a sufficient answer for it raised precisely the kind of questions which the SCM and ICF wanted to explore: could Protestants and Roman Catholics accept one another, not only recognizing the legitimacy of their different national aspirations, but also realizing themselves to be brothers and sisters in Christ? And, predominating in the students' minds, there were fundamental questions of social justice which evangelism did not begin to address. These issues were all discussed in the conferences already mentioned and in a book written by ICF members and published by the SCM Press in 1937, *Looking at Ireland*. The Introduction to this collection of essays acknowledges the

limitations of any reflection on the future of Ireland without Roman
Catholic contributors; the book therefore was addressed 'to Protestant Ireland'. What did the participants in these conferences and these
writers have to say to their fellow Protestants of Ireland, North and
South? What, more specifically, were their theological perspectives? In
considering these questions hopefully we will see more clearly the
underlying motivation of these spirits of the time.

Conferences and Writings

The Ireland's Hope conference, which was held at Queen's University
Belfast from 2nd – 7th January 1913, set the reflection on Ireland's
current situation and future firmly in the theological context of the
Kingdom of God. The aim of the Inter-Collegiate Christian Union,
which held the conference, was: 'To call Irish students to the knowledge of God in Jesus Christ and His discipleship in every department
of conduct that, united in Him, they may study the will of God for
modern life, and may hope to strive for the redemption of Ireland,
seeking to realize her mission in the Kingdom of God on earth'.[13]
Furthermore, in his introduction to the conference, T. M. Barker
echoed this aim when he declared: 'The salvation of Ireland, no
matter at what price, and our share in the work, are the objects of our
quest, seeking to realize her mission in the kingdom of God on
earth'.[14] The conference was based on the conception that in striving
for a better Ireland through tackling such major prevailing ills as
poverty, emigration, inadequate education, industrial exploitation,
political and religious intolerance and the problems distinctive to
rural and urban life, the Kingdom of God would be promoted and
'salvation' would be forwarded. One contributor, recognizing the
need for trust in God and reliance on the Holy Spirit, observed:

> The more we study the conditions of our country, and the more we
> look at the trend of events in others, the more we must conclude that
> Ireland's hope lies in her Social Regeneration. The real problems
> in Ireland are economic; but we cannot blind ourselves to the fact
> that the National Sins – Religious Intolerance and Political Suspi-
> cion – are at present, indeed, as they have always been, tremendous
> obstacles to progress.[15]

This reflection on furthering the Kingdom of God was accompanied
by an awareness of Ireland's ancient missionary tradition, but there
was a new recognition that the distinction between home and foreign

mission was becoming increasingly anachronistic: '. . . although it is becoming daily less common, there are many who distinguish between the two in order to set one in rivalry against the other. No such duality exists in the nature of things . . . Our task as Christians is to seek the kingdom of God, and that task is a unity.'.[16]

The awareness that God had a purpose for Ireland was a fundamental concept in the 'Towards a Better Ireland' gathering in Dublin in 1926. The same theological emphasis on Kingdom and social regeneration which characterized the 1913 conference was also clearly present here. Just as God had a special purpose for Israel, so too he had a purpose for 'all the peoples that are (his) creation and care; for each nation has its own meaning for mankind, its own task from the hand of the creator . . .'.[17] In this 1926 conference there was considerable emphasis on the problems of rural and urban life, as well as on the need for better educational provisions. It was essentially an attempt to be an Irish response to the 'Copec' conference in Birmingham and to the Stockholm Life and Work conference.[18]

The promotion of the Kingdom of God through mission expressed principally in social concern characterized the philosophy of these student gatherings. The years which had separated them had seen the partition of Ireland and the establishment of two States, but the 'Towards a Better Ireland' conference took little account of these particular developments; rather, that 1926 gathering concentrated more on the need 'to apply the principles emphasised at Birmingham and Stockholm to the particular conditions that prevail in Ireland'.[19] Accordingly, the speakers were chosen for their expertise in social and economic matters. The report of 'Towards a Better Ireland' shows a remarkably similar outlook to that of the 1913 conference, but one session during the four-day 1926 gathering was given over to the topic: 'Ireland: North and South'; the discussion appears to have been marked by a general conviction that partition was not the answer to Ireland's problems – it was a fact of life, but was regarded as of only temporary significance. The 'Towards a Better Ireland' conference, then, avoided any extensive discussion of what one today would regard as the most significant development in Irish life at that time – the division of the country into two separate jurisdictions. This avoidance of such a major issue does not appear to have been out of fear of its subject nature; rather, issues of economics and social justice were genuinely perceived as the really important ones.

The 1913 and 1926 conferences shared a very similar outlook and were based on very similar assumptions. The former concentrated more on the Home Rule issue than the latter did on that of partition, but both were essentially motivated by the Social Gospel.[20] The agenda was largely set by international Life and Work concerns.[21] The students related their concerns for the promotion of the Kingdom of God to what was actually happening to the people of Ireland as a result of their divisions and in terms of such issues as housing, education and working conditions. But the question of partition, or indeed of violence in Ireland, did not concern them as much as their vision of greater social and economic justice. Therefore they did not succeed in fully contextualizing their theology. The 1926 conference could have engaged in a more critical analysis of the national issues facing Ireland as a whole, North and South. These young people were indeed aware of the need for reconciliation across the religious and cultural divisions, but they were ultimately more interested in the social issues: the real problem in Ireland was one of economics.

The desire to face the social problems of rural and urban Ireland in these gatherings of 1913 and 1926 is striking. At the former, there was a remarkable description of rural life throughout the country:

As the train from Dublin to Belfast passes through Meath one sees pasture lands as far as the eye can reach, where 'the bullock has made a solitude and called it prosperity.' And again on the uplands of Armagh one sees little patches of fields huddled together in hopeless confusion where human beings try to make a home and find it poverty. No one who has travelled West past Athlone into Connaught can ever forget the cruel pathos of the sight of these hovels dark and dismal, with one window stuffed with rags, the home, so-called, of old men and women and little children, who exist in circumstances under which it has been said a central European goat would die of hunger. No one can imagine the hopeless desolation of the deserted towns and straggling villages, each of them, 'the centre of nothing but a mental bog.' No one can picture to himself the awful resignation that has found a home in the eyes of the Irish peasant, the ghost of a great despair.[22]

Ireland desperately needed investment and industry. Industrial development had, however, been mainly confined to the north-east and, as F.S.L. Lyons notes, 'over the most of Ireland the conditions for speedy or successful industrialisation simply did not exist'.[23] The adverse conditions, according to Lyons, included the rapid decline in the population after the Famine, poverty, the land system and insecurity of tenure in particular, the 'frequently disturbed state of the country', lack of raw materials, and costs of transportation. There was neither an

adequate economic base for any significant process of industrialization across the country, nor did the Irish population in general possess
the financial resources to purchase industrial products. As Lyons has
suggested, the railways were a mixed blessing in that while they
brought goods to rural Ireland and provided a means for transporting
goods and livestock from rural areas, they also provided for emigration 'with equal ease'.[24]

However, despite their lack of competence in modern agricultural
methods, the farmers of the emerging 'peasant proprietary' of the
turn of the century were slowly bettering their standard of living. L.M.
Cullen, who has investigated the social and economic background to
the development of the modern Irish experience, draws particular
attention to the significance of an emerging greater variety in diet and
has noted how in the second half of the nineteenthth century agriculture in Ireland was becoming increasingly commercialized, with half
of agricultural output being exported.[25] Nonetheless, he observes:
'The rural classes tended to suffer from the process of commercializa-
tion of their production which carried it to the towns'[26] and, regarding
the diversification in the Irish diet, shows how this ameliorated the
possible effects of famine, but still did not 'put Irish society securely
beyond the threshold of starvation'.[27]

As for the urban situation, the eighteenth century had seen the
considerable development of such centres as Cork, Dublin, Armagh
and Belfast. Of eighteenth century Cork J.C. Beckett writes: 'Its
importance was based on the export of provisions . . . By the end of the
century, Cork was one of the busiest and handsomest seaport towns in
the British Isles.'.[28] Of eighteenth century Dublin he writes: 'To this
period belong most of the buildings that give the city its distinctive
architectural character: the Parliament House, the Custom House,
the Four Courts, much of Trinity College, the mansions of the nobility,
many of the most graceful of the parish churches.'.[29] Equally, Armagh
city was transformed during the eighteenth century; under Primate
Richard Robinson (Archbishop, 1765-1795) many fine new buildings
were erected. Beckett notes how Belfast also was significantly developed in this period.[30] However, the nineteenth century was to bring
sweeping changes for Belfast with the growth of manufacturing
industry, especially linen, shipbuilding and engineering: 'The el-
egance and dignity that the town acquired . . . (in the eighteenth
century) were to be swamped by the rapid and uncontrolled expansion of the next century'.[31]

Major issues relating to city, town and country were thus understandably to the fore during the first decades of this century in the

reflection among Irish students on the future of Ireland. How could rural areas be developed? What were the ethics of the private enter- prise which led to so much hard labour and such low wages, while at the same time reaping rich rewards for industrialists?

The 'Ireland's Hope' and 'Towards a Better Ireland' conferences faced these issues with theological commitment. The need for more equal social conditions and in particular for the development of education, was clearly emphasized.[32] The Churches were called to point the way in such social circumstances, for direction was urgently required.

If the theological conceptions which lay behind the thinking of the 1913 and 1926 conferences were centred in the Kingdom of God, the mission of the Church and the demands of social justice, with what conception of the Church itself did the participants operate?

A distinctive feature of the 'Ireland's Hope' and 'Towards a Better Ireland' conferences is the absence of resolutions calling on the Churches to take particular actions. The students were reflecting and did not consider themselves as a pressure group. Rather, they were unpretentiously aware that, one day, they themselves would occupy positions of leadership in Church and community; education was for leadership. Barker declared at the 'Ireland's Hope' gathering: 'It is a great task that we have set before us . . . It would indeed be folly, but for two things; men and women, who are preparing for responsible positions in the world, must in honesty make such an attempt when our position, or the want of position, leaves the mind open and the life supremely free.'.[33] Nevertheless, the sort of Church for which they hoped was characterized by at least the three marks of prophecy, mission and unity.

Their conception of the role of the Church as prophetic was clear. Their whole intention and ambition was to respond in their own way to the need for a Christian voice of prophecy in the circumstances of their day and with a view to the future. There was, they passionately believed, a Christian contribution to be made to the debate about Ireland's future. The Church had a mission, not only to foreign peoples, but also to the Irish people. That mission was bound up with the Social Gospel which they extolled, but this did not entirely minimize the significance of the individual for, as one contributor to the 1913 conference emphasized, the times presented a challenge to the individual in terms of 'Knowledge of the facts; Courage in facing the problems; and Faith in the necssary basis for success'.[34] Further- more, in the spirit of the 1910 Edinburgh Missionary Conference, the Birmingham 'Copec' conference and the Stockholm Life and Work

Conference, the mission was to be a shared one: Ireland already suffered too much from the effects of religious division and intolerance.

In pursuing its prophetic role, in engaging in mission that was relevant to the spiritual and material needs of the Irish people, and in striving to overcome hatred and prejudice, the Christian outreach would forward the Kingdom of God itself. In their own terms, there was here a seeking first of the Kingdom (Matt. 6:33).

Those who participated in these early conferences were to make a further contribution to the discussion of the Churches' role in contemporary Ireland with the publication in 1937 of the book *Looking at Ireland* (addressed to Protestants, as we have noted above). This book, which consisted of essays by members of the Irish Christian Fellowship, included within its scope the subjects of the nature of Protestantism and its potential contribution to the new Ireland, Liberty in Ireland, Christianity and Culture in Ireland, and Reunion among the Irish Churches.

The awareness of the international as well as the national need for healing, the condition of the Churches, the witness of Protestantism, and the need for an acceptance of diversity and for freedom, were all remarkably brought together by the contributor to *Looking at Ireland*, Fred Rea:

> What the world needs today is the power to live together. Economically, industrially, intellectually, spiritually – on every plane of existence – the world is crying out for some force to bind its life in one. As yet Protestantism has offered no way out. How can we dare to speak of unity and brotherhood to a world perishing through lack of community, if the Churches are suffering from a like malady – and Ireland most of all? Community must be established on a national scale and on an international scale, if the nations are not to destroy each other. But can community be achieved without loss of freedom? Will the individual not be lost in the State, and the indiviidual State lost through the Super-State? Is it possible to build a community, world-wide in scope, yet preserving the freedom of thought, diversity of expression, spontaneity of action and inwardness of authority which is the right of each several member? As followers of Him who prayed that 'they all may be one', we believe such a community is possible.[35]

Rea asserted that Protestants had to engage in a fundamental reappraisal of Protestantism itself; there was a need 'to discern between the shadow and the substance, the label and the thing itself', for Protestantism had many enemies within itself – ecclesiasticism, rationalism and fundamentalism all 'obscured the true witness' of Protestants.[36]

For Rea a fundamental of Protestantism – 'the doctrine of personal freedom' – could be applied to the contemporary situation in Ireland. This principle had much to say about 'discussion, education, toleration, democracy', and Rea demanded: '. . . is the spiritual integrity of Protestantism dependent upon its political ascendency?'.[37] The 'enemies within', already mentioned, challenged the very principle of freedom at the heart of Protestantism, and Rea warned that 'We must not be beguiled into thinking that, with political autonomy, freedom has been achieved.'.[38]

Permeating this and other contributions was the affirmation of cultural diversity. Another writer asked: 'Christ 'caught hold' of the life of His day and country, of the culture of His people, at every point . . . Are we Christian people of Ireland 'taking hold'?'.[39] Theologically the implications of the incarnation itself were here being worked out in relation to the clash between the two traditions in Ireland, nationalist and unionist, for the incarnation supremely speaks of God's identification with humanity, even in the particularities of historical and cultural context. In Christ the historically formed divisions between human beings are transcended and overcome. This also provided a clear message to the Churches in their relations with one another. James Rutherford, upon whose work we will reflect more fully below, wrote in *Looking at Ireland*:

> The mission of the Christian Church, however, is not a purely defensive one. It does not exist merely to fight *against* sinister forces, but to create an entirely new order of things, to break down not only the barriers which separate man from God, but those which separate man from man, to permeate all their relationships – political, economic and personal – with the spirit of Christ, to transform and Christianize the world of human affairs.[40]

The theological concerns of the Kingdom of God, the mission of the Church to the whole person, the ability of the Gospel to unite humankind in a bond of peace, all were directly expounded by these thinkers. Yet, how were such forthright expressions received in the Churches themselves?

Religion, culture, tradition, politics and national aspiration all were inextricably bound up together in the debate about Ireland's future, but the Protestant and Roman Catholic Churches were – as we have seen in Chapter I – unable to stand apart from the popular associations

of religion and nationality. Protestantism was synonymous with unionism, but not only because of fear of domination by Roman Catholicism
and an alien culture in a new Ireland; in Ulster in particular there was
also a deep awareness that the link with Britain had considerable
economic benefits. The advance of industrialization in the north-east
required the link with Britain for a sound economic environment, for
the development of export opportunities and for the protection of
jobs. Thus the harsh realities of religious intolerance and economic
survival provided a powerful combination which separated Roman
Catholics and Protestants in the most fundamental ways.

On the other hand, we have also seen how the Protestant Churches
began at this time to relate to one another in new ways – how they
began to explore possibilities of reunion and established the United
Council in 1922 as a vehicle for co-operating and witnessing together.
Yet all the time there was the great religio-political divide between
Protestants and Roman Catholics, between unionists and nationalists,
which proved insurmountable. The Protestant students and young
graduates had, nonetheless, identified the issues with clear theological perspectives and many of these thinkers were to become key figures
in the developing ecumenical movement in Ireland in later years.[41]

The SCM and ICF engaged in perceptive theological reflection on
many issues of the day relating to both Church and society. There was
a fundamental social orientation in their theology, and while they
were well aware of the problems of cultural, political and religious
division, their social philosophy distracted them from taking a more
direct and more critical approach to the issues of divided Church and
divided society in Ireland.

One writer, however, was particularly concerned with the subject of
reunion between the Protestant Churches, and especially between the
Presbyterian Church and the Church of Ireland: James Rutherford.
There are many personalities upon whose lives we could reflect in
connection wiht the SCM, ICF and the Reunion Movement,[42] but
Rutherford was a particularly ardent advocate of a United Church. He
gave numerous addresses, wrote numerous papers, and ultimately
penned a book, all in support of reunion. It is therefore appropriate
that we should devote some space to a consideration of his individual
life and his work in this area.

2. James Spence Rutherford: 1881-1942

James Rutherford was described by the Rev. R.K. Lyle in his memorial
address as 'of the big, tireless frame and strong kind face'. These

adjectives describe the inner Rutherford as well, for his mind had wide
horizons, his efforts in the service of Christ and the Church unwearied,
and his disposition marked by compassion and concern which did not
shrink from action. He made a distinctive contribution in the area of
our theme of inter-Church relations.

Before entering the ministry of the Presbyterian Church, James
Rutherford had worked in Harland and Wolff's in Belfast and had
intended pursuing a career in engineering. His call to the ministry
was clear, however, at the time of his mother's death in 1903. It was
perhaps typical of Rutherford that he responded to the loss of his
mother by offering himself for service, and especially service to the
sick and bereaved through the ordained ministry of the Church.
Following his theological education at Assembly's College, and a
year at New College, Edinburgh, he was an assistant minister at
Newtownbreda, for a time sharing accommodation with Forrest
Reid, the Ulster writer. Following a short army career in the First
World War as a stretcher bearer in the RAMC and a brief spell as a
locum minister in Comber, James Rutherford was appointed to
Warrenpoint Presbyterian Church in 1919. During his time there, the
first two women elders of the Presbyterian Church in Ireland were
ordained in his church. In 1927 he was called to Kingstown Presbyterian Church (Dun Laoghaire) where he remained until his final
illness; this move south gave him practical experience of living in a
minority situation, and with the majority Church. The broad pattern
of Rutherford's outlook, however, was undoubtedly formed before
this change in his life, but in Dun Laoghaire he saw at first hand the
many benefits which reunion would bring to the Protestant Churches
in the Republic.

From his earlier years Rutherford had been a lucid writer, and was
especially interested in the devotional life. In 1914 his *The Seriousness
of Life* was published by James Clarke & Co. of London; this book
contained twelve sermons, all preached at Newtownbreda, and an
'Essay on Preaching'. The subject matter of these sermons is a blend
of the practical and devotional, a combination which might be a
suitable description of the man Rutherford himself. Shortly after his
move to Dun Laoghaire, the same publishers brought out his *The Truth
of the Christian Faith* (1928). This book resulted from Rutherford's
constant desire to communicate the Christian faith, and while the
themes are deeply theological, the author indicates that they are
treated in such a way as to 'set down as simply and briefly as I can my
reasons for believing that Christianity is true'; it was through the
expression of personal conviction that Rutherford felt there could be

'a much stronger appeal than (through) the more formal defences of professional apologists'. The two further writings which he penned were published shortly after his death: *Learning through Suffering* and *Christian Reunion in Ireland.* Both had been in his mind for some time, but were the fruit of the six to eight months which he spent during his final illness in tranquillity at a small country farmhouse in Derryoge, near Kilkeel, where the family had often spent holidays. *Learning through Suffering,* which was originally published in 1942 and is currently in its 33rd impression, was designed as a spiritual aid to the sick, especially those in hospital, and is full of sensible advice and devotional material. It is a testimony to James Rutherford's deeply spiritual nature and his pastoral concern – another example of his innate determination always to *do* something constructive, to try to meet needs, and to react positively even in tragic circumstances such as were those in which he wrote.

Rutherford's final book, *Christian Reunion in Ireland,* which was published by the Irish branch of the Friends of Reunion (the Foreword is dated 1942) under the chief direction of Kathleen Huggard,[43] is of major interest to us in the context of our study of Irish inter-Church relations. Rutherford was by no means what we today would call a 'professional ecumenist'. He was in demand as a devotional speaker and was deeply involved in the work of the Presbyterian Church's Augmentation Fund which provided practical assistance to ministers in need, and of which he was convener. Yet Rutherford was an ecumenist, to use the more modern term, and was fully involved in the Reunion Movement. He had been a member of the Church of Ireland – Presbyterian Joint Committee on Reunion which was in existence from 1931 to 1934; he attended the 1937 World Conference on Faith and Order in Edinburgh. Fr. Michael Hurley has seen in *Christian Reunion in Ireland* the voice of the Irish Christian Fellowship echoed in Rutherford's words.[44]

During the 1930s Rutherford spoke to meetings throughout Ireland on the subject of reunion; the title of a paper which he gave to the Cashel Clerical Club in 1931 was to be the title of his last book: 'Christian Reunion in Ireland'. The subject which proved most difficult for the Church of Ireland – Presbyterian Joint Committee on Reunion was foremost in Rutherford's mind, namely, the ministry. In 1932 he wrote a paper entitled 'The Ministry and Sacraments of the Presbyterian Church' which was specifically directed at the question of episcopacy. Rutherford here affirmed the practical value of episcopacy but denied its necessity, and declared that Presbyterianism was, *de facto*, episcopal:

I would be the last to deny that much can be said in favour of modern diocesan episcopacy, from a purely practical point of view. What I deny is its *absolute necessity*, and I would urge members of the Church of Ireland to recognise that alongside the type of episcopacy of their own Church there has existed in this country for many centuries another type, which was the normal type through the period during which the Canon of Holy Scripture was fixed, and the Nicene Creed formulated . . . (S)ince the Reformation the Church of Scotland and the Presbyterian Church in Ireland have faithfully observed the rule of episcopal ordination. Their ministers, as we have seen, are in all essentials similar to the bishops of the 2nd century and have been commissioned to ordain . . . I conclude by pointing out the grave consequences arising out of a rigid adherence to the theory that under no conceivable circumstances can others than bishops commissioned by their predecessors ordain. I cannot do so better than by quoting a few sentences from the Bishop of Gloucester's book on *Christian Unity*: 'For the last four hundred years the Presbyterian Church of Scotland has been solemnly ordaining its ministers, and solemnly celebrating the sacraments, it has been conspicuous for theological learning and evangelical zeal with missionary activity. Yet we are asked to believe that its ministers are only laymen and its Sacraments are not Sacraments at all . . .'.[45]

This paper was studied by Canon T.W.E. Drury, a Church of Ireland figure closely associated with the Reunion Movement at the time, who asked why the Presbyterian Church was so called if it was really episcopal. Rutherford replied that Presbyterianism was a protest against the 'prelatical type' of episcopacy rather than against episcopacy *per se*.

In 1933 Rutherford was again in action on this question, for he reacted quite intensely to remarks made by the Archbishop of Dublin (Gregg) on the occasion of the election of the Bishop of Cork and reported in *The Irish Times*. The Archbishop was reported as saying that up to the time of the Reformation there had always been bishops. Rutherford wrote a full reply to the editor of the newspaper, indicating that:

The overwhelming weight of modern scholarship inclines to the view that, during the Apostolic and Sub-Apostolic periods, each individual congregation was governed by a plurality of 'bishops' or 'presbyters' – the term perhaps being used synonymously in the New Testament. Early in the second century this system gradually gave place to 'mon-episcopacy', – one chief officer in every church,

known as the bishop, assisted in his more spiritual functions by a
group of subordinate officials, known as 'presbyters', and in matters
of administration and finance by another group, known as 'deacons'. This type of episcopacy was something altogether different
from modern diocesan episcopacy.[46]

This letter of James Rutherford was not published in *The Irish Times*;
evidently the editor did not wish a lengthy correspondence to
ensue, but did suggest that Rutherford should speak on the matter
at a public meeting and promised that the newspaper would cover
his remarks.[47]

Rutherford had carried out considerable research before writing
Christian Reunion in Ireland. He was particularly interested in present-
ing the facts of the actual situation in which the Churches found
themselves. Through such an analysis, he felt, it would be realized that
reunion would be for the benefit of all, both for practical reasons as
well as for the spiritual fruits which would result.

It would be a mistake, however, to view this book as a plea for
reunion because of dwindling numbers in many parts of Ireland and
solely for the strength in numbers which a united Church would gain.
Rutherford had a clear vision of unity, and in Chapter V of *Christian
Reunion in Ireland* sets out his 'Suggested Outline for Reunion',
describing the 'Type of Union Contemplated':

(a) It is the will of Christ that his disciples should manifest their unity
     in Him to the world by their oneness in spirit, in faith, and in love.
     That unity cannot be made manifest so long as Christians are
     separated from one another by divisions which are largely heredi-
     tary and concerned with matters in no way essential to the faithful
     following of their divine Lord . . .
(b) The ultimate aim should be a Church with a broad and elastic but
     unified system of doctrine, of worship, of government and finan-
     cial administration, but this can only come slowly and gradually.
     It must not involve the absorption of any one Church by another,
     but rather the conservation of everything that is most valuable in
     the past traditions of all . . .

Rutherford envisaged that the Uniting Church would initially consist of
the Church of Ireland and the Presbyterian Church, but he constructed
his Outline in such a way as to permit the necesssary modifications should
other Churches, such as the Methodist, Congregational or Moravian
Churches, wish to participate in this journey into union.

As far as the ministry itself was concerned, James Rutherford proposed that the Presbyterian Church should appoint superintendents or bishops, with the clear proviso that the acceptance of this type of representative episcopacy did not involve the acceptance of any theory about its historic origin or sanction. Probably under the influence of the South India scheme, he proposed that bishops of both Churches should be present at ordinations.

Rutherford devoted Chapter II of *Christian Reunion in Ireland* to the question: Why leave out the Church of the Majority? He affirms in this Chapter that the Roman Catholic Church is 'a genuine part of the world-wide catholic Church of Christ'. He defends this assertion by indicating his experience of Roman Catholics over the fourteen years during which he had lived in Dun Laoghaire, and by recording his indebtedness 'to some of the greatest spiritual teachers of the Roman Church – to St. Theresa, St. Francis de Sales, Fenelon, Father Grou, and above all, to Baron von Hügel.'. Certainly during his time in Dun Laoghaire Rutherford did not separate himself from the majority community; indeed, he mixed freely with Roman Catholic clergy.

Yet Rutherford was aware of the reality that the only possibility of reunion with the Roman Catholic Church would involve complete surrender and absorption. He wrote at the end of Chapter II:

> The facts stand out too blatantly to be denied by any man who will look at them. Nor does the Church of Rome assume the role of an humble, weak-kneed apologist. She proclaims magisterially from the housetops those doctrines which she deems it necessary that all who would be her faithful children should accept without reservation. They may accept or reject her teaching, but if they wilfully reject it, they do so to their soul's everlasting damnation. As for Protestants whose minds have been warped from infancy, and who may be living according to the best light they have, the more liberal and charitably-minded Roman theologians are prepared to leave them to God's uncovenanted mercy. Those, however, who have been born and brought up in the light of the Holy Church, and who in manhood or womanhood are beguiled into serious heresy or disobedience to their lawful teachers can count on no such concession. Their fate is sealed – more hopeless and aweful than human mind can conceive.

Rutherford's Approach

How far was James Rutherford representative of Presbyterianism? What were his underlying ecclesiological assumptions? In reflecting on these questions we will attempt a summary critique of his approach.

In both Scotland and Ireland in the eighteenth and nineteenth centuries, Presbyterianism had suffered much internal division, but in the latter century there were effective steps taken to reduce division and to promote the unity of the Church in its Presbyterian expression. In Ireland, in the eighteenth century, the seceders separated from the Synod of Ulster over the method of appointing ministers and the issue of patronage, and later themselves split into two parts – a division which was healed in 1818, only twenty-two years before the final reconciliation of the Secession Synod with the Synod of Ulster. A different series of controversies had been continuing since the early 1700s – those surrounding the matter of subscription to the Westminster Confession of Faith. Ultimately these led to the breach of 1830 with the establishing of the Remonstrant Synod. The non-suscribers differed from mainstream Presbyterianism on the doctrines of Christ and the Trinity. In 1840 however, as we have noted, orthodox Presbyterianism was unified in Ireland with the establishment of the General Assembly of the Presbyterian Church in Ireland, and by 1900 there were just two Presbyterian Churches in Scotland: the Church of Scotland and the United Free Church (cf. also Ch. I, *ad loc.*).

Irish Presbyterianism therefore was familiar with questions of division and reconciliation in the Church. Already in 1844, despite very recent tensions between the Presbyterian Church and the Church of Ireland relating to State support for schools and matrimonial law,[48] the Presbyterian General Assembly sought closer co-operation with other Protestant Churches in Ireland and even suggested the establishing of committees in the Churches to deal with inter-Church affairs.[49] In 1871 the General Assembly made further overtures on Church Union; in 1890 the Moderator (Park) foresaw the 'blessed prospect' that 'the next half century will see a great movement towards Union amongst the Churches'; and in 1904, 1910 and 1919 the General Assembly again took initiatives to promote inter-Church co-operation and Church Union.[50]

Despite earlier difficulties and tensions between Presbyterians and the Established Church, such as those already mentioned, there was a clear recognition that the Church of Ireland was a Church with which Presbyterians could develop relations. It was a natural progression in Presbyterian thinking to move – as the General Assembly did – from concern for Presbyterian unity to the issue of union with other reformed Churches, and the comments of the Moderator in 1890 exemplified this attitude. Thus there was nothing really new in Rutherford's call for reunion between the Church of Ireland and the

Presbyterian Church – apart that is from his forceful and persistent approach; nor did he make any such claim of charting the uncharted. Yet his chapter in *Christian Reunion in Ireland* on 'Why leave out the Church of the Majority?' makes for rather disappointing reading; there is little of a positive nature here, beyond an affirmation of the importance of cultivating 'good relations'. Rutherford nonetheless declares that his aim in seeking reunion between the Presbyterian Church and the Church of Ireland was certainly '*not* to rally the forces of Irish Protestantism *against* the forces of Irish Romanism', and spells out why he regards the Roman Catholic Church as truly a part of the Christian Church. Rome, however, would demand total surrender to her teachings as a precondition of union and Rutherford mentions those doctrines which he sees as unacceptable to Protestants: Infallibility, the Mass, Mary as 'Mother of God', the Invocation of Saints.[51] In fairness to Rutherford, however, Rome's stance was indeed absolute and unequivocal and there were no realistic prospects of any significant advance in Protestant – Roman Catholic relations at the time.

James Rutherford was a man with a mission. He was totally and urgently committed to Anglican-Presbyterian reunion in Ireland and, rightly at the time, considered it impossible to contemplate any Christian reunion involving the Roman Catholic Church. He was a realist rather than an idealist and as such represented the thought and outlook of many of his time. It must also be affirmed that, despite the ways in which the Presbyterian Church initiated reunion moves at its General Assembly, the positive aspects of Rutherford's views on diocesan episcopacy would have been regarded with considerable suspicion in the Presbyterian rank and file. A natural campaigner, Rutherford was consistently enthusiastic in his efforts to promote reunion and his draft for the last chapter of his book on reunion concluded with an urgent call to immediate action.[52]

The enthusiasm of James Rutherford for his cause is unmistakable and the energies which he expended in promoting Protestant reunion are undoubted. He characterized the spirit of the age in so far as he was concerned with effective witness; this was a fundamental priority throughout the Reunion Movement from Edinburgh 1910 onwards. Rutherford was a Presbyterian, committed to his Church, but also prepared for and indeed committed to change. That readiness for change and that recognition of the need for change – both of which are found in abundance in James Rutherford – indicate a way in which the Churches still often find it hard to follow.

3. Social Philosophies; Christus Rex; the Mercier Society

Within the Irish Roman Catholic Church during the first half of this century there was a growing social movement parallel to, but very different in fundamentals from, the Social Gospel concerns in the Protestant Churches. This social movement nevertheless had some, albeit limited, implications for Protestant–Roman Catholic contact in Ireland in the 1930s and 1940s. It already had developed on the continent in earlier decades, in particular after Leo XIII's encyclical *Rerum Novarum* (1891) for which much of the preparation had been made by the Union of Fribourg, founded by the Bishop of Geneva (Mermillod, later Cardinal), as a research association for social issues; its first annual meeting was held in 1885. The Union of Fribourg's reports were supplied to Rome, and were passed by Leo XIII to Cardinal Zigliara who was preparing the text of *Rerum Novarum*[53]. This first 'social encyclical' condemned the abuses of capitalism, notably the concentration of wealth in the hands of very few, and the gross exploitation of workers. Yet *Rerum Novarum* rejected 'class struggle' in preference to 'class harmony', and emphasized the right to private property and enterprise – a theme which was linked to the individual's family responsibilities. Moreover, workers had the right to form labour associations.

The Roman Catholic social movement, known as Catholic Action, was encouraged by Pius XI (1922-1939); the organization known as 'Young Christian Workers', founded by the Belgian priest, Joseph Cardijn, was particularly commended by Pius XI as 'a perfect example' of 'specialized Catholic Action'.[54] The Catholic Action movement on the continent was the organized participation of the laity in promoting social progress, particularly after the ravages of World War I. It was especially vibrant in Belgium, Holland and France, while in Southern Europe it was more specifically under national, ecclesiastical control.[55]

J.H. Whyte has shown how the social movement in the Roman Catholic Church began to find tentative expression in Ireland already in the early 1900s through the rural co-operative movement and, in towns, through the charitable work of lay volunteers in the St. Vincent de Paul Society.[56] The fact that the social movement was slow to develop in Ireland was, according to Whyte, due to national and political concerns dominating in Ireland from World War I through the 1920s and, in the intellectual context, due to the Hierarchy's 'discouraging Catholics from entering the universities available before 1908, or to the State for refusing until then to establish a university which the Catholic bishops would accept'. Whyte continues: 'But wherever the responsibility lies, the fact remains that before the Irish Universities Act of 1908, it was almost impossible for a Catholic university-trained élite to emerge in Ireland.'.

Nevertheless, following Pius XI's encyclical *Quadragesimo Anno* in 1931 (forty years after *Rerum Novarum*), the social movement began to develop more definitely in Ireland. In 1931, just before the publication of this second great papal social encyclical, Fr. John Hayes founded the organization Muintir na tire as a co-operative project, but gradually it developed into a nationwide network of local guilds for improving social circumstances.[58] While Muintir na tire, as E. McDonagh has commented, lacked a 'penetrating social and economic analysis'[59], it was not exclusively Roman Catholic; many Protestants, including their Church leaders, were fully committed participants.

Lay involvement was fundamental to Catholic Action on the continent and in the social movement as it grew in Ireland. The Legion of Mary, founded by Frank Duff in 1921, was formed in order to meet the need caused by women not being admitted to the St. Vincent de Paul Society; it was first known as the Association of Our Lady of Mercy, but in 1925 adopted its Legion of Mary title, opening its first hostels during the 1920s.

The social encyclicals, *Rerum Novarum* and *Quadragesimo Anno* gave full papal endorsement to the social movement[60]; indeed they acted as catalysts for social action. The encyclicals themselves were not radical; they conceived of social justice being forwarded not through any fundamental restructuring of society – they directly contradicted the tenets of 'atheistic' and 'materialistic' socialism and communism – but through the mutual respect and co-operation of all classes in the interests of progress. This social movement gained its genius from neoscholasticism with the latter's return to Aquinas and regard for the Middle Ages; there was, in the social movement, a style of adapted medievalism. The social encyclicals were founded on the concept of 'natural rights', and ultimately on Natural Law. In his Lenten Pastoral of 1948, dealing with the Church's social teaching, Cardinal D'Alton declared: 'Time and again the Popes return to the necessity of making it feasible for workers to acquire property of their own. The right to property is based on Natural Law. It is linked with a man's rational nature, and with his dignity and other rights as a human person.'.[61] Here then was the foundation of the Roman Catholic Church's social teaching – the Natural Law. Neoscholasticism had brought with it a revival of Natural Law theory; Aquinas, in distinguishing between the divine law (revelation) and the natural law (perceived by reason), had described the latter's principal precepts as 'existence; self-preservation; the family; and education, society and (natural) religion'.[62] The new interest in Natural Law was both a concomitant of the neoscholastic movement, and later, as P.E. Sigmund writes, 'The excesses of the Nazi régime suggested the need for a higher standard beyond that of the positive law . . .'.[63] There was then a fundamental cohesion between Roman Catholic theology and the approach to social issues; that cohesion was supplied by the return to Aquinas. Here, naturally, there is a basic difference between the Roman Catholic social movement and the Protestant Social Gospel, which gravitated around Kingdom-theology and the idea of progress in history. While the Natural Law affirmed the ability of reason to perceive the just, divine order, the Social Gospel taught society's ability to progress towards the Kingdom through the radical application of Jesus' ethical teaching which, for the proponents of the Social Gospel, stood in direct contrast to the principles of capitalism.

In comparing the social teaching of the Roman Catholic Church as it developed between 1891 and 1931, and subsequently, with that of the Life and Work movement and the Social Gospel, we must recognize that papal social teaching led to much more concrete action than did the Kingdom-theology of the Protestants. In the social movement lay people were encouraged to respond in particular ways to particular circumstances, and they did so, as in Catholic Action on the continent and in such bodies as Muintir na tire and the Legion of Mary in Ireland. The social movement in Ireland led to much more practical fruits than did the Protestants' reflections – incisive though they often were – on Church, Kingdom and society. A contributory factor here undoubtedly was the fact that the Protestant Churches were divided; it was natural that the chief practical fruits of the ecumenical Life and Work movement tended to issue from ecumenical as opposed to denominational life. In Ireland the United Council took a particular interest in refugee relief, and this was also to be a major concern of the World Council of Churches after its formation in 1948.

Christus Rex

The Irish Roman Catholic bishops in the 1930s became more conscious of the need for the Church to respond to social issues and they increasingly made reference to the Church's social teachings, in particular the papal documents. In 1941 the promotion of discussion on social questions and of the Church's teaching was given further significant impetus from outside the Hierarchy by the formation of the

Christus Rex Society in Maynooth. This Society was given episcopal approval in October 1945 when the bishops also specifically sanctioned the Society's plans to hold Social Study Summer Schools for priests and to issue a journal.

The idea of forming such a society as Christus Rex originated with the students of Maynooth who had already been reflecting on social issues in the social study circles in college, and who wanted an organization which would keep them in touch with one another after their ordinations. The move to form Christus Rex was supported by the Maynooth professors P. McKevitt and C. Lucey (Professors of Catholic Action and Social Ethics respectively – Dr. Lucey was appointed Coadjutor Bishop of Cork in 1951 and became Bishop of Cork in the following year). Both McKevitt and Lucey were the joint editors of the Christus Rex Journal when it started in January 1947. The aims of the Society were defined as (a) to promote among Irish diocesan clergy the study of the Church's social teaching, and (b) to encourage and assist priests in all forms of social work.[64]

The early issues of the Christus Rex Journal reveal it to be principally concerned with promoting the official teaching of the Church, and articles are intensely loyal to the papal documents. Dr. Lucey wrote in the first issue:

> We, as Catholics, therefore, must not let ourselves be jockeyed into the position of defending reactionary monopolistic capitalism on the one hand, nor bureaucratic State capitalism on the other. We want private enterprise and property not for the few – be they private capitalists or State commisars – but for the many; if we would limit nationalisation, we would limit no less monopolisation by irresponsible individuals and combines of the nation's industries and resources. We do not – we cannot – stand over things as they are. We want social reform, but we want it the Papal Encyclicals' way, not the Marxist-Leninist way – or the Monopoly Capitalist way.[65]

A more faithful representation of the official social teaching of the Roman Catholic Church could hardly have been produced. Other writers contributed in a similar vein – such as McKevitt, the Bishop of Galway (Browne), Cardinal D'Alton and Dr. Alfred O'Rahilly (who also contributed to the weekly newspaper *The Standard* which regularly expounded the social teaching of the Roman Catholic Church). Two early articles in *Christus Rex* defended, with papal references, the involvement of priests in social issues.[66] Cardinal MacRory and Cardinal D'Alton were successively the first two patrons of Christus Rex.

If the theological orientation of the early Christus Rex was essentially papal and consistently dependent on Natural Law theology, there was also no hint of social concern being an issue on which the Churches could effectively come together for the good of the community at large. In fact there are references which clearly extol papal teaching in contrast to Protestant approaches to social issues. In January 1947, the Bishop of Galway (Browne) wrote: 'We cannot be sufficiently grateful for the clear guidance which the Popes have given Catholics in the last few years. It is only when we contrast it with the doubts, hesitations and helplessness of non-Catholic bodies that we can realize its value.'. Later that year, E. Boylan openly disparaged any concept of pluralism:

> The view is held, vaguely perhaps, but widely, that because there is a small body of non-Catholics in our midst, Catholic principles must not be used as the fount and origin of any policy affecting public and social life ... Catholics are usually faced with the problem of reaching their personal convictions by one set of arguments (Catholic ones), and of trying to find another set of arguments (non-Catholic ones) to present their case in public. It is a type of schizphrenia [*sic*] that produces results in public life just as crazy as those it produces in private life.[67]

While the social movement in the Roman Catholic Church in Ireland in the 1930s and 1940s was fundamentally confessional and in no really significant way crossed the divisions in Irish society, Christus Rex was to develop a more critical approach in the 1960s, when articles began to be concerned more with social analysis than with the interpretation of papal social teachings. This change in approach was marked and came at a time when there was much social planning taking place in Ireland, as elsewhere. *Christus Rex* changed its name in 1972 to *Social Studies*, stating: 'Through the use of sociological analysis it (the journal) aims at giving Irish society an awareness of itself and the world in which it exists.'. The Christus Rex Society had begun its annual Social Study conferences in 1953 (in Galway – Bishop Browne was an active participant); these too changed in emphasis during the 1960s, when the calls were for more, rather than less, State intervention – as in 1966 in the area of 'State Welfare'. The earlier Christus Rex Society and Journal were, however, marked by a confessional introspection which betrays theological stagnation, a lack of critical inquiry and analysis – and imagination – and an acute dependence on official documents. Yet, when it broadened its perspectives on social issues in the 1960s, it did so in the company of many of the bishops who also saw the need for State planning and intervention in such areas as land, education and the elderly.[68]

The Mercier Society

We have seen how the Legion of Mary was an important expression of the Roman Catholic social movement in Ireland, involving the laity in a compassionate social outreach. One significant initiative of the Legion had inter-Church implications: the formation of the Mercier Society.

In 1938 the Legion of Mary had held a series of 'retreats for non-Catholics' at Blackrock College. These were for any who had an interest in the Roman Catholic Church and wanted to inquire further. Under Dr. McQuaid, then President of Blackrock College, James Cummins had organized the retreats. Cummins was closely involved with the Legion of Mary and he and Frank Duff decided, after the series of retreats, to establish the Mercier Society with the motto, 'Towards Better Understanding'.

The format of these monthly meetings, which ran in Dublin from 1941 to 1944, was standard: a speaker, perhaps a member or an invited guest, alternately Protestant and Roman Catholic, would address the gathering and this would be followed by a break and informal discussion. Certainly, by all accounts, the meetings of the Mercier Society were harmonious and distinguished occasions. The fact that the Society was attended by intellectuals and addressed by scholars and senior churchmen gave it a seriousness which distinguished it from a mere convert movement. Fr. Michael O'Carroll has written of its membership and speakers:

> Among the people who came regularly or as often as duty allowed, there was a whole bevy of future bishops of different churches. We had Dr. Simms and Dr. R.P.C. Hanson, future bishops of the Church of Ireland – Dr. Rodney Coote, Anglican Bishop of Gambia, came when home from his mission, as his father Commander Coote was a regular member. Fr. William Barden, O.P., later Archbishop of Tehran, was with us; so was the future Bishop Joseph Carroll and the future Bishop Donal Herlihy.
>
> Let me give some names picked at random from the impressive membership: Frank Duff, Leon O Broin, Desmond FitzGerald (father of the Taoiseach), Lonan Murphy, President of the Vincent de Paul Society, Professor Theo Dillon ..., F.H. Boland, later

President of the United Nations General Assembly, ... John
Betjeman, ... the Rev. Michael Ferrar ... Lecturers from outside
the regular membership included Mgr. Arthur Ryan, of Queen's
University, Belfast, Dr. Billy Matthews, Dean of St. Paul's, ...
Christopher Hollis and Fr. Hugh Pope,O.P.[69]

James Cummins was an out-going person and an able Chairman;
Frank Duff was more able to engage in debate and spoke at every
meeting, addressing himself to whatever subject was being considered
– but as the Society developed, any idea of converts resulting from the
dialogue receded ever further into the background.

In his book on Frank Duff, T. O'Flynn has commented: 'The object
of the Mercier Society was to discuss matters of Faith with non-
Catholics with a view to bringing them into the Church. It was not
exactly Ecumenism according to the mind of Vatican II. But it was a
first step in that direction . . .'.[70] Indeed, despite its nominal link with
early ecumenism through its Mercier title (after Cardinal Mercier of
the unofficial Anglican-Roman Catholic Malines Conversations), the
Society was not intended as an ecumenical witness. Duff was the
quintessential Roman Catholic, deeply devoted to the Virgin Mary and
never tiring of zeal in promoting his Church and faith. The Mercier
Society followed the 'retreats for non-Catholics' and no doubt originally had a convert motivation. It preceded Belfast's 'Clonard Mission
to Non-Catholics' which originated in 1947.[71]

Nevertheless, the Mercier Society took on a life of its own, inspired
by the able and erudite people who actually came along. It was not
founded in anything like the spirit of the *nouvelle théologie* which
ultimately led to a new ecumenical outlook in the Roman Catholic
Church, but as the Society developed it grew into a real dialogue. Soon
it became suspect in the eyes of the Roman Catholic authorities.
Archbishop McQuaid became anxious about the proceedings, and Dr
O Broin recalls how two priests were sent to report back to the
Archbishop.[72] Eventually, the Society's case was considered in Rome
itself, and finally – based on the Vatican's ruling – an unfavourable
verdict was issued locally.[73]

The experience of the Mercier Society shows that there were indeed
those Protestants and Roman Catholics who wanted to engage in a
dialogue that was more than a promoting of their own beliefs; here
there were those who recognized that, diverse though their back-
grounds and approaches were, they were Christians together seeking
a way towards reconciliation in faith. The ecclesiastical authorities'
verdict reflected the prevailing ecclesiological assumptions of the

Roman Catholic Church: the way to reconciliation was through the Protestants' return to the fold.

The Mercier Society sprang from the Legion of Mary's concern to make Roman Catholic teachings clear to Protestants and thereby, attract them. There had been an energetic Protestant proselytising movement in Ireland in the nineteenth century, which D. Bowen has investigated in his books, *Souperism: Myth or Reality?* and *The Protestant Crusade in Ireland, 1800-1870.* Bowen shows how Protestant proselytism had contributed to the Pope's decision to send Ireland 'an ecclesiastic totally committed to the Ultramontane cause':

> The ecclesiastic who came as papal delegate and Primate was Paul Cullen. There is little doubt that one of the reasons for his coming was the phenomenal report of Protestant advances which had reached Rome. Nor is there much question that his policies during the 1850s were greatly influenced by ICM (Irish Church Missions) gains in Connaught and elsewhere.[74]

The Legion of Mary's initiatives in relation to 'non-Catholics' were, however, not in the spirit of a twentieth century response to such a past, but rather to the absolute claims of Rome which came with neoscholasticism, Vatican I and the 1917 Code: if the Roman Catholic Church was indeed the one, true Church then it was imperative that others be encouraged to return. The Legion itself was an expression of the lay social movement; the emphasis was on action, and Duff and Cummins responded to the felt need for an outreach to Protestants by taking action. [75]

CHAPTER 3

The Churches and Educational Legislation in Northern Ireland: 1923–1947

Our survey of inter-Church relations in Ireland inevitably brings us into the highly complex and politicized area of education and the Churches. This topic is so extensive that it could be the subject of a volume on its own. Here we will restrict ourselves to a period of just over twenty years, and to Northern Ireland in particular. In this chapter we will examine how the Churches' involvement in the education debates in Northern Ireland between 1923 and 1947 reflected the fundamental nature of their relationships and self-understanding. This area provides a useful 'test' of the Churches' theological and ecclesiological priorities, as well as a case-study in inter-Church relations. In Chapter VI, we will consider some of the more recent developments in education.

The Protestant Churches' educational interests in the 1920s were held in common to such an extent that a United Education Committee was able to be formed in 1924 to handle the Churches' negotiations with the Government in Stormont.[1] The successes of this United Committee in obtaining the 1925 Amendment Act, extra provisions in the 1930 Act, and places on the management committee of the new Stranmillis College, show the committee's ability to organize and campaign effectively.[2]

The 1923 Education Act

From shortly after the establishment of the State of Northern Ireland until the late 1940s, the Protestant Churches were involved in virtually continuous controversy with the Government over educational legislation; the Roman Catholic Church also was involved, although with different demands. The first debate surrounded the 1923 Education Act.

The new Northern Ireland Government's Minister of Education, Lord Londonderry (whose Department was established in June 1921), swiftly appointed a committee to report on the educational services

55

and to provide for any changes for their improvement. This committee, under the chairmanship of Mr. Robert Lynn, issued its final report
on 19th June 1923 and only three days later the Education Act (N.I.),
1923 received the royal assent. Clearly the report of the Lynn Committee could not have been given serious consideration. In fact its
recommendations were ignored in the new Act and it is clear that the
Government had its own priorities; it desired a completely secular
educational system. Clause 7 of the 1923 Bill defined the aim of the
new educational system as 'an education, both literary and moral
based upon instruction in reading and writing of the English language
and in arithmetic'; Clause 26 stated that 'the education authority shall
not provide religious instruction in any such public elementary school';
and Clause 66(3) provided that the religious denomination of appli-
cants for teaching posts should not be taken into account by the
education authority when appointing: '. . . nor shall the education
authority have power to require that the teachers appointed for or
holding office in any provided or transferred school shall be teachers
who belong to or profess the tenets of, or who do not belong to or
profess the tenets of, any particular church or religious denomination'.[3]

In his *Episode in the History of Protestant Ulster*, Dr. William Corkey,
convener of Primary and University Education on the Presbyterian
General Assembly's Board of Education (1917-1945) and a leading
apologist of the United Committee, recognized that the intentions of
the Act were against the wishes of the Churches:

> Though it soon came to be evident that there was no sympathy for
> a secular system of education by any class of the community in
> Ulster, yet the Government and, it was alleged, also some officials of
> the Ministry of Education, remained adamant in their determina-
> tion to thwart the will of the people and to accept no amendment
> of the new Education Act.
>
> In these circumstances the representatives of the Protestant
> Churches and the Committee of the Grand Lodge of Ireland took
> every opportunity to make the convictions of the people and their
> opposition to the Act known to the Government.[4]

The 1923 Act provided for the transfer of all schools in Northern
Ireland to local education committees, but the Roman Catholic
Church made it clear that it would not transfer any schools. Canons
1373 and 1374 were particularly relevant in this area: the former
defined all education as having a religious dimension, which would
not be possible in secular institutions, and the latter specifically

required Roman Catholic pupils to attend Roman Catholic schools.[5] The Protestant Churches agreed to transfer their schools, provided that simple 'Bible instruction' would continue to be given by the teaching staff *and* that there would be Protestant teachers for Protestant children.

These conditions were contrary to Clause 26 and 66(3) of the 1923 Act (see above), and the Government held that it was bound by the terms of the Constitution of Northern Ireland in the Government of Ireland Act, 1920.

Upon taking Counsel's opinion, two senior K.C.s (John Leitch and James Pringle) assured the Protestant Churches that, on the contrary, there was nothing in the Government of Ireland Act which compelled the Government to include the two offending clauses in the 1923 Act, and debar an Amending Act. Furthermore, the General Assembly was told, as Dr. W.E. Davison has recorded:

> . . . of those cases in which the Government was already in breach of their own interpretation of the 1920 Law, quoting cases of public funds being allocated to Roman Catholic Training Colleges, of afflicted children being sent to school in accordance with the religious persuasion of the parents, and the appointment of chaplains to teachers in training.[6]

On 5th March 1925 the United Education Committee of the Protestant Churches and the County Grand Loyal Orange Lodge of Belfast held a Six Counties Conference in the Presbyterian Assembly Hall and thus consolidated their united efforts to bring about an amendment to the 1923 Act. On the following day the secretaries of the United Committee and the Orange Order were invited to meet the Prime Minister, Sir James Craig (later Lord Craigavon), to discuss the situation.

The 1925 Education Amendment Act

The political position at this time was particularly delicate, for in 1925 the Boundary Commission was due to report and the Prime Minister intended holding a general election to present a united front of unionists and to show that they were not prepared to surrender any part of the territory of Northern Ireland. Unionist solidarity was essential, and this had a decisive influence on the education debate.

On 7th March it was officially announced that the Government would introduce an amending Bill, which resulted in the 1925

Education Amendment Act. The prohibitions in Clauses 26 and 66(3) of the 1923 Act were removed.[7]

A degree of confusion in relations between the United Committee and the Ministry of Education continued, however, until the following June. It seemed that the controversies about Religious Instruction and teaching appointments were not fully resolved. The United Committee of the Protestant Churches and the Belfast County Grand L.O.L. enquired of the Ministry of Education whether it would be prepared 'to approve of the following conditions being incorporated in Deeds of Transfer of Schools:

1.   That Religious Instruction shall be given by the teaching staff as heretofore on a programme to be approved by the persons or Body transferring the schools.
2.   That in the event of a teacher being appointed who on religious grounds is objectionable to the persons or Body transferring the School (or the persons transferring and the local School Committee), it shall be competent for the persons or Body transferring the school, on giving due and reasonable notice to the Education Authority, to terminate the lease of transfer.[8]

The Ministry replied, quoting Section 5 of the Government of Ireland Act, 1920, to the effect that public money could not be applied for the teaching of any particular religious beliefs or for paying salaries of teachers who had to be of a particular persuasion. Negotiations between the United Education Committee of the Protestant Churches and Lord Londonderry followed (also including representatives of the teachers' unions), and a compromise agreement was reached. Donald Akenson has summarized the terms:

> . . . first, in the future local education authorities were empowered to require that 'a programme of simple Bible instruction' be given in provided or transferred schools in the period set apart on the timetable for religious instruction. Secondly, this simple Bible instruction, although given during the hours set apart for religious instruction, was not to include denominational dogmas or catechetical points . . . Thirdly, the daily period specified on the timetable for the Bible instruction was not to be included within the hours of compulsory attendance by the children . . . teachers *were* to be compelled to give such simple Bible instruction as part of their educational duties. The fifth point was that the teachers were not compelled to give denominational instruction if the school

managers chose to use the religious time slot for specific denominational teaching instead of general Protestant instruction.[9]

While these agreed terms required teachers to give 'simple Bible instruction' on a non-denominational basis, it should have been clear that this would be unacceptable to Roman Catholics. The Roman Catholic Bishop of Down and Connor was later to declare: '. . . we cannot transfer our schools. We cannot accept simple Bible teaching. I wish to emphasize this point. Simple Bible teaching is based on the fundamental principle of Protestantism, the interpretation of sacred Scripture by private judgement.'.[10]

In 1928 the Lurgan Clerical Union protested to the Government that the Armagh regional education committee would not insert a clause in deeds of transfer requiring daily Bible instruction. This triggered a conflict between the Ministry of Education and the Armagh committee, the former urging that such a clause should be inserted to ensure the harmonious working of educational legislation. The debate subsequently widened, and in 1928 the General Assembly, following a series of presbytery resolutions, demanded a further amendment of the Education Act securing places for transferors' representatives on education committees, and ensuring that in every provided or transferred school, where parents of not less than ten pupils so desired, Bible instruction would be given. A deputation of the Protestant Churches and the Orange Order met the Prime Minister on 21st February 1929. The Prime Minister asked that a sub-committee of the United Committee should enter into detailed discussions with the Ministry of Education and promised that if an agreement were reached he would introduce the necessary legislation. In the following April a deputation of the Association of Northern Ireland Education Committees met Lord Craigavon and the Minister of Education and opposed the proposals of the United Committee.

The 1930 Act

In 1925 the Prime Minister had asked the Protestant Churches to accept the Education Amendment Act of that year and to monitor the progress of the administration of education for several years. In 1928 the Churches agreed that further amendment to the Education Act was necessary. A split between the Orange Order and the United Committee was exploited to the full by the Government, satisfying the former's demands by promising legislation to ensure the continuation

of Bible instruction in transferred Primary Schools, but failing to
satisfy the further demand of the Churches that they should have
places on education committees. A general election was called for
22nd May 1929, and the Churches did not press their demands.
However subsequently – after the election – the appointment of
representatives of transferors of schools to regional education committees was granted, being incorporated in the 1930 Education
Amendment Bill.

At the 1930 General Assembly the Board of Education reported the
main features of the Bill with 'gratification': Clause I dealt with the
representation of transferors on Borough and Regional Committees
and empowered the Ministry to appoint representatives of transferors
or trustees of schools on Borough and Regional Committees up to one
fourth the total number of such Committees. Clause II dealt with the
constitution of school management committees and enacted that one
half of such committees should represent the transferors of the school
and group of schools managed by such committees. Clause III dealt
with the appointment of teachers and with the powers of the School
Management Committee to select a list from which appointment was
to be made. Clause IV dealt with the giving of Bible instruction and
with the right of the parents to demand such instruction.[11]

The pleasure of the United Committee at the provisions of the 1930
Bill is indicated by the fact that the Methodist and Church of Ireland
secretaries both addressed the Assembly. The Rev. James Quinn
(Church of Ireland) declared: 'Few things have done so much in
recent times to unite the Protestant Churches in Northern Ireland as
the common action they had felt compelled to take in the matter of
elementary education.'.[12]

Donald Akenson has pointed out that the events leading to the
earlier 1925 legislation differed from those leading to the 1930 Act in
that in the former the Roman Catholic Church took no part in the
debate. Yet by 1928 Roman Catholic MPs were taking a full part in the
Northern Ireland House of Commons and the Roman Catholic
Church was by now more inclined to participate in discussions with the
Government to secure its own interests in educational matters.

The six northern Roman Catholic bishops claimed that hardship
was created in Roman Catholic schools because they were unable to
receive any grants towards the erection or equipment of new schools,
or for the expansion of existing schools, except on grounds which
were religiously unacceptable. If the Protestant Churches' demands
were to be met in an Amending Bill, it would only be just for Roman
Catholic demands also to be met.

The Ancient Order of Hibernians staged a number of mass demonstrations, bringing the Roman Catholic community's demands to the public attention in 1930. A group of twenty leading Roman Catholics met Lord Charlemont (Minister of Education in succession to Lord Londonderry, 1926), but no agreement was reached. The Bishop of Down and Connor (Mageean) threatened legal action if the 1930 Amending Bill were passed without concessions for Roman Catholics. Akenson comments: 'This threat was an astute move for. . ..there were serious doubts about the legality of requiring teachers to give simple Bible instruction',[13] and regarding the outcome of the debate writes:

> Finally, the sum total of all these Roman Catholic pressures – the threat of legal action, the campaign by lay politicians and journalists, the denunciations from the pulpit, and the development of a set of compromise proposals which made the Catholic Church appear reasonable and the government arbitrary – forced Lord Craigavon to grant a major concession. Speaking at an Orange Order luncheon at Warrenpoint on 8 May 1930 he announced that he would have an additional clause added to the education bill then before the Northern Ireland parliament, providing fifty per cent grants for the construction and expansion of privately managed elementary schools.[14]

Stranmillis

The only teacher training college in Northern Ireland at the time of the establishment of the State was St. Mary's, Belfast (for Roman Catholic women). Northern teachers who were not trained at St. Mary's received their training in Southern Ireland. The Ministry of Education proposed that provision be made in Northern Ireland for the training of teachers for service in elementary schools in Northern Ireland. With the closing by the Free State Government of Dublin's Marlborough Street training college (which Presbyterians attended) there remained only the Church of Ireland training college (Kildare Place, Dublin) for the training of Protestant teachers in Ireland.

Things were made more difficult in 1922 when changes were made to the curriculum of the Southern colleges which were deemed inappropriate to the needs of Northern Protestant teachers (including provision for the study of the Irish language and literature). Contingency arrangements were made between the Northern Ministry of Education and the Kildare Place College to provide for the training of all Protestant teachers for two years (1922-24). Lord

Londonderry's committee for the training of teachers for Northern Ireland, under the chairmanship of H. M. Pollock (Minister of Finance), quickly went about its task and provided such training through The Queen's University of Belfast and the Belfast College of Technology. Separate buildings at Stranmillis were ready in 1929.

Under the arrangements St. Mary's would receive grant aid, and Roman Catholic male students would attend Stranmillis. The Roman Catholic Church was not content with this latter arrangement and eventually the Government agreed to grant aid the training of Roman Catholic male students at St. Mary's College, Strawberry Hill, Middlesex.

In July 1928 the representatives of the United Education Committee of the Protestant Churches and of the Orange Lodges had included in their demands to Lord Charlemont that there should be representation of the Churches on the governing board of Stranmillis. In February of the following year, the United Committee officially requested of the Government as follows:

> Without demanding a Denominational Training College, we ask as a matter of justice that the conditions under which teachers are trained who are in future to be entrusted with the education of Protestant children be made as acceptable to the Protestant Churches as the conditions under which Roman Catholic teachers being trained are made acceptable to the Roman Catholic Church.[15]

In April 1929 Lord Charlemont promised Church representation on the management committee of Stranmillis. Nevertheless, following the 1930 Act and in view of strong Cabinet opposition (including Pollock), he declined to make this provision and suggested the formation of an Advisory Committee on religious training at Stranmillis.

According to Corkey, Charlemont said that the committee for the training of teachers would have resigned as a body rather than admit clerical representatives on the Stranmillis management committee. He therefore dissolved the Pollock committee in April 1931, appointed a full-time Principal of Stranmillis where previously this position had been held by the Professor of Education at Queen's University, and placed the management of Stranmillis directly under the control of the Ministry of Education, without any management committee.

The United Committee was not prepared to settle for only an advisory or consultative role in the affairs of Stranmillis College; it sought the reconstitution of the management committee with Church representation. In July 1931 the Cabinet made a compromise offer of three places for the Churches (Church of Ireland, Presbyterian and Methodist) on a management committee, to be taken 'only when, in the opinion of the chairman, a religious or moral matter was being considered'.[16] This compromise was also unacceptable to the United Committee.

The combination of strong support from the Orange Order and of the degree of uncertainty surrounding the future created by the Free State's commencement of measures to distance itself constitutionally from the United Kingdom (including the abolition of the Free State MPs' Oath of Allegiance to the Crown), led to the unionists' desire – once again – to close ranks as effectively as possible. Despite the protests of the teachers' unions, the settlement sought by the United Committee went ahead and three Protestant Church representatives were fully part of the Stranmillis committee of management constituted in July 1933.[17]

The lead up to the 1947 Act

The 1930 Education Act provided, for the time being, a settlement of educational legislation which was widely accepted. The next episode of conflict between Church and State on education opened with the discharging of the Rev. Professor Robert Corkey (brother of William Corkey) from his position as Minister of Education in 1944.[18]

The reasons which can be deduced for the dismissal of Professor Corkey set the scene for the debate which would continue for several years. The 1944 Education Act for England and Wales marked a fundamental reform aimed at contributing to post-war reconstruction. The great Butler Education Act secured secondary education for all, and it also made religious instruction obligatory. With educational reform so advanced in Great Britain it was clearly necessary for the Government of Northern Ireland also to embark on a course of reform. However, as William Corkey records,[19] senior officials at the Northern Ireland Department of Education had an approach to religious instruction which was different from that embodied in the Butler Act, and wanted a radical reform of the provisions in the 1930 Act for Bible instruction and the appointment of teachers.

Clearly there was a serious clash between these senior officials and Professor Corkey, the Education Minister. He was dismissed, and the reason given was that of 'inattention to duties'. Professor Corkey claimed that the real reason was that he was not prepared to support any new legislation which would in effect repeal the provisions of the 1930 Act with regard to religious instruction.

The General Assembly of the Presbyterian Church in 1944 unanimously expressed its confidence in Professor Corkey and its regard for
his work as Minister of Education, and recorded its 'indignation' at the
treatment which he had received. In the following year he was elected
as Moderator.

Professor Corkey's successor at the Ministry of Education was Lt.
Col. Hall-Thompson who, according to William Corkey, 'had earlier
supported Alderman Duff when he opposed the Protestant Churches
in their efforts to secure an Amendment to the secularising clauses of
the 1923 Education Act'.[20] The dismissal of Professor Corkey as
Minister of Education was felt by many to be scandalous, and the
choice of Hall-Thompson as his successor at the Ministry of Education
seemed to reveal the real motives behind his discharge from duties.

In 1944 the Church of Ireland's Northern Education Committee
requested that discussions between the Ministry of Education and
interested parties should take place before the publication of the
White Paper on educational reform. The General Assembly of the
same year issued a similar call, for discussions would provide 'an
opportunity to settle outstanding questions involved in Educational
Reform which might otherwise lead to later controversy'.[21] From
previous experience the Churches knew the importance of consultation before the Government's plans would enter the public domain.

The Government White Paper (1944)

Despite the fact that consultations were held between the United
Committee and the Ministry of Education, the White Paper which was
published on 11th December 1944 did not satisfy the former. The
United Committee was concerned, as ever, over the provisions for
religious instruction and now also over increased grants for the so-
called 'four-and-two' committee (maintained) schools. These schools
had management committees on which four members were nominated by the manager and trustees, and two by the regional education
authority. William Corkey, in a pamphlet published on the subject of
the White paper, described it as 'The Government's proposals to
repeal and nullify the guarantee for Bible Instruction contained in the
Education Act, N.I. (1930)'.[22] The Northern Ireland attorney-general,
J. C. MacDermott, declared that the religious provisions of the 1930
Act were contrary to the Government of Ireland Act, 1920, and that
'the transfer deeds written under the 1925 and 1930 Acts were illegal
if they included provisions compelling teachers paid with public funds
to give Bible instruction'.[23] This was a remarkable judgement, for the

1930 Act had been in operation for fourteen years and had received the approval of the legal authorities in Belfast and at Westminster – and many schools had of course been transferred under the terms of the 1925 and 1930 Acts.

The three main Protestant Churches felt utterly betrayed by the proposed new legislation and in 1944 their three Education Boards simultaneously issued the same statement declaring their opposition to the repeal of the provisions for Bible instruction in the 1930 Act, recalling that these provisions had been regarded as secure by those transferring schools to education authorities. The Churches were, however, willing to have a conscience clause and indeed never had opposed such an insertion.

An election was looming, and the United Education Committee sent a message to J. M. Andrews (former Prime Minister of Northern Ireland, and a supporter of the Churches) indicating that they would make the proposed educational legislation an issue during the election campaign. Following this message to Andrews and a meeting with unionist back-benchers, the Prime Minister pledged that the Government's policy was that 'the rights at present enjoyed by parents and School Management Committees under the 1925 and 1930 Education Acts will remain unaltered, subject to an agreed conscience clause to be formulated to meet the objection to compulsion on the teacher'. [24]

A meeting between representatives of the Protestant Churches and the Orange Order and the Prime Minister (Sir Basil Brooke), the Minister of Education (Hall-Thompson) and the Minister of Home Affairs (Warnock) was held on 1st June 1945 with the aim of agreeing upon a conscience clause. The agreed clause allowed a teacher to be excused from giving Bible instruction provided that the appointing body was satisfied that an application of a teacher to be excused was *bona fide*. However, the conscience clause which appeared in the Bill published on 28th September 1946 omitted the *bona fide* provision and required a teacher to be excused on request from conducting or attending collective school worship or from giving 'undenominational religious instruction'.

This about-turn by the Government caused bitter feelings and accusations of what amounted to deceit on the part of the Government. However, it did not come as a surprise when the Bill was published in September 1946, for the Minister of Education's intention not to honour the agreement reached on 1st June 1945 had become clear later that year, and in the 1946 General Synod (in May) and General Assembly (in June) resolutions were passed demanding that the Government hold to 1st June 1945 agreement. Later in the year large public protest meetings were held in Belfast, Bangor, Portadown and Londonderry. The Churches thought that the Government had unscrupulously allowed the public to understand that the agreement was intact through the general election in June 1945, but later had reneged.

The Protestant Churches were concerned by this change of heart on the part of the Government with regard to the agreed conscience clause; they were not content with an unconditional conscience clause because they feared that this might be abused by teachers who would not need to give an account of their reasons for seeking to be released from school worship duties or 'undenominational religious instruction' teaching. The Protestant Churches were also concerned by the Government's intention to repeal the provisions of the 1930 Act which allowed management committees of transferred schools the right to require candidates for teaching posts to be willing to give Bible instruction. A deputation including the Primate (Gregg) which met the Prime Minister on 4th October 1946 had requested that 'the appointing Committees in charge of transferred Protestant schools should have complete freedom in making appointments from qualified applicant teachers', but the Prime Minister replied that 'such a provision would be contrary to the Government of Ireland Act, 1920'.[25]

The provisions which appeared in the White Paper were, for other reasons, not welcomed by the Roman Catholic Church. Cardinal MacRory expressed his concern at the considerable extra expense which would be involved as a result of raising the school leaving age and the new primary/junior secondary school (intermediate) pattern.

The Roman Catholic bishops declared that 'four-and-two' committees were unacceptable to them; they feared that this would be a forerunner to the complete transfer of their schools. Instead, they demanded that Roman Catholic schools should receive one hundred per cent Government financial support, as was the case in provided and transferred schools. A compromise was struck and the Government agreed a rise in the grant for capital expenditure for all voluntary schools, and a rise in the maintenance, heating and lighting grant to voluntary primary schools and 'non-academic' secondary schools, from fifty to sixty-five per cent.

The 1947 Act

Despite all the protestations of the Churches, however, the Education Act received the royal assent on 27th March 1947 without the changes to the Bill which the Churches had demanded. The Government had stood firm.

In educational terms the 1947 Education Act was a major reform and provided a fundamental reconstruction of education in Northern Ireland to meet the needs of post-war generations. From the perspective of the Protestant Churches, we still see them working closely together (and with the Orange Order) in the debates which preceded the Act. William Corkey concludes his account of these controversies by pointing out the irony that, while the Government had held that it was against the Government of Ireland Act, 1920 to appoint a teacher on the basis of the candidate's willingness to give religious instruction, the 1947 Act empowered the Education Authority to appoint a teacher to give religious instruction, when none of the teachers in a particular school was prepared to teach this subject – exercising the teacher's right under the controversial conscience clause. Corkey held that this arrangement was unsatisfactory, but as Dr. W. E. Davison suggests, it is a pity that 'he did not live to see the considerable benefits arising (later) from the right to appoint 'specialists' to teach religion'.[26]

From the perspective of the Roman Catholic Church, however, the 1947 Act went some way (although not as far as the Roman Catholic Church wanted) towards financially assisting the 'voluntary' sector to develop along the lines of the new pattern of education in Northern Ireland.

In terms of relations between the Churches the situation remained the same as in the earlier education debates, i.e. the three main Protestant Churches campaigning together and in liaison with the Orange Order to protect Protestant interests, and the Roman Catholic Church campaigning to protect its interests. Protestants feared that if the willingness and suitability of candidates to give Bible Instruction in schools could not be taken into account when appointments were being made, then a situation could emerge where, in the extreme case, a Roman Catholic could be appointed to a one-teacher transferred or 'provided' school. Some Protestants interpreted the grants available to the Roman Catholic Church in the voluntary sector as a State endowment. Roman Catholics, on the other hand, felt that they should receive one hundred per cent grants for the construction of the new schools which would be required by the new 1947 Act. They were not prepared to transfer their schools; this was a fundamental principle. It is difficult to conceive that the Government can ever really have expected the Roman Catholic Church to transfer its schools; if such an expectation was seriously entertained, the Government was guilty of naïveté in the extreme.

Theological and Ecclesiological Implications

The education controversies in Northern Ireland between 1923 and 1947 show the Churches to occupy entrenched, sectarian positions. On the Protestant side there was a readiness to transfer schools, but only if Bible instruction and Protestant teachers for Protestant children could be guaranteed; the Churches were prepared to let the State relieve them of their financial responsibilities for education if these basic demands could be met. The fundamental theological assumption here was that Bible instruction was at the heart of the Christian witness, the place of the Bible being paramount in the theological orientation of all the Protestant Churches: the contemporary perception of Scripture at the time of these education controversies was of its absolute supremacy. Denominational dogma was also important to the Churches, but the Bible was the foundation of faith.

Experiences no doubt differed as to the effectiveness of Bible instruction in schools. Yet there would always be a fundamental dimension lacking, for the Bible is the Church's book; it is to be studied within the context of faith, which alone brings Scripture to life. To teach infants Bible passages may have been a pleasing exercise to some, but the philosophy thus embraced by the Protestant Churches hardly did justice to their high doctrine of the Bible as the Word of God to be received by faith. The Bible is not an independent, objective testimony, but finds its origin and its enduring power in the life of faith. This basic conception was effectively set aside by the Protestant Churches at the time of these education debates: 'simple Bible instruction' could be no substitute for the teaching of Scripture within the context of faith. Once a teacher set Scripture within such a faith context, in the classroom, he or she was immediately contravening the Government of Ireland Act, 1920 which prohibited the payment of teachers to promote particular religious beliefs. Indeed, it should have been clear that to teach Christianity in the abstract, and specifically without commitment, is to train pupils not to make a spiritual response, not to be committed, and not to profess any particular faith in Jesus Christ. The Presbyterian educationalists Robert and William Corkey, Primate Gregg, the epitome of the constitutionalist, and Primate D'Arcy did not seem to take these ultimately more important issues into serious consideration. The practicalities of the situation – the difficulty of maintaining Protestant schools in the voluntary sector, like the Roman Catholic schools, on account of there being different Protestant Churches – required the transfer of schools, and the Church leaders were preoccupied with these matters.

The shallowness of the theological commitment of the Protestant Churches stands in contrast to the resolute approach of the Roman Catholic Church which insisted on retaining its own schools. This was a curious reversal of the situation at the time of the introduction of Lord Stanley's national system of education in 1831 when, because of lack of resources, the Roman Catholic Church was prepared to accept the new secular, state system. This national system soon became denominational however, for as P. Corish notes: 'The key figure was the 'patron', who applied for a school and became its manager. In most cases he was the Catholic priest. Ironically, perhaps, the new state system restored to the Catholic church a great deal of the control over the primary school system which it had been in danger of losing over the previous fifty years.'.[27]

The sectarian nature of the events and debates of 1923-47 is illustrated by the way in which the Protestant Churches used political circumstances to advance their purposes – notably the general elections and the uncertainties created by developments in Southern Ireland in 1932 – and how the Protestant and Roman Catholic Churches used each other's cases to advance their own causes. Furthermore, events have clearly shown that in these debates the close co-operation between the Protestant Churches and the Orange Order was highly significant; without this alliance with the politically powerful Orangemen it is indeed doubtful if the Churches could have been so successful.

Of course the experience of Protestants in the Republic at this time in the area of education was one of considerable alienation, for the first priority after the signing of the Anglo-Irish Treaty in 1922 was the creation of a distinctive Irish national identity and in this the South's educational system was to be the major medium of Gaelic Revival. There was considerable resentment amongst Protestants at the imposition of Irish in the school curriculum; this was especially so when the Second National Programme of 1926 removed the parental right to veto either English or Irish as an obligatory subject in a school (the First National Programme of 1921 had afforded this right). These developments undoubtedly reinforced Protestant and Unionist feelings in Northern Ireland.

For all the Protestants' demands for Bible instruction, the biblical ministry of reconciliation was forgotten; for all the Roman Catholic Church's insistence on Christian education embracing the whole of the curriculum and the whole human being, the Christian imperative to a reconciled life remained unapplied in the face of fundamental religious, cultural and political division in Ireland.

There could hardly have been a greater challenge to the faith they sought to impart to their children than in the Churches' own relations with one another.

CHAPTER 4

Theological Concerns for Protestants: 1932-1963

1. The Historical Background

The three decades from the 1930s to the '60s form the focus of much conflict and change all over the globe: from pre-war depression to Holocaust, to the war itself, to reconstruction and expansion, to cold war and détente, to the Vietnam conflict, to Western affluence. Although living on the periphery of Europe, Irish people were deeply involved in the political, economic and social world-turmoil of these years. In this chapter we will survey the major theological concerns of the Irish Protestant Churches from 1932-1963 and the development of their relations with one another and with reference to the Roman Catholic Church. As a preliminary however, we shall note several of the major issues of these years in Ireland and in the wider world.

The War

During the 1930s, the subject of war was understandably coming to the fore in the minds of Christians as the threat of totalitarianism to human rights became clear. 'The Church, the Community (common life) and the State' was the theme of the 1937 Life and Work Conference held in Oxford. Referring to this meeting, Nils Ehrenström has written:

> Only slowly did Christians come to perceive that the rise of totalitarian systems had introduced a new era for the world and for the Church. It was the genius of Oxford 1937 that it seized on the central issue of the times, the emergence of the new State which is a parody of the divine society, the Church, and yet spoke to the new situation in terms of the unchanging assurances of the Faith.[1]

Bolton Waller, a Church of Ireland clergyman who had been active in the SCM and the Irish Christian Fellowship, and in the League of Nations itself, reflected on 'The Church and Political Systems' in a paper read at a clerical meeting in Dublin in 1936.[2] In this paper Waller addressed two questions related to Church and society: first, was there, or could there be, a political and social system corresponding to Christianity, and second, how did that system compare with actual social systems already in existence, especially those which were then competing 'for the control of mankind'? Here there was a theological reflection, coming from an Irish pen, on the Church in relation to the social order, including the rise of totalitarianism in Germany and Italy, and Soviet communism.

In keeping with the approach of Life and Work and the Social Gospel, Waller affirmed that Jesus spoke not so much in terms of the Church but of the Kingdom: '. . . in the Gospels the new society is more often described in what we might call political or social rather than strictly ecclesiastical terms'. Nevertheless, this new Christian community or society had never been fully realized in practice, although some nations were closer to the Christian ideal than others. Yet Bolton Waller recognized that there were now 'new political and social systems claiming to control the whole destinies of men and women'.[3] Both communism and fascism sought to control the lives of citizens absolutely, in the former case for the advancement of 'society' and in the latter for the advance of the powerful. Much despised though it was by many ideologues of different persuasions, representative democracy as found in Britain and America at least preserved freedom of speech and action, and the rights of ordinary people were recognized. There were shortcomings, but here was a political tradition most in keeping with the Gospel of freedom and service.

Waller's approach in this paper did not provide any radically new insights, but identified the issues – Kingdom, freedom and service – in a way which reflected the particular concerns of the day. He wrote at a time when very basic freedoms were threatened in Europe. It was as Britain faced a Europe with advancing totalitarianism and the threats to human rights posed by marxism and fascism alike that Waller extolled representative democracy as the political system most compatible with Christianity; such was the historical context which determined the fundamental priorities for Waller's study in Church and society.

The dangers which Waller and so many others had seen swiftly led to the harsh realities of world conflict. These were soon to be directly experienced in Ireland; German air raids affected life both North and South of the border. Despite the Free State's neutrality, German bombs fell in Carlow, Dublin, Kildare, Louth, Meath, Wexford and Wicklow, all during the first three days of 1941.[4] During the month of

April over 700 people were killed and over 400 were seriously injured in air raids on Belfast. On that occasion fire-brigades were sent North from as far as Dublin. In May a further 150 people were killed in more air raids on Belfast during which the shipyard and aircraft factory were both extensively damaged. In June thirty-four people were killed in Dublin's North Strand as a result of German bombing, and almost one hundred were wounded. The German Government expressed regret for bombing Dublin and compensation was promised. Although these bombing raids – even in Belfast – were not on the scale of that experienced in Britain, they nonetheless inflicted much destruction, injury and loss of life.

Not only were the people of Ireland – North and South – suffering as a result of these attacks and through the further loss and injury of relations who were members of the British Forces, but the activities of the IRA continued during the war years. Already in January 1939 the IRA, as part of its campaign, issued an ultimatum to the British Foreign Secretary, Viscount Halifax, demanding the withdrawal of British troops from Irish soil and in August of that same year five people were killed and seventy wounded in an IRA bomb attack in Coventry. Added to such trials, Irish people experienced considerable economic hardship as a result of the war. The United Council was concerned about unemployment, despite the amelioration resulting from the war effort, and the emergencies caused by the war impressed upon Christians the importance of mutual co-operation – although such co-operation was restricted for the most part to the Protestant Churches. Even in the face of such common suffering, Protestants and Roman Catholics remained fundamentally divided.

The war undoubtedly exacerbated the already existing problems of community relations and of relations between the Protestant and Roman Catholic Churches in Northern Ireland in particular. A major issue was that of conscription. The Protestant community desired to be included in the total war effort on an equal basis with the remainder of the United Kingdom. Unionist leaders therefore wanted conscription to include Northern Ireland, but the Government was soon made aware of the difficulties which this would raise in the wider community. The Roman Catholic bishops had been swift to condemn conscription, declaring that this would be to compel their people 'to fight for their oppressor'[5]; at an emergency meeting of the Dáil on 26th May 1940, de Valera, Cosgrave and William Norton (Leader of the Labour Party) registered their protest at the British Government's proposals to apply conscription to Northern Ireland. Protestants and Roman Catholics within Northern Ireland were thus driven further apart.

This spiral was reinforced by the issue of the ports, which caused friction between Britain and Eire. J.T. Carroll has written:

Ireland's refusal to hand over the ports to the allied cause was portrayed in the popular British press, and to a lesser extent in the American, as a stab in the back from a so-called friend at the hour of greatest need by causing the deaths of thousands of sailors bringing vital supplies across the Atlantic not just to Britain, but even to neutral Eire.[6]

At the same place, Carroll quotes from the Northern Ireland poet, Louis MacNeice, who expressed his sentiments on this particular matter in the poem, 'Neutrality':

But then look eastward from your heart, there bulks
A continent, close, dark, as archetypal sin
While to the west off your own shores the mackerel
Are fat – on the flesh of your kin.

Behind the specific issues which made for tensions in Anglo-Irish relations there lay the whole subject of the neutrality of the South. This fundamental rift, which expressed itself concretely in specific ways, only served to deepen the Northern unionists' resentment towards the South and towards their nationalist fellow-citizens. There was, then, during the war years a socio-cultural and an ecclesiastical retrenchment as political matters provided a focus for the expression of fundamental differences between the two communities – Protestant and Roman Catholic, unionist and nationalist – in Northern Ireland.

A cohesion in national life was discovered as the British people faced a common enemy during World War II; the war effort united men and women of every class and background. It was with this national spirit that northern Protestants in particular wanted to be associated, but the experience of Irish people as a whole during the war was one of alienation for, in national terms, they were on different pilgrimages. Today, still, the annual Remembrance Day ceremonies belong overwhelmingly to the northern Protestant community, and when they are observed in the Republic they can lead to sorry controversy. Thus the potency of national allegiance has challenged, and continues to challenge, the Christian Churches' affirmation of the power of the Gospel to overcome all barriers.

Post-War Developments in Education and Health

The immediate task facing everyone at the end of the war was that of reconstruction. While attention was naturally concentrated on the

European and wider world scenes,[7] the Churches at home remained concerned about social conditions in Ireland. The Committee on Unemployment, originally established by the United Council, was extended to include Roman Catholic members – a very early instance of Protestant/Roman Catholic official co-operation.[8] The Irish economy did not share the experience of the British post-war boom; P. Corish has written: 'The real Irish problem in the 1950s was economic depression'.[9] It was this depression that led to unemployment and to so many young Irish people leaving home to seek their futures elsewhere.

Part of post-war reconstruction in Britain was new social legislation concerning education as well as health and social security. The 1944 Butler Education Act provided for universal secondary education and the 1946 National Health Service Act led to the foundation of the health service two years later, entitling everyone to free medical care; the 1942 Beveridge Report had formed the basis for the new system of social security. Legislation in Britain was followed by the Northern Ireland Education and Health Acts of 1947 and 1948 respectively.

Both education and health provided for much Church-State controversy in Ireland – principally, education in the North and health in the South; in Ch. III we have considered the Northern Ireland education controversies. The course of the health debate in the Republic has been clearly set forth in J.H. Whyte's *Church and State in Modern Ireland* and in Dr. Noel Browne's autobiography, *Against the Tide* where he shows the power of the Hierarchy over the Cabinet. Browne writes:

> Later Costello was to say, 'As a Catholic, I obey my authorities.' MacBride was quoted as saying, 'Those in the government who are Catholics are bound to accept the views of their Church.' Mr. Costello shrugged off any claim he might have had to being Taoiseach in a sovereign government by the letter he sent to the Archbishop (of Dublin, McQuaid) saying that the government would readily and immediately acquiesce in a decision of the hierarchy.[10]

The Hierarchy's objection to the mother-and-child scheme, and to free health services in general, was that according to the Roman Catholic Church's social teaching it was primarily the responsibility of parents to provide for their children, and not for the State to interfere except in cases of need. Browne records that during the debate he was advised by a theologian – who remains anonymous – that the hierarchy was being careful not to indicate that the scheme was contrary to *moral* teaching, but only to the Church's *social* teaching. When confronting the Cardinal Archbishop of Armagh (D'Alton) with the inconsistency in accepting the state health provisions in Northern Ireland while resisting the development of social welfare in the South, Browne had to be content with the reply: 'We are prepared neither to apologise, nor to explain'.[11]

The Church-State controversies over education and health show the Protestant and Roman Catholic Churches to have been totally unconcerned about each other's needs. The Churches were intent on exercising whatever power they could in their own interests and these post-war developments in the social and political arena reveal in the Irish Churches a sorry self-interest.

During the war and post-war years, the Protestant and Roman Catholic communities continued to be alienated from each other through the divisive issues which the war raised for Northern Ireland, and in the post-war Republic Church-State relations over health provisions merely emphasized the confessional nature of the State. There had been in the mid-1940s what P. Corish has described as 'a kind of integralist movement' in Ireland, known as 'Maria Duce', which sought an exclusive recognition of the Roman Catholic Church in the Irish Constitution.[12] Whatever the constitutional position of the Roman Catholic Church, however, its effective power over Government policy in the health debate was clear.

2.   Church of Ireland – Presbyterian Discussions on Reunion

The immediate pre-war years were marked by both success and failure in the Reunion Movement in Ireland. We shall first consider the course of developments in the Joint Church of Ireland – Presbyterian Committee for Reunion before reflecting further on the theological and ecclesiological issues which were raised in this dialogue.

The Joint Committee[13] met three times in 1932 (January, April and September), but it was not long before fears arose about its terms of reference, particularly on the Church of Ireland side. The subject of the mutual recogition of the Lord's Supper 'as celebrated in either Church (as) the Sacrament instituted by Christ' caused considerable uneasiness as some felt that such a topic was strictly not within the scope of the Church of Ireland committee's terms of reference as laid down by the General Synod of 1931. The two sides were instructed to consider, sitting separately, whether 'both Churches should agree to recognise that the Lord's Supper as celebrated in either Church is in accordance with the original institution made by Jesus Christ'.[14] When the two committees reported at the third plenary meeting (in September) the Church of Ireland side proposed that, for the moment at least, doctrinal issues should be avoided and concentration should be upon more 'practical' lines. The Presbyterians, for their part, felt that the issue of the Lord's Supper should be 'held in abeyance' but that discussion could be held on intercommunion, reciprocal Church membership, joint worship, and the administration of the sacraments in the context of such joint worship.

The plenary joint committee requested a clearer definition of the 'practical lines' which the Church of Ireland side had preferred as the way forward. During the ensuing discussion 'it became clear that there was among the representatives of the Church of Ireland some doubt as to the terms of reference (given) to their committee by the Synod of 1931, in consequence of which it was decided, on the motion of Mr. J. A. Maconchy, that further discussion should be postponed until the General Synod gave an explicit expression of its mind upon the matter.'.[15]

These clearer terms of reference were supplied in 1933 when the General Synod authorised 'the Lord Primate's Committee to carry on 'free and unrestricted Conferences' with the committee apointed by the General Assembly, 'on the basis of the Appeal to All Christian People issued in 1920' and keeping in view the Anglican and Scottish Conferences now taking place'.[16]

When the Joint Committee for Reunion reconvened in December 1933, there were differing views about how to proceed. The Presbyterians proposed continuing to discuss the sacraments and intercommunion, while the Church of Ireland representatives proposed considering what steps should be taken to provide a common ministry, as part of a scheme of complete organic union (cf. the *Appeal to All Christian People*, section 7, Lambeth 1920), on lines parallel to those of the scheme in South India.

Despite this divergence at the December meeting, the following resolution was proposed by the Presbyterian member, the Rev. John Waddell, seconded by the Dean of Belfast (W.S. Kerr), and adopted by 24 votes to 3 (the Archbishop of Dublin, Gregg, requesting that his dissent be recorded):

The Joint-Committee on Re-union recommends the supreme Courts of the two Churches to declare that

Without prejudice to the convictions held by either Church as to the preferable forms and methods of administering the rite of ordination and the sacraments of the Church,

And without prejudice to any future arrangements that may be mutually agreed upon,

Each Church fully and freely recognises, as a basis for further progress towards Union, the validity, efficacy and spiritual reality, of both ordination and sacraments, as administered in the other Church.[17]

When this report came to the General Synod in May 1934, the Primate (D'Arcy), seconded by the Archbishop of Dublin (Gregg), successfully proposed that the joint discussions be suspended until the report of the conversations of the Church of England with the Church of Scotland was published and considered by the Synod. The 1934 General Assembly, meeting in the following month, however did recognize as 'a basis for future progress towards union, the validity, efficacy and spiritual reality of both ordination and sacraments as administered in the Church of Ireland', and re-appointed the committee to continue discussions with the Church of Ireland, when the Church of Ireland similarly recognized the 'validity, efficacy and spiritual reality of Presbyterian Orders and Sacraments'.

The joint committee was thus suspended, but the report of the Church of England/Church of Scotland discussions was available later that year and the Home Reunion Committee of the General Synod requested the Standing Committee to have copies of it circulated to all General Synod members.

The English/Scottish report was fully discussed in the English Houses of Convocation in January 1935. The Upper House of Canterbury commended it 'to the sympathetic and careful study of the Church', while the Lower House desired that the Episcopal Church in Scotland should first express its opinion on the report's proposals. The year 1935 also saw the publication of a report of a series of conferences between Anglicans and Free Churchmen in England (*A Sketch of a United Church*, SPCK). This also was received sympathetically in the Convocations of Canterbury and York. The report of the Church of Ireland's Home Reunion Committee in 1935 commented:

It is indeed noteworthy and we shall do well to take account of it that almost the whole of the attention of the northern and southern Convocations at their January meetings was engaged in Reunion questions in the three reports before them, the Anglo-Scottish, the Anglo-Finnish, and the Anglo-Free Church.[18]

Against this background, the Dean of Belfast (Kerr), seconded by Mr. John Bristow, proposed at the General Synod in Dublin that the Church of England/Church of Scotland Report – already circulated – should be commended for sympathetic study in the Church of Ireland, and that '. . . The Church of Ireland fully and freely recognizes, as a basis for further progress towards union, the validity, efficacy and spiritual reality of both Ordinations and Sacraments as administered by the Presbyterian Church'. The course of the debate in relation to this latter part of Dean Kerr's resolution at the 1935 General Synod has been vividly recorded by George Seaver in his biography of Archbishop Gregg.[19] Gregg, the Archbishop of Dublin, initially objected that the proper procedure was not being observed, but the Primate's assessor, Lord Justice Best – himself a member of the Church of Ireland's Committee for Reunion consulting with its Presbyterian counterpart – ruled that there was nothing deficient in the procedure being adopted and that 'it is not really in any sense an alteration in our standards of doctrine or discipline. It (Dean Kerr's resolution) merely intends to express a view on the nature of the Orders and doctrine of another Church, without in any way altering our own.'.[20] After further debate, Gregg, convinced that this was not the best way to *start* discussions with the Presbyterian Church, and with the support of the Regius Professor of Divinity at Trinity College Dublin (Dr. Oulton), proposed an amendment which would in effect 'defer' the discussions between the Church of Ireland and the Presbyterian Church. Following Dr. Gregg's proposal the Primate (D'Arcy) indicated his preference for the original motion of Dean Kerr, but that he would rather the Archbishop of Dublin's amendment be carried than that the original proposal be rejected. Finally Archbishop Gregg's amendment was passed, and the original proposal of the Dean of Belfast – later Bishop of Down and Dromore – was abandoned. The amendment read:

The General Synod have received the Report of the Joint Committee of Representatives of the Church of Ireland and the Presbyterian Church in Ireland presented to the General Synod, 1934, and have noted its contents with interest.

It has also had opportunity to consider the Report of the Committee appointed by the Archbishop of Canterbury to confer with the Representatives of the Church of Scotland.

It has also learned the conditions prescribed by the General Assembly on June 6th, 1934, if the Representatives of the General Assembly were to engage in further discussion upon the subject of Reunion in Ireland with the Representatives of the General Synod.

And it recognises with regret that the approach to the question of Reunion in Ireland along the lines of the Appeal to All Christian People (Lambeth, 1920) or of the Lambeth resolutions of 1930, offers no present prospect of success and that further joint consideration of this important question must accordingly be deferred until more promising methods of approach disclose themslves.[21]

The conditions prescribed by the General Assembly of 1934 for further Church of Ireland – Presbyterian discussions towards union were, as noted above, that the Church of Ireland recognize 'the validity, efficacy and spiritual reality of Presbyterian Orders and Sacraments'. It should be stressed that while it was the Church of Ireland that ended these discussions, the termination was unavoidable because of the Presbyterians' insistence that their conditions be met from the outset. The Church of Ireland would have continued the discussions 'along the lines of the Appeal to All Christian People or of the Lambeth resolutions of 1930'. The 1920 Appeal expressed the conviction that the visible unity of the Church would require 'A ministry acknowledged by every part of the Church as possessing not only the inward call of the Spirit, but also the commission of Christ and the authority of the whole body', and went on to declare: 'May we not reasonably claim that the Episcopate is the one means of providing such a ministry?'[22] Resolution 31 of Lambeth 1930 endorsed the 1920 Appeal, and this position underlay the subsequent Lambeth resolutions of 1930 on the Unity of the Church (32-47). In the case of the Church of Ireland – Presbyterian discussions on reunion, the Presbyterians clearly were not prepared to accept that there could be any real problems for Anglicans in relation to non-episcopal ordinations and the consequent structure of the ordained ministry in non-episcopal Churches.

The Presbyterian Church responded to the 1935 resolution of the General Synod in the same year:

Inasmuch as the General Synod of the Church of Ireland invited this Assembly to appoint a Committee to confer with a Committee of Synod on the subject of Church Union, and the Assembly accepted the invitation on the basis of an unrestricted conference, and

Inasmuch as such Conferences can be carried on only where

there is a frank recognition by both sides that the Ministries and Sacraments of each Church are true Ministries and Sacraments of the Church of Christ, and

Inasmuch as a small minority of the members of the Episcopal Committee declined to recommend to the Synod a declaration of the validity of Presbyterian Orders and Sacraments, and

Inasmuch as the General Synod declined by a majority to adopt this declaration, put forward by a majority of their own Committee, and similar to a declaration as to the Order and Sacraments of the Church of Ireland unanimously passed by our General Assembly in 1934, the Assembly, recognising that further negotiations seem at present out of the question, thanks the Committee on Church Union for its labours in the interests of Christian Unity, and discharges it.[23]

This resolution of the 1935 General Assembly appears to cast blame on the Church of Ireland for apparent inconsistencies in the deliberations of the General Synod with regard to these discussions. It reminds us that invitation to talks was initially made by the Church of Ireland; it reminds us that the basis of the conversations was to be free and unrestricted; it indicates that the General Synod rejected the motion which was supported by a majority of its own committee. Nevertheless, in fairness, it must be pointed out that the original invitation was to discussions based on the 1920 Lambeth Appeal, and that when the terms of reference were clarified by the General Synod in 1933, it was agreed that the discussions should still be based on that Appeal. The General Assembly seems not to have taken fully into account the implications of this basis in the Lambeth Appeal for this document clearly stressed the importance of the episcopate. By insisting on a declaration from the Church of Ireland on the 'validity, efficacy and spiritual reality of Presbyterian Orders and Sacraments' at the beginning of the discussions, the Presbyterian Church was placing the Church of Ireland in a most difficult position, for such a declaration would have seemed to imply that episcopacy was dispensable.

It has been noted that Primate D'Arcy, whom Gregg described as 'an ardent advocate of Reunion',[24] was in favour of the Dean of Belfast's motion at the 1935 General Synod. D'Arcy placed an emphasis upon the fact that, in the discussions which led to the Appeal to All Christian People, Lambeth 1920 'unanimously decided to drop all consideration of the question as to the nature of 'validity' in relation to orders and sacraments, and to substitute the concept of *Reality*'.[25] The Archbishop declared: 'The former is pure legalism; the latter is open

to the test of experience'.[26] Quoting from the Lambeth 1930 Report
on Unity, D'Arcy nonetheless noted:

> . . . we do not call in question the spiritual reality of the ministries
> now exercised in non-episcopal communions. On the contrary, we
> reiterate the declaration of the Lambeth Conference of 1920, that
> 'these ministries have been manifestly blessed and owned by the
> Holy Spirit as effective means of grace'. But, out of all this, it
> becomes manifest that there is at present 'no ministry which fully
> corresponds with the purpose of God.' Yet we are persuaded that
> the historic continuity of the episcopal ministry provides evidence
> of the Divine intention in this respect such as to constitute a
> stewardship which we are bound to discharge.[27]

It might be argued that, in view of Lambeth 1920 and 1930 and the
recognition of the spiritual reality of non-episcopally ordained ministries, the Presbyterian Church was not asking for too much of the
Church of Ireland when pressing for the recognition of Presbyterian
orders and sacraments ('validity, efficacy and spiritual reality'). Yet the
essential issue for the Church of Ireland was the preservation of the
episcopate. Had the Presbyterians not pressed their point and allowed
the Anglicans time to work out what the recognition of the spiritual
reality of non-episcopally ordained ministries implied, discussion
would doubtless have continued. In the episcopate, Anglicans – as
Lambeth 1930 declared – have a stewardship to discharge; the Lambeth recognition of the spiritual reality of non-episcopally ordained
ministries was not to be taken as a declaration that the episcopate was
dispensable: on the contrary, it was of 'divine intention'.

   The reunion discussions between the Church of Ireland and the
Presbyterian Church thus very quickly came to the issue which has ever
since been these Churches' major point of difference in union
discussions – the ordained ministry. Since the early encounters of the
1930s there have been advances in the relationship between these two
Churches and in 1974 the three main Protestant Churches recognized
one another's ordained ministries as 'real and efficacious ministries of
the word and sacraments'.[28] It is noteworthy here that the concept of
'validity' was dropped in the 1974 formulation in favour of 'reality', as
at Lambeth 1920 (see further on validity/reality below, and on the
Tripartite Consultation in Ch. VI).

   The main factor which led to the rather abrupt end of these
bipartite discussions in 1935 was a differing approach on the part of
the two Churches: the Presbyterian Church wanted a recognition of its

ministry at the beginning of the dialogue process, while the Church of Ireland took the view that a reconciliation of ministries could be a fruit, rather than the starting point, of dialogue. Just as the Presbyterian – Church of Ireland discussions broke down over the ministry, so too this proved a sticking point in the Presbyterian – Methodist dialogue (1937-1947) as the issue of ministerial itinerancy provided insuperable difficulties.

In the light of more contemporary ecclesiological perspectives, certain theological themes may be identified in this debate of the 1930s and made the subject of critical reflection. The first is the subject of 'validity' and 'reality' in relation to orders; second, there is the subject of episcopacy and 'divine intention'; and third, the subject of apostolicity.

(a) Validity, efficacy and reality

When Archbishop D'Arcy commented that validity is legalism while reality is open to the test of experience, he voiced a very understandable sentiment. In exploring the pre-Tridentine origins of validity and liceity as sacramental concepts, J. A. Gurrieri has noted three 'currents' which were of formative influence:

> (1) the discussions of marriage as a contract, and whether the contract and the sacrament were separable in marriage; (2) the relationship between ordination and jurisdiction (and *potestas*), especially in the controversies over simoniac ordinations; (3) the influence of St. Augustine in the development of sacramental theology, especially the concept of objective or symbolic reality (*res et sacramentum*), and the separability of the reality and the effect in a sacrament.[29]

However even by the time of the Council of Trent (1545-63), the language of validity, although firmly in place amongst the theologians, was 'not yet the language of the papal magisterium'.[30] It was current among Anglican as well as Roman Catholic divines; Richard Hooker (1554-1600) employed the term in a way which was subordinate to the principle of divine economy.[31] However at the Council of Trent, according to Gurrieri, the vocabulary of validity was theological 'newspeak':

> There was . . . no discussion of the 'validity' of a sacrament in the Middle Ages, in the sense we understand that term. A *sacramentum*

was *verum* or *falsum*; a sacrament could be rendered *irritum*, if it was accomplished/celebrated contrary to its authentic meaning or contrary to *leges irritantes*.

This is not to say, on the other hand, that the principle of validity was never employed in the medieval period, but only that its use did not extend to the sacraments *in genere* or to the substance of the sacraments.[32]

Only after Trent did validity come to be closely involved in the sacramental teaching of the Magisterium, and, writing in 1981, Gurrieri called for a fundamental reappraisal: 'A language which entered the back door of theology because of the controversies over the sacramentality of marriage, and which has no basis in ancient tradition, should not be found in any constitution for the Church as it is presently employed in the *Lex Ecclesiae Fundamentalis*.'[33]

A sacrament is said to be 'valid' when the outward signs are correctly observed; or, as B. Leeming writes, validity is enabled to be known (although is not caused) 'because of (the) fulfilment of certain conditions in the rite which confers it, namely, due minister, matter, form, and intention'.[34] Liceity, as distinct from validity, refers to the 'complex of liturgical rites and jurisdiction'.[35] Yet it is axiomatic that God's grace is not restricted to 'valid' or 'licit' sacramental channels; Christ is present in the Church, and it is this presence that transcends validity or liceity and that makes the whole Church the 'sacrament of salvation'. So validity as a sacramental term is complemented by that of efficacy. E.J. Yarnold succinctly expresses the distinction between these two terms when he comments that 'whereas a valid sacrament must be efficacious unless the recipient resists the grace, it does not follow that an invalid sacrament is inefficacious'.[36] A sacrament can be invalid but nonetheless efficacious.

The term 'validity' belongs, nonetheless, to a former age when the Churches were conscious of themselves in contradistinction to one another. We now live in the age of ecumenism – described by Archbishop William Temple in his 1942 Canterbury enthronement sermon as 'the great new fact of our era' – when the Churches are aware of themselves more in relation to one another. Today validity as an essentially denominational term in sacramental theology is an anachronism; if it is to be used at all, the concept must be extended and developed in relation to the whole Church, for validity, like apostolicity (see below), must be given a wider ecclesiological reference. When contemporary Anglicans or Roman Catholics attend eucharistic worship in a Presbyterian or Methodist Church, for example, they can recognize the consistent efficacy of non-episcopally ordained sacramental ministries; they are 'real', and it is this concept of reality that ultimately replaces that of validity as the appropriate standard in a new age of ecumenical as opposed to denominational Christian experience. Writing in 1968, M. Villain shows clearly the power of experience:

> And now that we have begun to assimilate (Vatican II's Decree on Ecumenism), who would dare to maintain that the fruits of preaching, of eucharistic understanding and of sanctity among our Protestant brethren are but something marginally equivalent to grace? The marvel of Taizé, to quote but one universally known case, would plainly contradict such an assertion. Let us say it frankly: those fruits mature within the universal Church, they spring from the 'sacramental' character which is mysterious by definition, always alive and always operative.[37]

This is the test of reality and experience; Villain's comments reveal the potential of experience to open up new horizons in understanding between Christians of different traditions. In Ireland we have our own Taizés – such communities as Corrymeela, Columbanus, Cornerstone and Glencree – in which the experiential is given space to influence attitudes. So in terms of sacramental theology it is clear that the former ideas of validity, which Gurrieri has shown to have originated not in theology but primarily in fourteenth century canon law, must now be fundamentally revised in the light of our new opportunities for common understanding and appreciation.

(b) Episcopacy and 'Divine Intention'

If validity is to be replaced by reality as the standard in identifying truly Christian ministries and sacraments, with due respect given to constitutional and legal issues surrounding the interchangeability of ministries, where does this leave the conviction of Roman Catholics, Orthodox and Anglicans that the historic episcopate must be preserved in any Church union?

In recent reflections on the *Final Report* of the First Anglican – Roman Catholic International Commission (ARCIC-I), the Anglican theologian Paul Avis has made telling comments on the subject of divine providence and Church order. The context of Avis's remarks lies in the *Final Report*'s conclusion that 'it is possible to think that a primacy of the bishop of Rome is not contrary to the New Testament and is part of God's purpose regarding the Church's unity and catholicity, while admitting that the New Testament texts offer no sufficient basis for this.'.[38] Avis comments:

> My objection is that to appeal to the will of God manifested through his providential ordering of history is to introduce divine right by the back door. If the papacy is the will of God, and we can know that it is, whether through Scripture or providence, woe betide all who resist his will. If it is the will of God it moves up in the hierarchy of truths from things indifferent to things fundamental, from matters that are subject to discussion to claims that are non-negotiable. It begins to impinge on the area of truths necessary for salvation.[39]

There is in these observations on papal primacy a real warning to all who would appeal to divine providence in defending a particular form of Church order; Avis asks if the Eastern Churches, the Reformation, the Old Catholics, Methodism are equally 'providential'. So, in affirming that the historic episcopate is of 'divine intention', episcopal Churches must recognize the weaknesses and pitfalls of any argument based on 'the will of God'. It is salutory to recall Hooker's view, based on the principle of 'economy', stressing God's freedom and sovereignty in the Church as fundamental ecclesiological principles.[40] Today Roman Catholics may believe that the papacy is God's will for the Church, and with them Orthodox and Anglicans may hold with every conviction that the historic episcopate is of divine intention and providence, and Presbyterians may believe that the Presbyterian order is divinely providential, but none of these beliefs may be absolutized in such a way as to unChurch the others, for God is sovereign in the Church and the ministry is given to serve the Church, not the Church to serve the ministry. Within the particular ecumenical context of organic union, the real test for any Church order lies in an evaluation of the ways in which it uniquely can serve the unity, sanctity, catholicity and apostolicity of the Church, and how well it can serve the Kingdom and aid the Church to be the sacrament of the Kingdom. In terms of these objectives, the importance of the episcopate is rightly being increasingly recognized in modern ecumenical dialogues.

(c) Apostolicity and Ministry

The Nicene Creed affirms the apostolicity of the Church. Included here is, of course, the ordained ministry, but by implication rather than by specific reference. The apostolicity of the Church's ministry is a consequence of the apostolicity of the whole Church; the Church is primary and the ministry is secondary, for the Church is given a ministry, not the ministry a Church. For E. Schillebeeckx, 'the apostolicity of a christian community implies the apostolic faith and an office which proceeds from the apostolic church'; so Schillebeeckx affirms that an apostolic Church issues in an apostolic ministry: 'The apostolicity of the community of the church . . . is the basis of the apostolicity or validity of the office of the church.'.[41] Moreover, Schillebeeckx declares the considerable 'ecumenical consequences' in thus relating validity of office to apostolicity, 'since and insofar as (the Roman Catholic Church) has recognized the apostolic and therefore ecclesial character of other Christian churches at the Second Vatican Council. This means that she has implicitly accepted, to the same degree, the validity of the office in the other churches.'.[42] The apostolicity of the Church lies in its fidelity to the apostolic witness to Jesus Christ; the Church's proclamation of Jesus Christ as Son of God, Saviour and Lord is the fundamental mark of its apostolic identity.

The importance of apostolic identity, in particular on account of Gnostic heresies, led the early Church to link doctrinal apostolic continuity with the visible 'apostolic succession' of bishops. Once again it is clear that apostolic ministry is essentially related to apostolic teaching about Jesus rather than to episcopal succession as it has been traditionally understood. In recognizing an apostolic ministry, the fundamental criteria lie in the teaching of the Church about Jesus, rather than in the visible structure of its ministry. Within the New Testament the Jerusalem and the Pauline traditions reveal fundamentally different structures of ministry in the Church.[43]

Apostolicity belongs to the whole Church; for Hans Küng, 'every individual member of the Church stands in (this) apostolic succession'. The apostolic succession belongs to each believer and Küng affirms that there is, more specifically, a prophetic and also a teaching 'succession', both within the context of the primary apostolic succession of the whole Church.[44] Apostolic succession today is no longer expounded as a simplistic, mechanistic chain linking the Church of today with the apostles and with Christ but, as Küng remarks, the 'chain' still poses 'an impressive sign of the unity, catholicity and apostolicity of the Church'.[45] The episcopal succession powerfully illustrates that continuity of Christian faith and Christian life linking the Church of today with the Church of the apostles and is a stewardship which episcopal Churches must guard. J. Remmers comments, nonetheless, that in limiting the notion of apostolic succession in the

Church to succession within the hierarchy, 'the Church (i.e. the hierarchy) is set over against the People of God'[46]; rather, the apostolic succession is 'a process of succession in the mission which lies at the core of the Church',[47] the mission which is the same from the apostles' time, proclaiming the one, apostolic faith in Jesus.

There are many implications for contemporary ecumenism – in Ireland as elsewhere – in these reflections on validity, reality, episcopacy and apostolicity. The pilgrim people of God in Ireland today can easily recognize one another as 'real' Christians, belonging to 'real' Churches, with 'real' ministries and 'real' sacraments; the implications for eucharistic sharing are obvious. The apostolicity of the Church has a direct New Testament reference to mission; so in a new appreciation of our common apostolicity there lies a significant impetus for unity-in-mission.

The Protestant Churches in Ireland in the pre-war years were unable to make progress on the mutual recognition of ministries. They were, however, working with concepts and approaches which by now have given way to broader perspectives. The full implications of these broader perspectives have still to be worked out in terms of the Churches' day-to-day relations with one another.

In the post-war years developments in Church relations in India were to be of particular interest to the Irish Churches. We shall now turn to the experience of post-war Church union in South and later North India and consider the relevance of those developments to the then contemporary Irish experience.

3.   The Churches of South India and North India/Pakistan

The inauguration of the Church of South India took place in September 1947 in Madras Cathedral. The Churches participating were: the Church of India, Burma and Ceylon (Anglican), the Methodist Church, and the South India United Church (a union of former Presbyterians, Congregationalists and Dutch Reformed). The chief ecclesiological and ecumenical significance of the new Church of South India lay in the fact that it was the first ecclesial reconciliation involving episcopal and non-episcopal Churches. The union was effected in accordance with the Tranquebar Manifesto of 1919 which had proposed four principles as a basis for union:

1.   The Holy Scriptures of Old and New Testaments as containing all things necessary to salvation;

2.   The Apostles' and Nicene Creeds;
3.   The two Sacraments ordained by Christ himself – Baptism and the Lord's Supper; and
4.   The Historic Episcopate, locally adapted.[48]

The parallel correspondence of this basis with the Lambeth Quadrilateral of 1888 is striking; the non-episcopal Churches realistically recognized that any union with the Anglicans would require the continuation of the historic episcopate. However, those clergy who had been non-episcopally ordained were not re-ordained, but all future ordinations in the new Church of South India would include the episcopal laying on of hands.

Protestants in Ireland took an interest in this union particularly on account of their connections with India through missionary activities. The Irish Methodist Conference in 1948 cordially welcomed the Scheme of Union and expressed 'thanks to Almighty God for the successful completion of negotiations'. The Conference resolved that minsiters of the Irish Conference then at work in South India, and who as from September 1947 became ministers of the Church of South India, should continue in good standing with the Methodist Church in Ireland. Similarly, Methodist ministers who had been serving in India with the Methodist Missionary Society were permitted to serve in the Church of South India.[49]

The Church of Ireland was more guarded in its response. In 1951 the General Synod asked its Church Unity Committee (the post-war, re-styled Home Reunion Committee) to examine the question of the relationship between the Church of Ireland and the Church of South India. The committee drew up an eight-point response, points 4 and 8 of which we note here:

4.   That the Church of Ireland being pledged to maintain inviolate the three orders of Bishops, Priests or Presbyters, and Deacons, holds that Ministers of the Church of South India who have not been episcopally ordained should not be regarded as having acquired any new rights or status in the Church of Ireland solely by reason of the fact that they are Ministers of the Church of South India.
8.   That we earnestly look forward to the time, which we hope will not be long delayed, when our Church of Ireland will be in full communion with the Church of South India.[50]

The committee was also asked, in the light of this C.S.I. episcopal/non-episcopal union, to consider the question of intercommunion with the Presbyterian Church in Ireland, and in 1952 reported: 'In view of the Declaration prefixed to the Constitution of the Church of Ireland we regret that we are unable to propose any action in the matter.'. The Declaration mentioned pledges, at Section I.2, the Church of Ireland to 'maintain inviolate the Three Orders of Bishops, Priests or Presbyters, and Deacons' and Section III affirms that the Church of Ireland will 'maintain communion with the sister Church of England, and with all other Christian Churches agreeing in the principles of this Declaration'. Thus, in response to the new Church of South India the Church of Ireland was unable to recognize those of its clergy who had been non-episcopally ordained, in such terms as to permit full or intercommunion.

Our reflections on the validity, efficiacy, reality and apostolicity of orders (above) have indicated the new situation which has emerged in the light of a fuller appreciation of what apostolicity implies and of what efficacy demands. Understanding in these areas has developed considerably since the formation of the Church of South India; were such a situation to emerge today there would undoubtedly be much more scope for eucharistic fellowship.[51]

The Methodist Church in Ireland welcomed the formation of the Church of South India; the Church of Ireland did so also, but was not prepared to enter immediately into a state of intercommunion; the Presbyterian Church in Ireland did not comment at all. What was the significance of the Presbyterian Church's silence?

We have already referred to the missionary connection between Ireland and India as one of the reasons why Irish Protestants took an interest in the South India developments. The Presbyterian Church's connections were, however, specifically with North India where the Irish Presbyterian Mission had been involved in the United Church of Northern India (mainly Presbyterian/Congregational, but later to be part of the very different Church of North India).[52] Although there are frequent references to the later United Church of Northern India in the General Assembly's Reports and Minutes[53], apparently the Presbyterian Church took the view that the C.S.I. had nothing to do with Irish Presbyterians – it was the Church of Scotland's missionary area. Moreover, the prevailing attitude in the Presbyterian Church would not have been sympathetic to the South India scheme.

There was some considerable discussion within the Irish Presbyterian Church over plans for the formation of the Church of North India (again, to be an episcopal/non-episcopal union). Already in the 1959 General Assembly there was a move to dissociate the Presbyterian

Church in Ireland from the proposed C.N.I. and to 'inform the Church Council of Gujarat and Kathiawar that we cannot approve of their entrance into such a Church, nor undertake any obligations, financial or otherwise, in connection with it'.[54] Although this move failed, the Assembly nonetheless declared that 'the Plan does not fully, positively, and unequivocally acknowledge the validity of the sacraments and orders of any Church which has not an episcopally ordained ministry'.[55] The General Assembly would not consider the North India Plan adequate for any union in which the Presbyterian Church in Ireland might be involved, but gave an assurance that if the Church in India felt that this was the best way forward, 'the Presbyterian Church in Ireland will endeavour to co-operate with the Church in India in the future as it has done in the past'.[56]

It is clear that Irish Presbyterians could not sanction either the South or North Indian methodology of union because both were felt to deny the 'validity' of the Presbyterian Church's orders and sacraments. Just as the Presbyterian Church had insisted on such a recognition from the start in its reunion discussions with the Church of Ireland, so too this priority influenced the General Assembly's approach to the two schemes for union in India.[57] Yet, as M. Hollis has commented in relation to the ordained ministry in the C.S.I., 'The original Tranquebar message had spoken of bishops in the historic succession exercising their ministry constitutionally. The fact of episcopacy was what was held to matter, 'not any theory as to its character'.'.[58]

The Church of South India thus tried to avoid passing judgement on any of the participating denominations as they had been constituted prior to the union, by refusing to define any particular interpretation of episcopacy. Hollis has observed that the concern was 'not that history ceases to matter, but that it ceases to dominate'.[59]

When the Church of North India was inaugurated in 1970, a different procedure from that of 1947 was followed. At one service episcopal and non-episcopal ministries were united. The Anglican Consultative Council commented positively:

In this (corporate act of worship), with grateful acknowledgement of God's grace already manifested in the Churches and their ministries when they were separate, there was a prayer of humble commitment to God that he might continue to all this favour and grant to each minister 'whatever of the fulness of Christ's grace, commission and authority' he might need for his further ministry. This corporate act, carried through with the laying on of the same hands on all without discrimination, provides the channels which

had traditionally been used for the bestowing of spiritual gifts by
God. But it includes no negative judgement on the past and clearly
expresses a common and continuing dependence on the grace of
God.[60]

The Lambeth Conference consistently encouraged the Churches of
India in their quest for union. In 1930, following the publication in the
previous year of the Plan based on the 1919 Tranquebar meeting's
'manifesto', the Lambeth bishops 'strongly desired' that as soon as
negotiations were successfully completed, 'the venture should be
made and the union inaugurated'.[61] However, upon its inauguration
in 1947, the Church of South India was not in communion with the See
of Canterbury, although all ordinations in the C.S.I. after its inauguration were to include episcopal laying on of hands. Nevertheless, just
over twenty years later the Lambeth Conference of 1968, reviewing
Anglican relations with the South Indian Church in the light of the
passage of time, asked the Churches and Provinces of the Anglican
Communion to re-examine their relation to the Church of South
India 'with a view to entering into full communion with that Church'.
The Church of Ireland finally did enter into such full communion in
1978, having previously – in 1974 – entered into full communion with
the Church of North India.

   The attitudes adopted by the Irish Churches towards these Church
union developments in India illustrate Irish theological and
ecclesiological priorities. The understanding of the ordained ministry
was directly, though not radically, challenged in North and South
India. In South India episcopally ordained clergy worked alongside
those who were non-episcopally ordained until the latter eventually
disappeared, while in North India the method of unifying these
ministries was innovative.

   Clearly, the Indian Churches perceived the inter-relatedness of the
Church's mission with its unity and renewal. These were indeed
missionary Churches and, as B. Sundkler writes, already from the mid-
nineteenth century they were deeply conscious of their interdepend-
ence:

Missionaries in different parts of India found about 1850 that they
needed to meet together in conferences in the interest of their
common work. Local or Provincial Conferences were held, for
Bengal in Calcutta in 1855, for North-West India in Benares 1857,
for South India in the hill resort of Ootacamund in 1858, for the
Punjab in Lahore 1862. These local efforts were followed by the first

General Missionary Conference for the whole of India, held in Allahabad in 1872, where 136 missionaries took counsel together.[62]

We have already seen how the South Indian Plan of Union originated at the Tranquebar meeting in 1919, which itself illustrated the force of the Edinburgh Missionary Conference of 1910, and of the 1888 Lambeth Quadrilateral, in providing impetus for union. These missionary Churches of India were from the start aware of the need for close co-operation in planning missionary strategy, and soon came to recognize that mission demanded unity.

The Irish Churches were, of course, in a completely different situation; they were long-established and numerically and financially strong. There was therefore not the same sense of urgency about their mission – they could afford disunity. From this India-Ireland contrast it is clear that for mission and unity to bring renewal through a complementary and creative tension, there must first be a sense of the urgency of mission.

In their historical and religio-sociological context, the Irish Churches in this century have not sensed in any fundamental way the need for common mission in Ireland. At the time of the formation of the Churches of South and North India/Pakistan, in 1947/1970, the Irish Churches – in stark contrast to the Indian Churches – were individually self-sufficient: they could not repeat either scheme in Ireland because there was no sense of an urgent need for unity-in-mission. Self-sufficiency and complacency were the enemies of mission, unity and renewal in Ireland, while the urgency of mission impelled the Indian Churches to chart new courses for ecclesial reconciliation and Church union.

The themes of unity and mission, however, were to be kept at the forefront of thinking within the Irish Protestant Churches through the deliberations of the new World Council of Churches. While the religious divide was slow to be crossed or challenged in any fundamental ways, the Irish Churches were forced to reflect on new perspectives coming from abroad: this applied in different ways to both Protestants and Roman Catholics. Such an interchange between world and national developments in ecumenism (here, in relation to Ireland) in its own way illustrated the creative and renewing power of the fundamental mark of the Church as local and universal. Yet precisely how were the first meetings of the W.C.C. relevant to Christians in Ireland? How faithful were Irish Protestants to the imperatives of the world ecumenical movement? How did they relate the theological insights of ecumenism to praxis in Ireland?

4.   The Irish Churches and the W.C.C.: 1948-1963

The First Assembly of the World Council of Churches at Amsterdam
in 1948 was described in the report of the United Council in the
following year as marking 'a new epoch in Christian history'. Churches
throughout the world had invested many hopes in the new World
Council; representatives of 145 Churches and from forty-four nations
took part in the Amsterdam Assembly for which preparations had
been in hand since the 1937 World Conferences on Life and Work,
and Faith and Order in Oxford and Edinburgh respectively. The First
Assembly's Message to the Churches provided a reflection on the
imperative of Christian witness to God's redemptive purposes for the
world and to a just social order:

> Our coming together to form a World Council will be vain unless
> Christians and Christian congregations everywhere commit them-
> selves to the Lord of the Church in a new effort to seek together,
> where they live, to be His witnesses and servants among their
> neighbours . . . We have to learn afresh together to speak boldly in
> Christ's name both to those in power and to the people, to oppose
> terror, cruelty and race discrimination, to stand by the outcast, the
> prisoner and refugee. We have to make the Church in every place
> a voice for those who have no voice, and a home where every man
> will be at home.[63]

There was here a striking affirmation of the Church as a pilgrim
people united for mission, powerfully engaged with the struggle of the
poor and the oppressed, and in a partnership between the local and
universal community of faith. There was indeed a need for a *World*
Council, but only if it were to enable Christians, where they were, to
witness to the imperatives of the Gospel. Thus, in a direct response to
the Amsterdam Assembly, the United Council in Ireland sponsored an
'Irish Amsterdam' conference specifically to relate the themes of the
First W.C.C. Assembly to the Irish experience. This method was also
pursued after the 1954 Evanston Assembly and the 1963 Montreal
Faith and Order Conference.

While the Irish Amsterdam affirmed that 'visible unity is God's
purpose for the Church',[64] reunion was undoubtedly conceived of in
inter-Protestant terms. No Roman Catholics were present (nor had
there been Roman Catholic representation at the Amsterdam Assembly itself), and it was understandable that Protestants would think in
Protestant terms. Yet there was no affirmation that the search for

visible unity would require dialogue with Rome; indeed the conference declared that, because of the rigid attitude of the Roman Catholic Church regarding mixed marriages, social mixing between young Protestants and Roman Catholics was rendered 'dangerous'. There was a need for youth conferences to bring young Protestants together. Furthermore, the mission of the Church was conceived of principally in terms of evangelistic outreach. With regard to the social order, the dangers of marxism (atheism, materialism, oppression) were highlighted, although it was recognized that Christianity and marxism both opposed economic injustice and affirmed the brotherhood of all mankind. Nevertheless, the Irish Amsterdam meeting registered serious reservations about increased State control and State welfare provisions in Ireland, in terms that strangely echoed Roman Catholic social teaching:

> While it is recognized that controls and limitations are in some degree necessary in present circumstances, yet such governmental controls can lead to a loss of sympathy and of the human touch in social relations. So, with the State taking over health and other services, provision must be made consciously for the maintenance of voluntary effort and personal interest in social problems . . . Generosity, kindness, consideration, self-sacrifice and the other Christian virtues need scope and exercise, and especially so in a world which presents us with the new de-personalising tendencies of legislation in this age of machines and of a new mass life.[65]

In terms of the divisions in Irish society the Irish Amsterdam meeting had little to say. There was no challenge to the Churches to demonstrate how human barriers are overcome in Christ, other than a call for the promotion of mutual understanding between North and South and for 'friendly personal contacts' and an interchange of viewpoints on political issues in the spirit of goodwill. The full implications of such a call could, however, have been made the subject of much more reflection.

The second W.C.C. Assembly, at Evanston, Canada in 1954, with the theme 'Christ the Hope of the World', was similarly followed by an 'Irish Evanston' (2nd – 6th January 1956). This gathering – like the Irish Amsterdam – was concerned that discussion should be carried further at local level; the Irish Evanston recommended that the United Council should appoint an Organising Secretary specifically to forward this purpose. It was, however, for its consideration of the 'Tensions in Ireland' that the Irish Evanston marked an advance on the Irish Amsterdam; there was a more direct and specific approach to the divisions of Church and society in Ireland.

Three areas of tension were highlighted: the issue of partition; relations between the member Churches of the United Council; and between the Roman Catholic Church and the other Churches. In an introduction to this section, the report of the Irish Evanston declared:

> To speak of Jesus Christ as the hope of the world is to say something directly to the Irish situation. For it calls in question at once the pretention that identifies the policy of any single group with the ultimate good of the country . . . We say to the Churches represented here, and to those not represented, that in setting our hope upon Christ alone, a way of Christian reconciliation is open to be explored which will be reflected in our whole national life.[66]

Unlike the Irish Amsterdam, the Irish Evanston directly challenged the social and religious divide and the assumptions associated with division in Ireland. With regard to partition, there was a 'refusal to listen to one another' and no group could 'evade responsibility for a share in creating the suspicion and bitterness which underlie the political problem'. For the Irish Evanston the Churches in Ireland had a particular responsibility to bear witness to reconciliation. There was an urgent need to form local councils of Churches, but tensions between the Protestant and Roman Catholic Churches in particular clearly posed a much more fundamental challenge. The conference declared:

> The basis of our concern is the need for constant and ever renewed submission of the Church to the judgment and correction of Jesus Christ as Lord. This humble submissiveness is the only spiritual safeguard against ecclesiastical tyranny and arrogance in all the churches. Desiring to share all the riches of Christ given to our fellow-Christians, we regret that the Roman Catholic Church isolates herself from the rest of the Christian Church in our common attempt to understand the Word of the Living God to this day and generation.[67]

The mission of the Church (or Churches) in Ireland was here seen not only in terms of the evangelistic outreach – as at the Irish Amsterdam – but also more radically in terms of facing and challenging the contemporary Irish situation with all its divisions, suspicions and resentments. There was, at the Irish Evanston, an affirmation of tolerance, pluralism and diversity, and a growing awareness that Christians in Ireland had to be able 'to share all that is true in the religion of our neighbours'; they shared an allegiance to Christ but differed in their expressions of this allegiance, and they shared the same island. The Irish Evanston was one of the first inter-Church gatherings to face such issues realistically.

Delegates to the Irish Evanston recommended that a part-time officer of the United Council should be appointed to interpret the Evanston message and the ecumenical movement in general to the Churches in Ireland; by 1958, the Rev. T. Carlisle Patterson had been appointed. Mr. Patterson, a Presbyterian minister, was to be instrumental in developing interest in local councils of Churches and in the formation of the Churches' Industrial Council, as well as promoting Christian Aid Week throughout Ireland. While the original constitution of the United Council included a commitment to form local councils, this aspect of its work was to be disappointing. The fundamental difficulty was a general lack of interest, a contentedness with the *status quo* in the Churches, and the absence of any urgent sense of the Churches' common mission to the Irish people.

The New Delhi Assembly of the W.C.C. in 1961 again emphasized the importance of ecumenical work at local level. Despite the difficulties which this faced in Ireland, even between the Protestant Churches alone, by the early 1960s local councils of Churches in Strabane, Belfast, Bangor, Dun Laoghaire and Limavady were affiliated to the United Council, and councils in Dublin and Ballynahinch were soon to follow. In 1962 plans were in hand for a shared church for regular united worship between Methodist, Presbyterian and Church of Ireland people in Shannon New Town, and by that year there were over thirty centres in Ireland where Christian Aid Weeks were organized. There was no 'Irish New Delhi', and that W.C.C. Assembly's emphasis on 'all in each place' was not given any imaginatively new expression in Ireland beyond the gradual development of local councils of Churches and schemes of co-operation between the Protestant Churches.

The striking factor in these developments in Irish inter-Church relations in the early 1960s is the fact that they were, of course, inter-Protestant. The Irish Protestant and Roman Catholic Churches on the eve of the Second Vatican Council lived in almost total isolation from each other and there is no evidence to suggest that – apart from the very few – Protestants and Roman Catholics thought of themselves in any real sense as the one people of God. However, as J. H. Whyte notes, the goodwill of the Irish Government – in contrast to the attitude of the Roman Catholic Church – was shown particularly clearly during an unfortunate episode in 1957 at Fethard-on-Sea in Co. Wexford, when Church of Ireland people were 'boycotted' by local Roman Catholics on account of a dispute concerning the children of a mixed marriage.[68]

The New Delhi Assembly's emphasis on the unity of the local Church, followed by the Montreal Faith and Order Conference (and an Irish Montreal), followed finally by the 1964 Nottingham Conference,[69] all gave impetus to the renewal of union conversations between the Protestant Churches in Ireland. The Presbyterian, Congregational and Methodist Churches entered into union discussions in 1963, and the Presbyterian Church had extended an invitation, with the approval of the other two Churches, to the Church of Ireland to join the talks. J.M. Barkley has commented: 'The Synod's reply was not quite satisfactory in that it merely established three sets of bipartite talks.'.[70] With the entry of the Church of Ireland into the dialogue process, the Congregational Union withdrew. Although the Congregationalists had agreed to the invitation going to the Church of Ireland, they were in the end not prepared to discuss union with an episcopal Church. The resulting three sets of bipartite conversations merged in 1968, and the three Churches adopted a Declaration of Intent affirming their 'intention to seek together that unity which is both God's will and his gift to the Church' – an affirmation which echoed the New Delhi Assembly's definition of the unity which the Churches sought (see further Ch. VI Section 2).

We can relate certain developments in Irish inter-Church relations during the period 1948-1963 to the ecumenical witness of the World Council of Churches. However, in so far as the Protestant Churches linked mission and unity, it was with a limited perspective; the connection was largely understood in terms of co-operation in evangelism, although the Irish Evanston made challenging suggestions about facing the real religious and political tensions in Ireland. The Protestant Churches, on account of the Roman Catholic Church's stance, were unable to do other than explore possibilities for closer co-operation and union among themselves, and even here progress was slow. It is only with the advent of the Second Vatican Council and the spirit that preceded it in certain quarters in Ireland that more – although by no means many – Irish Protestants and Roman Catholics began to meet in a religious context and so gradually to become more aware of themselves as together forming the one people of God on a pilgrimage of self-discovery and towards liberation from the constraints of their different religious, cultural and national identities.

CHAPTER 5

The Second Vatican Council and the Irish Experience

1. Background to the Council

The Second Vatican Council, announced by Pope John XXIII on 25th January 1959 and opened by him in October 1962, added a new dimension to inter-Church relations throughout the world. Although termed 'ecumenical' it was nonetheless confessional, but its important significance for the Roman Catholic Church also implied a wider significance throughout the Christian world. It had this wider significance because the Council engaged in fundamental reflection on the nature of the Church and on the relationship between the Roman Catholic Church and other Churches. Here the Dogmatic Constitution on the Church (*Lumen Gentium*) and the Decree on Ecumenism (*Unitatis Redintegratio*) are of prime importance, but other Constitutions also had particular implications for ecumenism – those on the Sacred Liturgy (*Sacrosanctum Concilium*), on Divine Revelation (*Dei Verbum*) and on the Church in the Modern World (*Gaudium et Spes*). Those on the Sacred Liturgy and Divine Revelation were the full-fruits of the liturgical and biblical movements, affirming first the need for liturgical reform, and second, the critical study of Scripture and the ministry of the Word; *Gaudium et Spes* reflected the influence of the *nouvelle théologie*'s openness and positive attitude to the secular world. The Second Vatican Council was a vindication of much progressive thinking which had expressed itself in individual writers and theologians. It was John XXIII's *aggiornamento*, the renewing and modernizing of the Church to meet its mission in the modern world.

The origins of Vatican II go deep into the history of the Church in this century, and indeed further into the past. It will be necessary for us to examine briefly the context in which the Council took place and its historical antecedents. Following this background survey, we will proceed to a consideration of the Irish Churches in relation to the historical processes which led to Vatican II and in relation to the Council itself.

Modernism and Liberal Protestantism

In the nineteenth and early twentieth centuries, Protestant theology was dominated by the liberal theologians. Liberal protestantism was a force in both philosophical theology and in biblical studies. In the former, F.D.E. Schleiermacher (1768-1834), G.W.F. Hengel (1770-1831) and A. Ritschl (1822-1889) were of formative influence, while F.C. Baur (1792-1860) and D.F. Strauss (1808-1874) led in the area of biblical studies. The liberal theologians contributed their own individual approaches, but their school of thought was generally characterized by a basic questioning of traditional concepts in a way which reflected the legacy of the critical approach of the eighteenth century Enlightenment or Age of Reason, and the influence of modern science. The post-Enlightenment world demanded such a critical methodology. The biblical scholars of the liberal tradition advocated the 'scientific' study of Scripture, by applying to it the criteria of investigation which until then had been reserved for secular texts.

Modernism is the term which refers to the liberal Roman Catholic movement of the late 1800s and early twentieth century; it was countered by neoscholasticism which tried to determine both concept and method in Roman Catholic thought. Modernism was diffuse, representing a style of approach to philosophical, theological, historical and biblical studies. There were thus certain parallels with liberal protestantism, but there were also important conceptual differences. Liberal Protestants were particularly concerned with the investigation of Christian sources, while modernists stressed the concept of development in Christian history. Alfred Loisy, the author of the modernist classic, *L'Évangile et l'Église* (1902), understood the Church as developing from the Gospel and disputed Harnack's static conception of Christianity. Further, Gabriel Daly has shown how for George Tyrrell, liberal protestantism . . .

. . . by its rejection of the eschatological (or, as he preferred to put it, the apocalyptic) dimension of the Gospels, had removed the transcendent element from Christian revelation. It filled the resulting vacuum with an immanent humanism that lacked the angularities, the tensions, and the heart hunger of a drive towards transcendence expressed in apocalyptic imagery. 'The whole tendency of liberal protestantism is to minimise the transcendence by establishing a sort of identity of form between this life and the other.' 'Heaven and the Kingdom of Heaven are in our midst; they are the spiritual and moral side of life.'.[1]

In 1907 modernism was officially condemned by the Vatican in the Decree *Lamentabili Sane Exitu* and in Pius X's encyclical *Pascendi Dominici Gregis*. Measures were taken to counter the modernist 'heresy', but a development had commenced which could not be reversed. With regard to biblical studies in particular, we may note the establishment in 1890 of the progressive École Biblique in Jerusalem, under the Dominican M-J Lagrange. Although the Pontifical Biblical Institute, founded by Pius X in 1909, was initially much more conservative in outlook – indeed part of the anti-modernist programme – it did become another centre of positive scholarship: the leadership of Augustin Bea during the years 1930-1949 was a formative influence in this respect. Writing in 1966 C. Stuhlmueller could comment: 'Almost every Catholic biblical scholar today is a graduate either of L'École Biblique or the Pontifical Biblical Institute.'.[2] Nonetheless, the insights of the modernists were slow to be taken up, and the modernist crisis brought forth a conservative reaction in the form of neoscholasticism – the return to Aquinas which was imposed throughout the Roman Catholic Church. We have already seen in Chapter II how, for example, Roman Catholic social teaching as expressed particularly in the 'social encyclicals' *Rerum Novarum* and *Quadragesimo Anno* (1891 and 1931) was grounded in the neoscholastic outlook, and we have seen the essentially ultramontane complexion of the Irish Hierarchy in the 1920s and 1930s. It was this conservatism, which was so rigidly and systematically enforced in canon law, theological instruction and ecclesiastical appointments, that only gradually gave way to the modern and more open outlook characteristic of the Second Vatican Council.

Bible and Liturgy

Pope Pius XII reigned from 1939-1958. With his pontificate is associated the encyclical which specifically endorsed the critical study of Scripture and which recognized the need for scholars to use all the proven skills at their disposal in expounding and interpreting the Bible: *Divino Afflante Spiritu* (1943). Nevertheless, there were those who still clung to the more rigid, conservative form of Roman Catholic biblical studies and during the pontificate of John XXIII the critical biblical approach was under some scrutiny. Yet the approaching Second Vatican Council was to confirm the approach pioneered within the Roman Catholic Church by the modernists and endorsed by Pius XII in 1943. The biblical movement had been gaining ground since the late 1800s and was closely allied to the rise of the criticial study of Scripture in the Protestant world. Within the Roman Catholic Church it was slow to gain acceptance, but finally did so with the authority of the Vatican Council's Dogmatic Constitution on Divine Revelation:

> III,12: Seeing that, in sacred Scripture, God speaks through men in human fashion, it follows that the interpreter of sacred Scriptures, if he is to ascertain what God has wished to communicate to us,. should carefully search out the meaning which the sacred writers really had in mind, that meaning which God had thought well to manifest through the medium of their words.
>
> In determining the intention of the sacred writers, attention must be paid, *inter alia*, to literary forms for the fact is that truth is differently presented and expressed in the various types of historical writing, in prophetical and poetical texts, and in other forms of literary expression. Hence the exegete must look for the meaning which the sacred writer, in a determined situation and given the circumstances of his time and culture, intended to express and did in fact express, through the medium of a contemporary literary form. Rightly to understand what the sacred writer wanted to affirm in his work, due attention must be paid both to the customary and characteristic patterns of perception, speech and narrative which prevailed at the age of the sacred writer, and to the conventions which the people of his time followed in their dealings with one another.[3]

The first draft of the preparatory Theological Commission's text of the Constitution had been rejected and a new text subsequently prepared. R.A.F. MacKenzie has commented that the revised text (which with further revision and alterations became the document *Dei Verbum*) did not distinguish between Scripture and tradition as separate sources of revelation and was 'less philosophical, more biblical and historical', with notably more stress being laid on modern methods of interpretation.[4]

Parallel to the developments in the approach to traditional dogma and Scripture was the growing desire, already from the nineteenth century, for the laity to participate more actively in the worship of the Church. The role of the spectator would no longer satisfy the lay person who was becoming accustomed to an increasingly egalitarian society and to participating more relevantly in secular affairs.

In the nineteenth century the liturgical movement found its roots in the rich Benedictine worship, influenced by the Abbot Prosper

Guéranger of Solesmes. At the beginning of this century it was encouraged by Pope Pius X through his instructions on Church music and frequent communion, and in 1947 Pius XII officially recognized the movement in his encyclical *Mediator Dei*.

The gathering strength of the liturgical movement in the Roman Catholic Church (as in the Protestant and Anglican Churches) together with a new emphasis on the place of the laity in the life of the Church, led to particular importance being attached to the liturgy in the agenda of Vatican II. The movement for liturgical renewal and reform was a fact of the times, in the same way as the critical approach to Scripture amongst scholars was a new 'fact'. The Constitution on the Sacred Liturgy, promulgated on 4th December 1963, was the first completed work of the Council.

The liturgical movement, like the biblical movement, came to full fruition in the Second Vatican Council. Both were deeply influenced by attitudes in other Churches and contributed fundamentally to the changing outlook of the Roman Catholic Church with regard to other Christian communions.

Towards the Dogmatic Constitution on the Church and the Decree on Ecumenism

The Church is the all-pervading theme of Vatican II. Avery Dulles has recalled that 'in 1959, when John XXIII announced his intention of convening an Ecumenical Council, it was generally surmised that the coming Council would deal with the Church as its major theme'.[5] This expectation, Dulles suggests, was due to the fact that Vatican I had enacted only four of the planned fifteen chapters of the Constitution on the Church of Christ. In addition to this incomplete work there was the lack of balance for which Vatican I was criticized, and equally – if not more important – there was a growing movement demanding a new openness to Scripture, in the Church's worship, and towards Christians of other traditions. The pressures of the times were as significant a factor as any when Paul VI, in his encyclical *Ecclesiam Suam* (1964), emphasized that the Church was 'the principal object of attention' of the Council.[6]

Exponents of the new theology, pleading for a positive relationship between Church and world, were unwittingly preparing the ground for Vatican II. Bill McSweeney has written:

'Ironically, the new theology received its most systematic elaboration, not in Germany, where Catholic scholars were least inhibited by an inquisitorial Curia, but in France; it was from French theologians that the most compelling challenge to official orthodoxy originated and was sustained in the theological debates which culminated in the Second Vatican Council.'[7]

The new theology, associated principally with France and expounded by such well-known writers as Paul Couturier, Marie-Dominique Chenu, Yves Congar and Henri de Lubac, was a significant factor in the developing of a more positive attitude in Rome towards the other Churches.[8] These writers were influenced by the biblical and liturgical movements, as well as by the rediscovery of patristics which was particularly strong in France, and were pioneers whose insights challenged the Roman Catholic Church to look beyond its own confines to the witness of other Christians and to the positive elements in the life of the secular world.

Lumen Gentium and *Unitatis Redintegratio* did not, however, amount to a total reversal of the Vatican's approach to the ecumenical movement. While marking a greater openness to others, they recognized only degrees of ecclesialness in Churches not in communion with Rome. Thus *Lumen Gentium* could declare:

> This Church (the sole Church of Christ), constituted and organized as a society in the present world, subsists in the Catholic Church, which is governed by the successor of Peter and by the bishops in communion with him. Nevertheless, many elements of sanctification and of truth are found outside its visible confines. Since these are gifts belonging to the Church of Christ, they are forces impelling towards Catholic unity.[9]

The Decree on Ecumenism, promulgated on the same day as the Constitution on the Church (21 November 1964), while warning against 'any frivolous or imprudent zeal',[10] called 'all the Catholic faithful to recognize the signs of the times and to take an active and intelligent part in the work of ecumenism'.[11] Thus, K. McNamara commented in 1966:

> ... the Catholic Church has now deliberately committed itself to ecumenism, recognizing it as fully conformable to, indeed demanded by, the meaning and spirit of the Church of Christ. It has seen that its own future is profoundly linked to the progress of ecumenism. As it faces the challenges that lie ahead, it knows that the development of a truly ecumenical spirit – and for the Catholic

Church, as for every Christian Church, this is much more than a matter of goodwill towards other Christians – will be a measure of its success and a test of its fidelity to the will of Christ.[12]

This document, the Decree on Ecumenism, recognized the special position of the Eastern Churches and of the Anglican Communion as a communion 'in which Catholic traditions and institutions in part continue to exist'.[13] This basic ecclesiological principle of Vatican II, which has been termed 'degrees of ecclesialness', requires our specific consideration.

Vatican II's Ecumenical Ecclesiology

The ecclesiology of Vatican II in its ecumenical context is character-ized by the assumption, set forth in *Lumen Gentium* (cf Sections 8 and 15) and *Unitatis Redintegratio*, that the Church of Christ has been fully preserved in the Roman Catholic Church, while other Churches possess, to different degrees, ecclesial elements; their ecclesialness is seen as measurable against the standard of Rome. McNamara has written: 'The strict, exclusive identification of the Encyclical *Mystici Corporis* (1943) of the body of Christ with the Roman Catholic Church is here modified and allowance made for the genuine ecclesial character of other Christian bodies'. Nevertheless, the ecclesialness of these 'other bodies' is 'in varying degrees incomplete and defective'.[14]

All Churches are, no doubt, incomplete and defective in so far as sin is present; the constant need for renewal and purification in the Church was recognized by Vatican II. Yet is it possible to be *ecclesially* incomplete or defective?

In the New Testament, the *ecclesia* is the Christian community, the new People of God – an important theme of the Second Vatican Council. This New Testament Church is also an eschatological com-munity – again a theme of Vatican II – which, as Hans Conzelmann has written, 'on the one hand expects the consummation of salvation in the future, while on the other hand it already sees it effective in its midst, in the work of the spirit'.[15] The means of entry into the Church is by baptism. Rudolf Bultmann affirms that baptism is 'the indispen-sable condition for admission to the Congregation' and notes how in the *Didache* and in Justin Martyr's *Apology*, it is the prerequisite of participation in the eucharistic celebration.[16]

Vatican II's Decree on Ecumenism refers clearly to the new life of baptism, comparing Col. 2:12 – 'For you were buried together with him in Baptism, and in him also rose again through faith in the working of God who raised him from the dead.'. Baptism is therefore referred to in the Decree as 'a sacramental bond of unity linking all who have been reborn by means of it'.[17] However, the Decree then qualifies this statement by asserting that baptism is 'only a beginning' and that it looks forward to 'a complete incorporation into the system of salvation' and finally to 'a complete participation in Eucharistic communion'.[18] Yet, if baptism is the point of entry into the Church and incorporates into Christ, it is hardly *only* a beginning but provides a sacramental bond of immense significance. Baptism, without doubt, incorporates into Christ; this is indeed implicit in the documents of Vatican II as well as, for example, in the W.C.C.'s New Delhi definition of the aim of the ecumenical movement ('all in each place who are baptized into Jesus Christ'[19]), and more recently in the W.C.C. Faith and Order Commission's *Baptism, Eucharist and Ministry* document:

> Administered in obedience to our Lord, baptism is a sign and seal of our common discipleship. Through baptism, Christians are brought into union with Christ, with each other and with the Church of every time and place.[20]

Clearly baptism marks the point of entry into the Church; it is a beginning, but a highly significant one. It is thus not possible to speak in terms of an ecclesial body being 'partially' the Church, for it is not possible to be 'partially' in Christ: Christ cannot be divided (cf I Cor. 1:13).

The Dutch theologian, G.C. Berkouwer, who was invited by John XXIII to be an official observer at the Vatican Council, has approached this subject from another New Testament perspective. Referring to Pope Paul VI's mention of 'sheep that are wandering outside the sheepfold' in his speech at the re-opening of the Council, Berkouwer comments:

> Is such a distinction biblically allowable? *Does the Lord have sheep who are not part of His flock?* Could John the evangelist conceivably have had in mind sheep who were outside the door? His very definition of the sheep includes the fact that they are *inside* the door, that they *hear* the Shepherd's voice and *follow* him, that they are the sheep for whom the Good Shepherd lays down his life (John 10: 1-18). The picture of sheep that are outside the sheepfold – i.e. the Church – is, biblically considered, an inner contradiction [n. John 10:16 refers to 'other sheep' but these refer to the future and to the history of salvation, and have no bearing on the sheep outside the visible

Church at any given time.] The Shepherd, the sheepfold, and the sheep are uncompromisingly united each with the other so that to use the dialectic of sheep inside and sheep outside the fold is to use a biblically unwarranted device. The image of the sheepfold is parallel to that of the ark, both of which are equally sharp and clear. One can only be inside or outside the fold, inside or outside the ark, and to be inside is to be saved and to be outside is to be lost.[21]

Vatican II's ecumenical ecclesiology therefore cannot be said to be consistent with the New Testament's conception of what it means to be 'in Christ' and with the implications of baptism. There is no sustainable foundation for the concept of the 'partial' Church for there is 'one Lord, one faith, one baptism' (Eph. 4:5). The one Lord is Jesus Christ, the one faith is in him as the Son of God and Saviour, and the one baptism is the seal of union of the baptized with the Lord and with the whole body of Christ. Vatican II was biblically orientated it is true, but the Council's ecclesiology in particular remained over-developed and could not be described as biblical in its fundamentals. In the New Testament the Church is expounded in such terms as the new Israel, the Kingdom, and in terms of Christ himself; this contrasts with an essentially juridical approach which still permeates Vatican II's ecclesiology.

We have in this section surveyed the background to the Second Vatican Council and reflected on some of its documents. We now turn to the specifically Irish experience and ask how the biblical, liturgical and ecumenical movements were reflected in the life of the Irish Churches, and in particular the Roman Catholic Church, prior to the Council and in the immediately post-Conciliar years.

2. Towards Vatican II: The Irish Experience

The formation of the Glenstal Liturgical Congress, at which English and continental liturgists were often present, and of the Irish Biblical Association already in the mid-1950s (see further below) were signs that the world-wide liturgical and biblical movements found expression within Irish Roman Catholicism. Yet it cannot be claimed that Ireland made any major contribution in the earlier stages of either movement. This, however, may be contrasted not only with the ecumenical vision of the nineteenth century Roman Catholic bishop James Doyle of Kildare and Leighlin but also with a readiness on the part of many Roman Catholics in Ireland to enter into the spirit of

Vatican II as it approached and as its significance gradually became clearer through the study of its Decrees and Constitutions. Dr. John Armstrong, Church of Ireland primate from 1980-1986 and a life-long ecumenist (a founding father of the Glenstal and Greenhills conferences), noted this receptiveness especially among Roman Catholic religious who, as opposed to the parochial clergy, had more time to reflect and were more visionary in their thinking.[22] In particular, the pre-Vatican II years saw the establishment of the two progressive Roman Catholic journals, *The Furrow* and *Doctrine and Life* under the editorship of J.G. McGarry and Austin Flannery respectively. The contribution of these journals in broadening intellectual horizons was highly significant. The editors of a recent *Festschrift* to Fr. Flannery have commented: '. . . in so far as Ireland was not totally unprepared for the *bouleversement* of Vatican II, or totally unaware of the significance of its proceedings, this was almost entirely due to these two journals and their editors'.[23] J.G. McGarry, the founder and editor of *The Furrow*, was Professor of Pastoral Theology at St. Patrick's College Maynooth from 1939-1969 and was a master of the art of preaching and communication; he was renowned for his appearances on Telefís Éireann's 'Outlook' programme. The journalist Cormac MacConnell interviewed him for an article in *The Irish Press* in 1972 (19th July) and quoted his subject's poignant words which were not without a characteristic touch of humour: 'When I am preaching, I try to find the shining phrase which illuminates some experience of their (the congregation's) own . . . I think some priests perhaps don't over-estimate the capacity of a congregation to understand but perhaps do over-estimate their own ability in conveying the message.'.

McGarry's interest in preaching was to be seen in *The Furrow*, in which regular sermon notes appeared, but in a broader sense *The Furrow* itself was a new departure in communication within the Church. Professor Enda McDonagh, in an important review of his work, has written of McGarry's purpose 'of renewing the Irish Church pastorally, in mind and activity', and in an appreciation of Canon McGarry wrote:

In Irish terms *The Furrow* played a providential role in preparing for the Second Vatican Council before that council was even conceived. The theological, liturgical, ecumenical and pastoral concerns of the council had already surfaced in *The Furrow* in the 'fifties and were to receive fuller and deeper consideration in its pages in the 'sixties and 'seventies.

By a judicious combination of borrowing abroad and stimulating home production, Gerry McGarry, as editor, helped to enlarge the vision of the Irish Church and deepen its understanding to a greater degree than perhaps any other single individual in this generation.[24]

While, as Professor McDonagh has indicated, *The Furrow* did not confront socio-political issues in any fundamental or persistent manner,[25] there is no doubt that it was ecumenically pioneering. In 1963 a special Unity Octave number was issued with writers from the four main Churches. In paving the way for the Second Vatican Council in Ireland it made the most significant contribution, however, by its fresh and open general approach and ethos. The very title, *The Furrow*, came from the journal's motto, taken from Jeremiah 4:3 – 'Yours to drive a new furrow, nor sow any longer among the briars.'. Thus McGarry was instrumental in promoting renewal in the Church. This renewal which he – and Flannery – enabled, touched upon the whole spectrum of Church life and experience in Ireland. The Archbishop of Tuam (Cunane), paying tribute to Canon McGarry after his death in a road accident in 1977, said: 'In the days before the Second Vatican Council he contributed more than most to preparing people for renewal within the Church. There was no element of renewal within the Irish Church of which Canon McGarry was not a leading and inspired advocate.'.[26]

J.G. McGarry's purpose was to assist renewal so that the Church's mission could go forward in the modern era. As a pastorally committed priest and theologian he recognized that renewal required an effective channel of communication. The type of renewal which he established was significant because it was, above all, contemporary. With mission and renewal firmly coalescing in his thought it was natural that ecumenism should come to the fore. This was an area in which *The Furrow* made important advances, for regular contributions from members of other Churches became a marked feature, especially from the 1960s. McGarry's renewal had wide horizons; just as *The Furrow* pioneered in Irish ecumenism, so there was an implicit recognition of diversity in the Church, although the full implications of ecclesial diversity were not and still have not generally been fully recognized. *The Furrow* was given an international dimension by the contributions from abroad, especially from continental theologians whose articles appeared in translation. Here McGarry saw that the local Church in Ireland could find renewal only through exposure to the outside world and to the thought of theologians from other environments with new insights to share. *The Furrow* was, from its first number in 1950, on a journey of challenge and exploration; neither it nor *Doctrine and Life* ever was apologetic in the style of the early *Christus Rex*, nor did either journal ever follow the comparative style in ecumenism such as was characteristic of the earlier Mercier Society, but both represented the searchings of a pilgrimage into a new age of Church life.

The approach of these two adventurous journals was, however, an exception to the general attitude amongst Roman Catholics in Ireland towards other Churches. In the 1950s and early 1960s the Roman Catholic Church still regarded Christians of other traditions strictly as *extra ecclesiam*. Writing in 1954 Bishop Stephen Neill could declare: '. . . there is a deep incompatibility between the Roman Catholic ideals of unity and those professed by all the other Churches'[27]; the way to unity was through a return to Rome. The position of the Roman Catholic Church in relation to other Churches was treated of in two encyclicals of Pope Pius XII, *Mystici Corporis* (1943) and *Humani Generis* (1950). In the former, despite the fact that it came in the same year as the forward-looking *Divino Afflante Spiritu* (on Scripture), the Church was defined in exclusive terms as 'the Holy, Catholic, Apostolic, and Roman Church'.[28] In the latter encyclical, *Humani Generis*, there was no relaxation of any of the prevalent official attitudes, although the Holy Office's Instruction of the previous year had permitted restricted ecumenical contact.

William Conway (later Cardinal Archbishop of Armagh) commented on this 1949 *Instruction of the Holy Office on Religious Unity* in the very reserved terms of a canon lawyer, unenthusiastic about ecumenical encounter. He interpreted the purpose of the document as dealing with the 'problem' arising 'from the fact that there are, at the present time, many millions of people who profess belief in Christ but who are actually cut off from the Church of Christ. The divine mission of the Church 'to preach the Gospel to every creature' applies to these non-Catholics no less than to the millions of 'non-Christians' who are also outside the Church.'. Regarding 'round-table conferences', Conway commented: 'There is the danger that Catholics, in accepting merely equal rights of speaking at the meeting, may give the impression that they accept the principle that the Catholic Church is on an equal footing with other religious bodies.'. He pointed out that 'the Instruction contains no direction or recommendation, express or implied, that such 'round-table' conferences be authorized or attended. It reminds local Ordinaries of their duty to do all in their power to further the return of non-Catholics to the Church, but it leaves it to each local Ordinary to decide what means are practicable and prudent in his own diocese.'.[29]

Conway himself was closely involved in the training of Irish priests and had a great influence on a generation of clergy. His attitude at the time did not give any priority to the demands of ecumenism and his approach is in stark contrast to that of McGarry.

A considerably more hopeful outlook was evidenced in Fr. P.J. Devine's comments on the 1949 Instruction in an article in *The Furrow* of January 1956; he described it as 'something very positive and an advance on the previous *monitum* (1948), which reserved all contact to the Holy See'. Fr. Devine concluded his article by referring to the Church Unity prayer octave:

> If we all really enter into the spirit of the Octave, there is no doubt that one of the fruits would be less bigotry and more sympathy and understanding between all Christians, a nearer approach to the 'one fold and one Shepherd''.[30]

The ecclesiological perception of William Conway, as opposed to P.J. Devine, here betrayed a characteristically conservative view; there was no hint of a changing situation and an opening for new relationships.

The promulgation of the Dogma of the Assumption of the Blessed Virgin Mary in November 1950 was widely regretted by those outside the Roman communion. The Church of Ireland bishops issued a pastoral letter to be read in all churches on Sunday 10th December. Signed by the Archbishops of Armagh and Dublin (Gregg and Barton) on behalf of the House of Bishops, the letter declared:

> By its various enlargements of the ancient Catholic Creed to contain the twelve new articles of Pope Pius IV's creed, the two new articles of Pius IX in 1854 amd 1870, and this new dogma of 1950, the Roman Catholic Church is shutting itself further and further away from the rest of Catholic Christendom into being a self-enclosed corporation – a sectarian organisation, governed by its own private and self-determined Rule of Faith, which those who are content with the ancient Rule of Faith and the Primitive Church Order, can only reject as heretical.[31]

The Church of Ireland bishops felt clearly, and strongly, that the new dogma was erroneous, and they affirmed the faith of the primitive Church as definitive. The statement however expresses a regret that the Roman Catholic Church should choose to place such an obstacle of faith between itself and the rest of the Christian world; there was thus an ecumenical perspective to their response. The dogma itself illustrated the Roman Catholic Church's self-understanding as possessing a monopoly of Christian truth.

The traditional position of Roman Catholicism with regard to other Christians is, understandably, echoed in many articles in contemporary journals of the period in Ireland. We have already seen, in Chapter II, how the Mercier Society in Dublin and the Clonard Mission in Belfast in the 1940s were founded essentially out of a convert motivation, although were to develop into a more open dialogue between Protestants and Roman Catholics. While in certain quarters there was such a growing openness, however, the overwhelmingly prevalent approach of Roman Catholics in Ireland was to look for the return of Protestants to the 'one, true Church'.

These observations are not to suggest that while Roman Catholics saw those in other Churches as in need of conversion, other Christians did not hold similar views about Roman Catholics. If Rome envisaged unity in terms of 'return', equally very many Protestants could envisage Christian unity with Roman Catholics only through their embracing the Reformation faith. There can be no doubt that this was the prevailing attitude on both sides of the religious divide in Ireland in the 1940s and 1950s, as in earlier years.

J.H. Whyte has been able to show, however, that historians are apparently in unanimous agreement that 'towards the end of the nineteen-fifties, Ireland as a whole, and not just Irish society in its religious aspect, passed some kind of turning-point'.[32] In showing that there is even agreement on the nature of this turning-point, Whyte records:

> Mr. (Donald) Connery speaks of a move from inertia to ferment. Mr. (Alan) Bestic notes more frankness of discussion and less sensitivity to outside criticism. Mr. Charles McCarthy says that 'there has been a remarkable change in our society in recent years, a growth of frankness, a growth of moral maturity'. Mr. T.P. Coogan says: 'In the last few years an enormous psychological change has occurred in Ireland. The conviction that things could be improved has dawned on a people conditioned to believe that they could only get worse'. Mr. Garret FitzGerald speaks of 'a transformation of the economy of the Republic and, most important of all perhaps, a transformation of the outlook of the Irish People'.[33]

This general change in Irish attitudes and outlook was ultimately to be given additional impetus through the advent of R.T.E. television broadcasting in the Republic and was not without a bearing upon the new situation which was dawning for the Church with the advent of the Second Vatican Council. Ireland was, to an increasing extent, receptive to new ideas and to change.

In the Unity Octave issue of *The Furrow* in 1963 – itself an important event – Abbot Joseph Dowdall noted the change in the title of the votive Mass for Unity from *Ad Tollendum Schisma* to *Pro Unitate Ecclesia* in 1961, and Fr. Denis Faul wrote frankly about the state of ecumenism in Ireland:

> At the beginning of a survey of recent Catholic ecumenical work, honesty makes one admit that before the accession of Pope John XXIII on 28 October 1958 any individuals or groups of Catholic religious or laity engaged in ecumenical work were regarded by many of us here in Ireland as good-natured eccentrics. Then overnight leaders exchanged friendly visits and we were forced to recast our thoughts. It is time now to do our ecumenical homework. . .[34]

A definite interest in ecumenism was further evidenced amongst Irish Roman Catholics at this time in three publications in particular: M. Hurley's *Towards Christian Unity*, E. McDonagh's *Roman Catholics and Unity*, and K. McNamara's *Christian Unity* (the 1961 Maynooth Summer School's papers). To varying degrees these publications displayed ecumenical openness. The booklet by Fr. Hurley, who has become one of the foremost Roman Catholic ecumenists in Ireland, was a highly competent survey of the ecumenical movement which he categorically affirmed as not just for those outside the Roman Catholic Church, but was a movement 'created and maintained by Catholics and non-Catholics'; Hurley was countering the view that ecumenism was the work of those outside the Roman Catholic Church, to find their way back to Rome.[35]

A similar approach was adopted by all the speakers at the Maynooth Summer School in 1961. The breadth, and depth, of the ecumenical subjects covered was illustrative of the profound seriousness with which ecumenism was being considered within the Roman Catholic Church in Ireland. The lecturers, eminent and accomplished churchmen and theologians from Britain, Europe and America, as well as Ireland, were however all Roman Catholics. It is remarkable how the papers – three years before Vatican II's Constitution on the Church and Decree on Ecumenism – reflect what today would be described as a conservative interpretation of the Council's ecumenical theology. In clearly pre-Conciliar tones (this was indeed prior to the Council), the Bishop of Pittsburgh (J. Wright) could compare the Reformation

Churches' search for reunion with Rome with the parable of the Prodigal Son; F. Clark (of Heythrop College, Oxford) envisaged Anglican-Roman Catholic reunion in terms of a uniate relationship involving those Anglican Churches which at the time were most 'Catholic', ultimately finding sufficient agreement with Rome to enter into this kind of relationship. Comparing such a development with the South Indian Church, Clark suggested:

> If Evangelical Anglicans in South India, under the pressure of changed circumstances and in the presence of a pagan majority, could sink their old differences with Nonconformists and could enter an inter-denominational merger with former Presbyterians, Congregationalists and Methodists, why should it be out of the question that a body of Anglo-Catholics in some other part of the world could decide to seek communion with the Catholic Church and its Sovereign Pontiff, either by complete integration or by the formation of a new 'uniate' rite? Such a development might in time have far-reaching effects throughout the Anglican Communion, and eventually (who can tell) even in the Church of England itself.[36]

This approach was fully compatible with K. McNamara's contribution in which he extolled the concept of 'vestigia Ecclesiae', or the 'partial Church', upon which we have reflected above. More positively, McNamara and J. Höfer (Paderborn) referred to the significance of baptism among the 'separated brethren', the latter indicating that although Protestants were 'separated from us by historical forces and dogmatic reasons' they were nevertheless 'united with us through Baptism and faith in Jesus Christ, the Son of God, our Redeemer'[37] – a position which was being repeatedly expounded at the time by Cardinal Bea.[38] Again, P. J. Hamell, in a balanced account of the ecumenical movement in the 20th century, noted the particular significance of Orthodox membership of the W.C.C.[39]: 'In the World Council of Churches the Orthodox claim to be the true and sole Church of Christ and that Christian Unity involves a return of all to Orthodoxy.'.[40]

The implicit point, that if the Orthodox could do this, why could not the Roman Catholic Church, was not elaborated. However, this was a point which Enda McDonagh discussed further in his *Roman Catholics and Unity*; he wrote: '. . . it would seem that in principle there is nothing to prevent the Roman Church from becoming a member of the World Council. Such membership would not of itself compromise her claims to be the one true Church of Christ', although McDonagh felt that the W.C.C. and many Roman Catholics were not prepared for such a development.[41] Referring to the importance of prayer in the ecumenical movement, he continued:

> . . . although Roman Catholics believe that they have all the essential unity willed by Christ, they do not know how or when that unity will be fulfilled in others. They (Roman Catholics) abandon themselves to Christ's will and without any insincerity or yet any relinquishing of what they have from Christ, pray as He taught us all to pray – that the Father's Will be done.'.[42]

It must be emphasized that in the course of the ecumenical experience of the subsequent twenty-five years, these individual authors have expressed their thoughts with ever increasing openness and have contributed in remarkable ways to the development of Irish ecumenism and to the Churches' common ministry of reconciliation. Nevertheless, the general approach to be found amongst Roman Catholics in Ireland on the eve of the Vatican Council was marked not only by a growing readiness on the part of some for ecumenical dialogue, but also – as might be expected – by a relatively fixed, traditional Roman Catholic ecclesiology. There was undoubtedly a new openness, as evidenced in the journals, in the developing theological reflection at Maynooth and in specific writers. Although this was still a pre-Conciliar situation there were definite signs of the *aggiornamento* and more developed ecumenical commitment which was to come; the authority which these new approaches received in the Council's documents was to give further impetus to ecumenical reflection, and action, in Ireland.

Three final instances of the developing ecumenical experience in Ireland as the Vatican Council commenced its deliberations are to be noted. On 7th November 1962 Professor McNamara addressed the Methodist Junior Ministers' Conference at Cloughjordan, Co. Tipperary. In an account of this occasion he displayed a readiness for dialogue combined with a reserved ecclesiological perspective:

> In my address I referred to the special conditions in which Catholics engage in ecumenical discussion. Unlike other groups, for whom the eventuality of a change in the structure of their Church may not be excluded, Catholics can envisage reunion only as taking place within the framework of their own communion. At the same time it is possible to display the ecumenical virtues of courage and renunciation by being prepared for reforms within the Catholic Church

which do not endanger any essential part of its life and structure but nevertheless remove genuine obstacles to reunion.[43]

Although very measured in its tones, this account cannot conceal the highly significant nature of that meeting between a Roman Catholic Professor from Maynooth and Methodist clergy in 1962. It was a remarkable occasion for its time, and the fact that it took place at all was of infinitely greater importance than the actual content of the exchanges which were made possible. It was a cordial meeting of churchmen across a great divide.

In that same year, 1962, the Church of Ireland officially issued a prayer for the Second Vatican Council,[44] and when Pope John XXIII died in the following year, the Presbyterian General Assembly, which was in session when the Pope's death was announced, stood in silence as a mark of respect. The Moderator, the Rev. Dr. W.A. Montgomery, declared: 'The death of Pope John is a matter for sincere regret to all Christian people. In him the graces of a Christian have been made apparent to all.'.[45]

In the January 1963 Unity Octave issue of *The Furrow*, to which we have already referred above, a Symposium on Church Unity was published with contributions from a Presbyterian, a Methodist, an Anglican and a Roman Catholic. The Rev. J.L.M. Haire (later Moderator), the Presbyterian contributor, paid tribute to the Abbé Couturier, for it was 'due to him more than to anyone else that a week of prayer for Christian unity is observed, not only by his own Church but by almost all the Churches, Protestant, Orthodox and Anglican, which belong to the World Council of Churches'.[46] He also drew attention to the new signs of co-operation between Protestants and Roman Catholics in Belfast, in the Churches' Industrial Council, 'where union leaders connected with the Churches seek for ways of improving employment and industrial conditions', and to the fact that for some time there had been co-operation between the governing bodies of grammar schools, and between Roman Catholics and Quakers in the area of refugee relief.

In this issue of *The Furrow*, the Roman Catholic contributor, Fr. Michael Hurley, wrote of the Unity Octave:

Prayer for those of our brethren in Christ who are not in full communion with us is the chief means at our disposal for filling our hearts with love and charity towards these separated brethren and thereby emptying them of all that pride and prejudice, all that arrogance and antipathy, or worse still of all that apathy and indifference by which we hinder the fulfilment of God's will for the unity of His people. Prayer is a mediation of love; its cause as well as its effect. Our prayer for others expresses our love for them but also nourishes and deepens it.[47]

Given these beginnings of outreach between Roman Catholics and Protestants, there can be no doubt that there were significant signs of ecumenical 'movement' in Ireland. Especially for Roman Catholics, however, all eyes were now fixed on Rome and the work of the Council.

3.   The Response to Vatican II in Ireland

During a visit to Ireland in 1985 Cardinal Jan Willebrands, President of the Secretariat for Promoting Christian Unity (established by Pope John XXIII in 1960 under Cardinal Bea in preparation for the Council) reflected on the subject, 'Twenty Years Since Vatican II', recalling how at the opening of the second session of the Council in 1963, Pope Paul VI set forth his presentation of the goals of the Council. These were summarized by Cardinal Willebrands under four headings: the nature of the Church, the renewal of the Church, the restoration of unity among all Christians, and dialogue between the Church and the modern world. Most significantly, Willebrands stressed how ecumenical concern had been pivotal in the whole work of the Council:

> It was, so to speak, a crucial and central point on which the Council's other three goals converged, and which in turn presupposed and called for them. To speak of the restoration of unity you must first work for a more precise definition of the Church, one which will make due allowance for the ecclesial reality of other Christian communities. So too the hopes for unity were closely linked to the renewal of the Church and with the needs of the modern world, and thus imposed the duty of a common witness to all Christians so that the Gospel could be more effectively proclaimed in a way that would meet the real and often tragic need of our day.[48]

Given this centrality of the ecumenical concern, it is all the more appropriate to ask how the Council influenced ecumenical life in Ireland and what its ecumenical fruits were amongst Irish Christians.

The Decree on Ecumenism was promulgated by the third session of Vatican II (Sept. – Nov. 1964), but already in June of 1964 a major,

unofficial ecumenical step had been taken in Ireland with the convening of the first Glenstal Ecumenical Conference. Although there had
already been other more informal meetings between Roman Catholics and Protestants, Glenstal 1964 was marked by what Joan Turner
has described as 'a sense of going into the unknown'.[49]

Discussion at the first Glenstal Conference was on the theme of
liturgy, with particular reference to Vatican II's Constitution on the
Sacred Liturgy (December 1963), and papers were presented
by Roman Catholic, Anglican, Presbyterian and Methodist speakers.[50]
The world-wide liturgical movement had found expression not only
in the Roman Catholic Church in Ireland through the Glenstal
Liturgical Congress, but also in the Church of Ireland Parish and
People movement. Closely related to the English Parish and People,
it organized national and regional liturgical conferences in
Ireland between 1952 and 1962, when many of the leading figures
became members of the Church of Ireland's Liturgical Advisory
Committee (which drafted the Alternative Prayer Book of
1984). Deans Gilbert Mayes and Charles Gray-Stack provided a link
between the new meetings at Glenstal and this earlier Anglican
movement.

Two years after the Glenstal Conference was founded, the first
Greenhills Ecumenical Conference was held at the Greenhills Presentation Convent near Drogheda. Like Glenstal this became an
annual occasion, being held during the Week of Prayer for Christian Unity, but relationships have developed more easily at Glenstal,
which has been residential, than at the one-day Greenhills meeting.
Both Glenstal and Greenhills have featured specially invited speakers on a chosen subject and maintained a high standard of reflection. Although numerically limited, they have provided a focus of
wider ecumenical life in Ireland, as distinct from the work of officially structured bodies, and they have served as a constant and
regular encouragement for committed ecumenists. Both undoubtedly are to be seen as having been enabled, to some extent at least,
by the Second Vatican Council. However, even without the formal
authority of the Conciliar decrees they, or similar meetings, would
surely have emerged as an expression of the growing openness
towards ecumenism on the part of many Roman Catholics in Ireland even before the Council, as also of many Protestants who
desired such ecumenical growth. The real test of the Council, however, is surely to be found in the degree to which the Roman Catholic Church officially and institutionally identified with Vatican II's
new approaches to the whole area of ecumenism. The leadership

which the Council gave was particularly intended to be the basis for new initiatives throughout the Roman Catholic Church, under the authority of its local Hierarchies.

Returning from the Council to Dublin in 1965, Archbishop McQuaid could declare:

> Now is our work completed, in union with the Pope our decrees were drafted, voted on and proclaimed. One could not but feel that God the Holy Ghost had guided our deliberations. You may have been worried by much talk of changes to come. Allow me to reassure you. No change will worry the tranquility of your Christian lives. As the months will pass, gradually the Holy Father will instruct us how to put into effect the enactments of the Council. With complete loyalty as children of the one true Church we fully accept each and every decree of the Council.[51]

The Council, however, had been all about change and modernisation – *aggiornamento* – in the Church, and Archbishop McQuaid's words appear as an ominous attempt to pacify the Church and to reassure Roman Catholics in Ireland that there would, in effect, be need for little change in their lives and in their Christian experience.

While the Church of Ireland could welcome the Decree on Ecumenism as encouraging 'many members of (the Roman Catholic Church) both clerical and lay to express their interest in what other Churches are thinking and doing',[52] and while, for example, the Rev. J.C. Breakey could declare at the 1963 General Assembly, 'We cannot afford to hold aloof from this historic Church (the Roman Catholic Church), but when a hand is stretched out to us, we must grasp it in the spirit of Christian faith and love',[53] there was to be little immediate effect on Church relations in Ireland. As Alan Falconer wrote in 1985, reflecting on the fruits of Vatican II in Ireland, and recognizing Protestants' hesitations in committing themselves to the 'ecumenical pilgrimage', progress in ecumenical awareness within the Roman Catholic Church in Ireland has been limited: 'In the field of theological education, for example, little explicit attention has been paid to the life, thought and practice of other Christian traditions or to inter-church theological approaches. In attitudes towards society, little joint deliberation is evident.'.[54] In elaborating on both of these points, Falconer refers first to a study by C. O'Mahony, 'Education in Ecumenism of the Roman Catholic Clergy in Ireland', which revealed 'remarkably little action or interest in this with the exception of one seminary in the south east'. Regarding the lack of joint deliberation on social issues, Falconer notes in particular those of divorce, abortion and the Forum report.[55]

More immediately after the Council, however, two semi-official developments within the Roman Catholic Church in Ireland were to have increasing ecumenical significance: the formation of the Irish Theological and Biblical Associations in 1965-66. These were 'semi-official' in so far as their constitutions were approved by the Hierarchy. The ITA was originally proposed by priests engaged in teaching theology, who felt 'that there is a special need at the present time for an Irish Theological Association to study and discuss matters of particular interest to teachers of theology'.[56] This proposal was approved by the Hierarchy, together with a draft constitution. Conversely, the formation of the IBA (then styled the Catholic Biblical Association of Ireland) was suggested by the Hierarchy itself. Invitations were sent 'to professors of Scripture and others with a Licentiate in Scripture' to attend a meeting to establish the Association.[57] Fr. J.A. O'Flynn of Maynooth had been requested by the Hierarchy to arrange for this meeting, which took place at Maynooth in February 1966 with Monsignor P. Boylan in the Chair. Cardinal Conway addressed the meeting personally, affirming that both the ITA and IBA 'could do very important work in harvesting the fruits of Vatican II'.[58] Both Associations first admitted Protestants to associate membership, and then as full members; the Catholic Biblical Association changed its name to the Irish Biblical Association in 1968 (an earlier IBA had been formed in 1955 as a private and unofficial meeting).

The ecumenical dimension to theological work had already been reflected in the pages of the *Irish Theological Quarterly* which had been revived in 1951 and was edited at Maynooth. Particularly from the late 1950s its concerns included ecumenism, although it was not until the late 1960s that the work of Protestant contributors began to appear.[59] Roman Catholic theologians in Ireland had seen the value and importance of dialogue and exchange with one another, and the need to take Protestant theological perspectives into account. Vatican II's clear affirmation of ecumenical discussion, particularly amongst experts and specialist theologians, enabled the Hierarchy to approve such contact as was proposed, and was developed, in the ITA and IBA. Section 9 of the Decree on Ecumenism was particularly relevant in this connection:

We must come to understand the outlook of our separated brethren. Study is absolutely required for this, and should be pursued with fidelity to truth and in a spirit of good will . . . Of great value for this purpose are meetings between the two sides, especially for discussion of theological problems, where each can deal with the other on an equal footing. Such meetings require that those who take part in them under authoritative guidance be truly competent. From dialogue of this sort will emerge still more clearly what the true posture of the Catholic Church is. In this way, too, we will better understand that attitude of our separated brethren and more aptly present our own belief.[60]

In terms of institutional Church relations, however, it took rather longer for specific developments to emerge in Ireland. In 1970 the Irish Council of Churches (formerly the United Council) and the Roman Catholic Church formed a 'Joint Group on Social Problems', although paradoxically this group was not to tackle problems directly related to the Troubles, but was to advise the Hierarchy and the I.C.C. and its member Churches 'on the role of the Churches in Irish Society on such matters as world poverty, employment and housing conditions, drug addiction, alcoholism etc.'. A report on *Violence in Ireland* was undertaken by the Joint Group only with special permission (and was published in 1976). Clearly, the *raison d'être* of the Joint Group was not to give consideration to the Troubles, but simply to be an exercise in working together. In its first report this purpose was admitted:

> As anticipated, the Group normally operates through working parties which it appoints to undertake specialist work in certain fields. In each of the three working parties already appointed (Drug Abuse, Alcohol among Young People, Housing) there are about twenty members, drawn fairly evenly from both parts of Ireland, and only three or four of whom are members of the Joint Group . . .
>
> In normal times the work of the Joint Group would have been acknowledged as important for the life of the nation as a whole and the Churches' place in that life. In the context of the present upheaval, however, it might appear to some that we have been concerning ourselves almost with trifles. It is nonetheless astonishing that we have met at all – in view of the disintegration going on around us – and have continued to do so regularly not only in the group itself, but also in its working parties.[61]

The 'Ballymascanlon Talks', however, were to have a much broader frame of reference. Eight years after the close of the Vatican Council, the first Irish 'Inter-Church Meeting' was held – at the Ballymascanlon Hotel, Dundalk (26th September 1973).[62] In its report of 1974 the

Irish Council of Churches described this meeting as 'an enormous step forward for inter-Church relations in our country', and was confident that 'the experience of the past few years helped to bring it about'. This was a reference to the Troubles which had erupted in 1968; there can be no doubt that the Churches were convinced of their obligation to witness together, in some way, in the face of growing sectarianism and violence.

At the first 'Ballymascanlon' in 1973 there were sessions on (1) Church/Scripture/Authority, (2) Social and Community Problems, (3) Baptism/Eucharist/Marriage, and (4) Christianity and Secularism. Four working parties were formed on these subjects, and the final reports of these working parties were presented at the third Ballymascanlon Conference, on 23rd April 1975. The Ballymascanlon process was undoubtedly given urgency by the Troubles and as a witness against sectarianism, but as a venture in ecumenical reflection on important theological subjects it appears more as a dialogue furthering – for the Irish Hierarchy – the theological imperatives of the Vatican Council such as were anticipated by Pope Paul VI's four goals for the Council (see above). Indeed, when the establishment of the Inter-Church Meeting was being considered, it was Cardinal Conway who suggested that the range of issues to be discussed should be extended beyond practical, divisive matters, as the I.C.C. had initially suggested, to include specific theological subjects.[63] Furthermore, the 1975 report of the Inter-Church Meeting's working party on Church/Scripture/Authority in particular was to illustrate the Roman Catholic participants' reliance on the documents of Vatican II. (See Ch. VI further on the Joint Group and the Inter-Church Meeting.)

The ecumenical experience in Ireland surrounding the Vatican Council suggests several ways in which the preparations for, and the decrees of, the Council were of influence. First, as a result of the mediation in Ireland – through such journals as *The Furrow* and *Doctrine and Life* – of new theological approaches particularly evident on the continent, Irish Roman Catholics were being unintentionally prepared for the coming Council. Vatican II itself emphasized the need for 'competent' ecumenical dialogue, and there had been historic visits of Church leaders to Rome,[64] as well as official observers from other Churches present during the Council. As a result of the Council, the Vatican embarked on a series of international ecumenical dialogues, co-ordinated through its Secretariat for Promoting Christian Unity.[65] In Ireland, as we have seen, the Roman Catholic Hierarchy approved the formation of the Irish Theological and Biblical Associations, with Cardinal Conway specifically relating these to the process of renewal called for by the Council. The Glenstal and Greenhills Conferences contributed in an unofficial but highly competent way to the promotion of ecumenical dialogue in Ireland. Finally, the Irish Council of Churches/Roman Catholic Church Joint Group on Social Problems and the Ballymascanlon Inter-Church Meeting were, for the Roman Catholic Church, conducted within the framework for ecumenical development affirmed, elaborated and endorsed by Vatican II. The Council's authoritative summoning to ecumenical action has been reflected in the Irish Roman Catholic Church's sustained commitment to the Ballymascanlon process. While there have been public perceptions of Ballymascanlon as a failed attempt to promote peace in Ireland and to overcome practical differences between Roman Catholics and Protestants, these have been founded on a mistaken understanding of how the Roman Catholic Church must understand the process, namely as a theological dialogue, including discussion of moral and social issues, in response to the Conciliar decrees. It is by accident of history that this encounter takes place within, and has been given added urgency by, the wider Irish contemporary context of violence, sectarianism and alienation.

Given this historical coincidence, however, the Inter-Church Meeting faces an added challenge which it may not neglect, and a more obvious responsibility to improve wider Protestant – Roman Catholic relations through tackling specific practical issues, and overcoming them as a witness to the reality of reconciliation not only as a pastoral concept but – more important – as a truly possible experience.

CHAPTER 6

Aspects of Church Relations Since 1968

The late 1960s were unsettled years in many different parts of the world. In 1968 the assassinations of Martin Luther King and Robert Kennedy, only three years after President Kennedy himself was assassinated, were a shocking indication that there were festering resentments beneath the successful surface of American society. Although peace talks between North Vietnam and the United States were opened in Paris in May 1968, the war in Vietnam remained a constant horror, leading to many demonstrations in capital cities. The Russian invasion of Czechoslovakia was a cruel blow to reform. Student riots in 1968, particularly notable in Paris, were a violent expression of the frustration and anger of young people rejecting establishment authoritarianism and sensing the need for a more just social order. In its Message, the Fourth Assembly of the World Council of Churches at Uppsala, Sweden in 1968 recognized the confusion of the times: 'We hear the cry of those who long for peace; of the hungry and exploited who demand bread and justice; of the victims of discrimination who claim human dignity; and of the increasing millions who seek for the meaning of life. God hears these cries and judges us.'.[1]

In Northern Ireland attempts by the Prime Minister, Terence O'Neill, to develop co-operation between North and South, symbolically expressed most clearly in the visit of the Taoiseach, Mr Sean Lemass, to Stormont in 1965, were to raise resentments and fears among unionists,[2] and the outbreak of the Troubles in 1968 came as a violent expression of frustration and alienation. The Civil Rights Movement, as an expression of the minority community's feelings, was to be replaced by the intimidation, violence and terror of the IRA which gradually came to dominate the nationalist people, especially in Londonderry, West Belfast, Newry and South Armagh.

The years since 1968 have witnessed an ever-increasing polarisation between the Protestant and Roman Catholic communities in Northern Ireland, but they have also brought certain advances in official inter-Church relations. Such advances cannot be said to have contributed significantly to inter-community relationships in general but they

have been real, although limited, advances for the Churches themselves. Such developments in Church relations have been in part a
natural progression from beginnings related here in preceding chapters, encouraged by the gradual progress of the world-wide ecumenical movement. They have also been in part enabled by the Second
Vatican Council and, to a not inconsiderable degree, were given
added stimulus by the recognition that in a divided society the
Churches must witness to reconciliation, justice and peace. However,
Dr. Eric Gallagher has affirmed that it is impossible to point to any
specific fruits of the advances in inter-Church relations in terms of
improved community relations, and admits that it is no real comfort
to recognize that, but for these advances, things could have been
worse.[3] The situation doubtless would have been worse, but only
careful analysis and reflection in the future will enable us to measure
with any real accuracy the implications for community relations
provided by the positive trends in ecumenical life in these years.

In their book, *Christians in Ulster: 1968-1980* (OUP, 1982),
E. Gallagher and S. Worrall recount in detail the experience of
the Churches in the Northern Ireland conflict. This book charts the
course of events until 1980 and was written by two distinguished
churchmen who themselves were closely involved. We do not intend
to repeat their work here; there is no need to do so. Rather, we will seek
to identify the major developments in inter-Church relations in
Ireland since 1968 and focus our attention on some of the specifically
theological concerns of the Irish Churches: the Gospel in the face
of sectarianism and violence; the resumption of union discussions
among the Protestant Churches; the Ballymascanlon process, with
particular reference to mixed marriages; and recent inter-Church
developments in education. We will continue to search for the theologically motivating factors and try to identify the theological and
ecclesiological implications of the way in which inter-Church relations
in fact developed.

1. The Churches, the Troubles and the Gospel

The first effect which the outbreak of the Troubles had on official
relations between the Churches was to drive their leaders together.
The months from January to April 1969 witnessed the steady worsen-
ing of an already extremely serious situation: in January a People's
Democracy march from Belfast to Londonderry was attacked by
Loyalists at Burntollet; later that month Brian Faulkner resigned from

the Cabinet and a major split developed within unionism – in the February general election there were pro-O'Neill and anti-O'Neill candidates, with the pro-O'Neill faction still retaining the majority. Serious disturbances erupted in Londonderry in April and Capt. O'Neill resigned as Prime Minister. This rapidly deteriorating situation continued, with rioting in Belfast and Londonderry resulting in the arrival of troops in August. The Churches were powerless to stem the tide of rising sectarian conflict and violence.[4]

As Gallagher and Worrall record, a joint meeting of the Irish Council of Churches Executive Committee and the leaders of the three main Protestant Churches issued a call to the Government for an inquiry into the causes of unrest and the way it was being handled; there was also a public denouncing of the Burntollet incident and the joint meeting resolved to approach Cardinal Conway, 'suggesting the time was ripe for some form of continuing consultation regarding the developing unrest, with its implications and opportunities for the Churches'.[5] The response from the Cardinal was positive; the Irish Hierarchy's 1969 *Directory on Ecumenism*, summarizing and highlighting certain particularly significant aspects of the first part of the Vatican's 1967 Directory, had expressed the hope that the new movement among Irish Christians to live in harmony and peace would 'grow and become even more permeated by the love and truth of Christ'.[6] In response to the I.C.C.'s overtures, an Ad Hoc committee was established, with two members nominated by the Cardinal and one each by the Primate, Moderator, Methodist President and the I.C.C. Executive.[7] This Ad Hoc committee was replaced shortly afterwards by regular joint meetings between the four Church leaders. As Gallagher and Worrall comment: 'Joint statements, meetings and television appearances became commonplace.'.[8]

In the summer of 1970 the Churches agreed to the formation of the Irish Council of Churches/Roman Catholic Church Joint Group on Social Problems. This was a response to the need for the Churches, in a threatened society, to witness to co-operation across religious divisions on matters of common concern. As we have already seen in Chapter V, the Joint Group was established – from the Roman Catholic perspective – within the terms of the Decree on Ecumenism of the Second Vatican Council and was a response to the new ecumenical commitment of the world-wide Roman Catholic Church. As we have also noted, the Joint Group was not, however, to tackle problems directly relating to the Troubles but was to advise the Hierarchy and the I.C.C. and its member Churches on more general social isses. Thus the studies pursued by the Joint Group reflect a reluctance to confront the political and social problems arising from alienation and unrest; the responsibility for this does not lie with the Joint Group itself, but with the Churches which defined and controlled the Group's work.[9] The 1976 study, *Violence in Ireland,* was undertaken only by 'special delegation'.

The Irish Council of Churches commented on the formation of the Joint Group: 'In the light of the history of Protestant/Roman Catholic relations in Ireland, and particularly in view of the political situation in 1970, few could have anticipated that the member Churches (of the I.C.C.) would have had no difficulty in agreeing to the proposal, but this in fact proved to be the case.'.[10] This was, however, a limited initiative. While many were seeing ecumenism increasingly as an imperative for the Churches – in the face of fundamental social alienation – this step of the Churches was hesitant and very tentative; there were still far more for whom ecumenism was a threat to the cherished *status quo* and who, at a time of political polarisation, saw religious *rapprochement* as compromise.

The formation of the Ballymascanlon Talks, which were first held in 1973 (see also Ch. V), was another result of the Irish Churches' desire to be seen to co-operate when community relations were worsening; but it was also, for the Roman Catholic Church, a response to the new ecumenical commitment brought about by Vatican II. In their book entitled *Ballymascanlon,* Cardinal Cahal Daly and Stanley Worrall recall the sense of enthusiasm and excitement surrounding the first Inter-Church Meeting, and reflect on the way relationships developed within the Meeting:

> Subsequent Ballymascanlon conferences have not had the same sense of novelty. But the meetings have matured . . . As respect and trust have grown, so too have frankness, sincerity and honesty of discussion come more and more to mark the exchanges. The truth is indeed spoken, but it is spoken in love, listened to in humility, responded to in respect for sincere convictions.[11]

The Ballymascanlon process has enabled the Churches to reflect together on important theological questions, as in the working parties on Church/Scripture/Authority and Baptism/Eucharist/Marriage, as well as on issues facing the Churches in contemporary society, such as 'secularism'. Yet the extent and influence of these discussions were necessarily limited on account of the infrequency of meetings until 1984, when there was a re-structuring of the Ballymascanlon process.[12] Again, there has been a certain 'ecclesiastical remoteness' about the talks. However Roman Catholics in particular, at the time when the meetings were beginning, were finding their way ecumenically. More recently the Inter-Church Meeting has recognized the problems created by the infrequency and 'remoteness' of meetings; the 1984 restructuring replaced the Steering Committee with a new Inter-Church Committee with two working departments – on Theological Questions and on Social Issues.[13] The Inter-Church Committee and its departments pursue their work between more regular, major Inter-Church Meetings. In addition to this, there have been plans to develop 'regional' Inter-Church Meetings (the first of which was held in Ballina, Co. Mayo in 1988). These new developments are signs that the members of the Inter-Church Meeting have been aware of the limitations of the Ballymascanlon process and have tried to make some improvements.

2. Protestants and Reunion, Again

Reunion discussions between the Church of Ireland and the Presbyterian Church had broken down in 1935 on the subject of the ministry and Presbyterian-Methodist discussions between 1937 and 1947 were brought to a standstill over the issue of ministerial itinerancy. However, against the background of the 1961 New Delhi W.C.C. Assembly's emphasis on local ecumenism and the 1964 Nottingham Faith and Order Conference's commitment to reunion, bipartite discussions between the Church of Ireland, the Presbyterian and Methodist Churches were established in 1964 and merged to form the Tripartite Consultation three years later, starting work on 9th January 1968. On 10th March of that year a Declaration of Intent was published and was subsequently adopted by the participating Churches.[14] This Declaration committed the Churches to a quest for unity without any predetermined conception of what exact form a United Church might take, but recognized that there would be 'changes' for all.

The Tripartite Consultation thus set about its work with an open mind as to what might emerge. In 1970 the Consultation submitted a Study and Questionnaire to each of the three Churches involved in the discussions. These were considered by local synods, councils and presbyteries, and an extensive summary of the findings of each Church was reported in 1971. The Questionnaire required each Church to consider the positive aspects, and the deficiencies, of the form of ministry and government in its own tradition as well as in the other two Churches. The results showed a willingness to discuss Church Union, but also a strong attachment in the Churches to their own distinctive features. The Churches wanted closer relations, but did not want to lose their individual identities.

Two years later the Tripartite Consultation produced its major report, *Towards a United Church*.[15] This document set out the background to the discussions and recorded the agreement reached on Divine Revelation and Scripture, the Church, the Sacraments, the Creeds and Later Historical Statements of Belief, and the Ministry. The publication of *Towards a United Church* was followed by the Churches' own reflection on its contents, which included a working basis for a United Church. In 1975 the Consultation could report on the Churches' findings, noting in particular the fears of the Presbyterian Church with regard to the type of episcopacy recommended, as well as with regard to the doctrine of Baptism. In the following year the A.P.C.K. published a review of the Tripartite Consultation's work by a leading Church of Ireland ecumenist: *Journey Towards Union* by Dr. S.G. Poyntz, secretary of the Conversations from 1968-76, then Archdeacon of Dublin and subsequently Bishop of Cork (1978-87) and of Connor (from 1987).

The 1973 proposals suggested that a new United Church should retain the historic episcopate; its ordained ministry would consist of 'Bishops and Presbyters', and associated with this ordained ministry, the Church would 'recognize' Deacons, Ruling Elders, Local Preachers, Class Leaders and Lay Readers. The report envisaged a United Church bringing together the major traditions of the three Churches; it attempted to include all that each Church wanted, but in the end it did not prove possible to resolve the difficulties which the Presbyterian Church had concerning the historic episcopate.

Sensing that the Consultation was not making any substantial progress, the representatives of the three Churches decided in 1978 to ask their governing bodies for clear terms of reference. A definitive report had been produced, but the Consultation had been left in 'mid-air' when no steps were taken by the Churches. The Consultation asked the Churches 'to indicate clearly to us if they wish us to formulate proposals for: 1) a full mutual recognition of ministries; 2) a form of federation; 3) organic union.'.[16] At the next year's General Synod, General Assembly and Methodist Conference, the Consultation's request was considered. Assembly and Conference voted on the three options, while the General Synod simply accepted organic union without voting on the other two. The feeling at Assembly and Conference as to what the immediate objective of the Consultation should be can be gauged by the voting pattern. Each option was voted upon as follows:[17]

	For		Against		Abst.	
	G.A.	M.C.	G.A.	M.C.	G.A.	M.C.
1. Organic Union	203	97	166	33	52	4
2. Federation	233	96	147	22	49	10
3. Recognition of Ministries	388	135	9	1	24	0

Professor Barkley has noted in relation to these voting statistics: 'The Consultation surveyed these replies and concluded that the climate of opinion did not seem to suggest a readiness to consider a Scheme of Union at present.'.[18] On the immediate objective there was thus a difference of some substance between the Church of Ireland and its partner Churches. Ecclesiologically, the Church of Ireland was, and remains, committed to the view that both a federation of Churches and an interchangeability of ministries fall far short of the ideal of visible unity.

In 1974, however, there had been some advance on the question of ministry. In that year the Tripartite Consultation had proposed to Synod, Assembly and Conference that a declaration of the mutual recognition of the ordained ministries of the three Churches as 'real and efficacious ministries of the Word and Sacraments' would be a valuable contribution towards unity. The following resolution was passed by the three governing bodies in 1974:

> . . . We recognise the ordained ministries of our three Churches as real and efficacious ministries of the word and sacraments through which God's love is proclaimed, his grace mediated, and his fatherly care exercised. We also recognise that our three Churches have different forms of church order and that each of us continues to cherish the forms which we have inherited . . . [19]

In a document produced at the Tripartite Consultation the implications of this resolution were set out:

> It . . . implies a readiness to recognise the reality of the ministries of our three Churches, not simply within their own ecclesial bodies, but within the whole Church of Christ. At the same time it does not imply in our present divisions a constitutional right to minister in the Churches other than the one to which each minister belongs.[20]

In our discussion of the earlier reunion negotiations, in Ch. IV, we have considered the theological implications of the terms 'validity', 'efficacy' and 'reality'. The General Synod of 1935 had not been prepared to recognize the 'validity, efficacy and spiritual reality of Presbyterian order and sacraments'; the 1974 resolution nevertheless recognized both Presbyterian and Methodist ordained ministries as 'real and efficacious'. A step forward was taken, but what would such 'recognition' mean in terms of inter-Church relations?

As subsequent events have shown, this resolution did not provide the desperately needed breakthrough. Although Anglicans could regard Presbyterian and Methodist ordained ministries as 'real and efficacious', non-episcopally ordained clergy cannot be interchangeable with those who are episcopally ordained. Yet the 1974 'recognition' by the Church of Ireland of the reality and efficacy of Presbyterian and Methodist orders and sacraments undoubtedly led to much more eucharistic sharing between the Churches.[21]

Despite this modest advance, however, the Consultation drifted for several years and, as we have seen above, the request for clearer terms of reference in 1978 did not result in any fresh inspiration for its work. In the 1980s the broad agenda of the Consultation was a recognition of the fact that its work would have to be an extended process of growing together and that there were many ways of approaching the search for unity.[22]

These Tripartite discussions were being held against the background of a changing climate of opinion, politically and ecclesiastically. The general enthusiasm for reunion in the late 1960s gradually faded and in Northern Ireland the experience of the Troubles brought not only a political drift to the right, but also greater conservatism in the Churches. In 1980 the Presbyterian Church withdrew from the World Council of Churches[23] and when Pope John Paul II came to Ireland in 1979 there was only a limited ecumenical dimension to his visit, the Presbyterian Moderator, Dr. Wm. Craig, declining to join an ecumenical delegation to meet the Pope (although the Clerk of Assembly, Dr. Weir, headed a Presbyterian delegation). In 1988 the Presbyterian Church was the only one of the three Churches participating in the Tripartite Consultation to reject proposals for a new Joint Theological Working Party to succeed the Tripartite Consultation and in the following year the Church of Ireland and the Methodist Church established a bi-partite group.

If at national level the Churches were unable to take any definite steps towards reunion through the Tripartite Consultation, there was nonetheless an increasing number of local ecumenical schemes in Ireland. It was to this area that the Tripartite Consultation, in conjunction with the I.C.C., turned its attention in 1983.

Local Resource-Sharing

A major study of local co-operation between the Irish Churches was carried out in 1975 by I.J.E. Knox (Univ. Hull/ISE B. Phil. dissertation). Since then the subject has been given special consideration by the Tripartite Consultation and the Irish Council of Churches. In 1983 two regional conferences were held for those involved in local schemes. The first was held at St. Andrew's, Knockbreda, Belfast and the second at Gurteen Agricultural College, Roscrea, Co. Tipperary. This initiative arose from the Tripartite Consultation's 1983 five-point programme which had the purpose of 'continuing the process of growing together and mutual understanding' (see note 22).

The first steps in official local resource-sharing in Ireland were taken by the Presbyterian and Methodist Churches in 1953 with the launching of the Taughmonagh project in Belfast. This was followed five years later by a project in Braniel. These schemes were described as 'federal'; each Church has one minister and is 'in association' with both the Presbyterian and Methodist Churches. Co-operation developed further when a scheme of Presbyterian/Methodist 'alternating ministries' was first introduced at Christ Church, Limerick in 1973. While 'federation' suited new areas, the alternating ministry scheme was intended to advance co-operation particularly in small but established congregations, this being particularly relevant to the situation in the Republic.

There were certain factors which encouraged the development of joint projects. In 1952 the World Conference on Faith and Order, held at Lund, Sweden, challenged the Churches to ask themselves first, whether they were sufficiently eager to enter into dialogue with other Churches and, second, whether they should not 'act together in all matters except those in which deep differences of conviction compel them to act separately'.[24] Then, in 1964, the British Council of Churches' Nottingham Conference formally encouraged the sharing of resources (the conference was aptly entitled 'Unity begins at Home'). Four years later the Lambeth Conference recalled the importance of the Lund suggestion and stressed the need for attention to be paid to local ecumenism.[25] That year, 1968, coincidentally saw the participation of the Church of Ireland in a joint-church at Glengormley (with the Methodist Church).

The Second Vatican Council's Decree on Ecumenism provided a new situation in which the Roman Catholic Church was now able to engage in planned resource-sharing with other Churches, albeit only in exceptional circumstances. Certain problems, such as the presence of the reserved sacrament, still present themselves particularly when places of worship are being shared. Knox has drawn specific attention to the provisions of the Vatican's General Directory on the Pastoral of Tourism[26]; this document recognized the appropriateness – in the light of the Ecumenical Directory – of sharing places of worship with other Christians and of directing non-Roman Catholics to their clergy and places of worship. Planned resource-sharing at the local level in Ireland does not often involve Roman Catholics but there are specific instances of this, e.g. the community church in Dingle, Co. Kerry, and university and hospital chaplaincy co-operation. However, while official schemes are not numerous, there is no doubt that there is much co-operation between Protestants and Roman Catholics in the Republic in particular, and in parts of Northern Ireland.

In his dissertation of 1975 Knox made certain observations and comments on the then current situation. A major theme in his conclusions was the need for better ecumenical planning, for sponsoring bodies and for a national consultative committee. While it cannot be said that ecumenical planning has developed greatly in the intervening years, it should be noted that the two 1983 regional conferences, to which reference has been made, also expressed the view that a national co-ordinating and consultative body would be of value. This result from the two conferences led to the Tripartite Consultation bringing a motion to the General Synod, General Assembly and Methodist Conference in 1985 calling for the formation of such a national body; the Consultative Committee for Local Schemes of Co-operation was duly constituted in that year. Irish delegates to the British Council of Churches had been aware of the work of the English Consultative Committee and some desired to see an Irish counterpart.

The Irish Consultative Committee's terms of reference defined its purpose under three headings: (1) Review of existing schemes; (2) As a result of reviews, the provision of guidelines for future schemes; (3) Advise on covenants where these are desired at local level. There was some concern in the Presbyterian Church that covenants should not be forced in any way, that the committee should be clearly defined as advisory in nature, and that the term Local Ecumenical Projects (the accepted term in Britain), because of the word 'ecumenical', would not be acceptable. Thus, in its terms of reference the advisory capacity of the consultative committee is explicitly stressed, the committee is only to advise on covenants when they are desired at local level, and its title substitutes 'Local Schemes of Co-operation' for 'Local Ecumenical Projects'.

Despite these initial reservations on the Presbyterian side, illustrative of the theological trend to the right, the Consultative Committee was formed by the three main Protestant Churches and provides the best opportunity of ensuring proper ecumenical planning, particularly for new and also sparsely populated areas. It is one major development since I.J.E. Knox's study of 1975. Another development has been in the area of worship. Knox commented:

> Worshipping together does reinforce the sense of community that is already there. There could be more development towards Church of Ireland/Methodist united worship if problems of ministry and the Eucharist could be worked out. One solution might be if more churches followed the example of Christ Church, Shannon and drew up a common order for the Communion, which would be the basis for a Sunday service.[27]

In 1986 the Tripartite Consultation finalized an agreed Order of Service for the Holy Communion, based upon the 'Lima' liturgy of the World Council of Churches. This common order was for use 'on ecumenical occasions, in uniting congregations and in any of the Churches'[28] and could provide a useful basis for meeting local needs in shared churches.

While the Protestant Churches were able to make some advances in their relations in the 1970s and 1980s, notably the 1974 Tripartite resolution on ministries and the establishment of the Consultative Committeee for Local Schemes of Co-operation, this can only be described as relatively modest ecumenical growth. During the 1970s and 1980s, however, the Protestant Churches were also developing their relations with the Roman Catholic Church, as we have seen, through the Ballymascanlon process. We now turn to two specific areas of Protestant – Roman Catholic relations which have been particularly sensitive: mixed marriages and education.

3.   Mixed Marriages[29]

At the April 1975 meeting of the Ballymascanlon Conference, a working party on Social and Community Problems recommended 'the appointment of a small joint standing committee to report annually to the Churches on such general trends in Church practice concerning mixed marriages as appear to involve difficulties or misunderstandings calling for resolution or clarification'. This significant proposal was a recognition that the Inter-Church Meeting would lack all credibility, certainly on the Protestant side, if the issue of mixed marriages were not discussed realistically. There was thus established an Irish Council of Churches/Roman Catholic Church Joint Standing Committee on Mixed Marriages, which submitted its first report to the Churches in 1977.

A revision of the Roman Catholic Church's rules on mixed marriages took place only more than fifty years after the decree *Ne Temere*, to which we have referred in Chapter I. In 1966, Pope Paul VI issued the Instruction *Matrimonii Sacramentum*. While this removed the reference to the Roman Catholic party's duty to try to convert the non-Roman Catholic, it still made provisions relating to canonical form and the Roman Catholic upbringing of any children. However, *Matrimonii Sacramentum* did make provision, in serious circumstances, for dispensing with the obligation for a mixed marriage to be conducted in the presence of an authorized priest (i.e. in accordance with canonical form), and if the non-Roman Catholic could not agree to any children of the marriage being brought up as Roman Catholics appeal could now be made to Rome.

In 1970 Paul VI's *Matrimonia Mixta* further revised the nature of the promise upon which the issuing of a dispensation from the 'impediment' of mixed religion was conditional: the Roman Catholic party was now required to do all in his or her power to have any children brought up in the Roman Catholic Church and no promise was required of the other partner. *Matrimonii Sacramentum* did not fully reflect the spirit of Vatican II's Declaration on Religious Freedom and Decree on Ecumenism; in particular, if persons and communities had the right to 'social and civil freedom in matters religious' (Declaration), and if there was indeed a baptismal 'sacramental bond of unity' (Decree), promises from the non-Roman Catholic partner in a mixed marriage were inappropriate. *Matrimonia Mixta* constituted a further advance.

It is clear that the major developments since *Ne Temere* are in the areas of the upbringing of any children of a mixed marriage and in the provisions relating to canonical form. With regard to the former, Fr. George Wadding has written:

> ... the obligation not to expose one's own faith to danger is absolute; but the obligation to baptize and educate the children in one's own faith is qualified. The manner and extent of its implementation will depend on the circumstances of a given inter-Church marriage.

In fairness, at this stage, I should point out that not every bishop nor every hierarchy has interpreted the expression '*all in one's power*' precisely as I have done. Some interpret the words in much the same way as the older documents, requiring practically a *guarantee* that the children *will be* baptized and educated as Catholics.[30]

It is quite correct that there is variety in the interpretation of regulations; the 1974 International Consultation on Mixed Marriages held in Dublin under the auspices of the Irish School of Ecumenics noted the fact that there were more liberal interpretations in other countries. Wadding, in the same article, quotes from a Statement of the Swiss Hierarchy:

> The Roman Catholic partner promises after discussion with the other Christian partner, to do for the Catholic baptism and Catholic upbringing of the children *what is possible for him consistent with respect for the religious convictions of the non-Catholic partner and without prejudice to the marriage union*[31]

Matrimonia Mixta was followed in Ireland by the Irish Hierarchy's Statement on Mixed Marriages (October 1970), the Directory on Ecumenism (1976) (cf. Part Six), and the Directory on Mixed Marriages (1983). The 1983 document is the Irish Hierarchy's detailed set of local laws, as provided for in *Matrimonia Mixta*. Based on *Matrimonia Mixta*, it takes account of the two previous Irish documents, but is intended 'to give a fuller explanation of the Catholic position and thus endeavour to remove certain misunderstandings that have arisen, to give more detailed guidance for the clergy in dealing sympathetically and consistently with mixed marriage couples, and to assist the couples in meeting their responsibilities as positively as possible'.[32]

Mixed Marriage Rules and Inter-Church Relations

There is no doubt that strict Roman Catholic regulations governing mixed marriages have been the cause of much resentment on the part of the Protestant community, particularly in the Republic. The First World War and the heavy losses sustained by the Protestant population in Ireland, a low fertility rate and consistent emigration all led to a steady reduction in the number of Protestants. The *Ne Temere* regulations were yet another factor which threatened the strength, if not the very existence in some parts of Ireland, of the Protestant community. So already in 1911 J.A.F. Gregg could write in his vehement attack on *Ne Temere*:

It is a crying shame that men with Protestant names should let their children who ought to be strengthening our community grow up as Romanists, giving their Protestant blood and brain and energy to a community which would drive us out of the land if it could . . . Mixed marriages tend to rob us of the next generation, and we need to band ourselves together to stop the leakage. Parents need not throw their children into unnecessary association with Roman Catholics either in school or in society. If the barrier is broken down or even weakened, those who played together as children will quite naturally say when they grow up, 'If you let us play together then, why should we not marry now?' Keep up the distinction, I would entreat you. Make the idea of marriage with a Roman Catholic as much out of the question as a marriage within the prohibited degrees. Make it the first idea with your children that marriage with a Roman Catholic is not for them; that such a marriage cannot be entered into on fair and equal terms, but only on terms of shame and dishonour.[33]

These words were strong indeed; there was no equivocating. Later, in 1948, in somewhat softer terms, the Lambeth Conference could also issue a clear warning to Anglicans the world over against 'contracting marriages with Roman Catholics under the conditions imposed by the modern Roman Canon Law, especially as these conditions involve, among other things, a promise to have their children brought up in a religious system which they cannot accept'.[34]

The new light of Vatican II influenced official Roman Catholic policy with regard to mixed marriages and, as we have noted, the years 1966 and 1970 brought revisions of the regulations (*Matrimonii Sacramentum* and *Matrimonia Mixta*) which, while far from satisfying Protestant demands, nonetheless constituted moves forward.

In 1976 the Presbyterian General Assembly noted the 'substantially more liberal provisions' of *Matrimonia Mixta*. In January of the previous year, however, the Church of Ireland bishops, noting the 'deep spiritual concern' within the Church of Ireland with regard to mixed marriages, issued an 'Instruction on procedure with regard to Mixed Marriages', requesting clergy to follow a series of guidelines. In particular, this document stressed that no Church of Ireland clergyman should accept an invitation to participate in a mixed marriage service in the Roman Catholic Church unless he had been assured 'that the 'pro viribus' clause in Norm 4 of the existing Moto Proprio regulations, which says that the Roman Catholic partner must make a sincere promise to do all in his or her power to have all the children baptized and brought up in the Roman Catholic Church, will not be so interpreted as to exclude the partners from exercising freely their responsibility in conscience regarding the baptism and upbringing of any children of the marriage', and unless arrangements for joint pastoral care 'recognizing the equal responsibility of both Churches and the equal responsibility of both partners for the religious upbringing of the children' were agreed.

The establishment of the Ballymascanlon Joint Standing Committee on Mixed Marriages provided an on-going opportunity for the Churches to learn about one another's approaches and to voice any dissatisfaction which might be felt by either side. The lines of communication were open and were seen to be open, for this subject – on account of general concern among Protestants and indeed some Roman Catholics – simply had to be at the top of any fully inter-Church agenda. No doubt, the working party which had suggested the formation of this body at the 1975 Inter-Church Meeting[35] had been considerably influenced by the major International Consultation on Mixed Marriages which was held in Dublin in 1974. That Consultation gave 'pride of place' to *praxis* over against *theoria*. In his Introduction to the book based on the work of this gathering, Fr. Michael Hurley writes:

> The difficulties involved in marriages between Christians of different denominations pale into insignificance when seen, as they must be, in the perspective of the vast challenges and problems which the churches face today in every sphere of life and not least with regard to the future of the institution of marriage itself. These mixed marriage difficulties, however, deserve careful consideration because they are at present preventing the churches from addressing themselves together, more credibly and effectively, to the larger issues of our time.[36]

In the course of the Irish Hierarchy's preparations for its 1983 Directory on Mixed Marriages – the local regulations for Ireland under *Matrimonia Mixta* – Cardinal O Fiaich invited the members of the Protestant side of the Joint Standing Committee on Mixed Marriages to submit their views on how mixed marriages should be treated both within the terms of *Matrimonia Mixta* and from their own perspectives. In the Church of Ireland's submission, this invitation was recognized as 'an encouraging and a kindly gesture'. This submission went on to recall Pope John Paul II's words addressed to Protestants during his visit to Ireland:

May no Irish Protestant think that the Pope is an enemy, a danger
or a threat. My desire is that instead Protestants should see in me a
friend and a brother in Christ.[37]

On this, the Church of Ireland members commented: 'We look
forward to the concrete fulfilment of this generous assurance in that
area where Protestants have the strongest and most obvious reasons
for feeling that their community is threatened and where they feel obliged
to adopt defensive attitudes which can easily be mis-interpreted.'.[38]

The discussions at the Joint Standing Committee may well have
contributed to the generally conciliatory tone of the text of the 1983
Roman Catholic Directory, but did not make any real impact in terms
of the actual regulations contained in the Directory. Upon its publication in 1983, the Church of Ireland bishops stated in the course of
their preliminary comments:

On the central issue of the Promise we find that two phrases have
been added to the form of words used in the Directory of 1976 – 'as
God's law demands' and 'as God's law also requires' (7.1). Neither
of the phrases is found in the formulation of the promises in
Matrimonia Mixta or in *The Code of Canon Law*. One can only
conclude that the object of this change is to underline the imperative nature of the Roman Catholic partner's duty; to add weight to
the obligation, and to exclude any possible sense of choice or option
for the partners in the religious upbringing of the children. We do
not know where in God's law there is support for a promise to ensure
the Roman Catholic upbringing of all the children of a mixed
marriage . . .
       . . . The basic thrust of the Directory appears to be the claim that
the Roman Catholic Church alone 'has been endowed with the
fullness of the means of salvation.' It is this very claim that Anglicans
cannot accept.[39]

The present situation

The Roman Catholic rules governing mixed marriages in Ireland are
clearly set out and are readily available in the published 1983 Directory. The interpretation of the rules leaves scope for flexibility, as
individual bishops have the power to grant dispensations. For example, the declaration which the Roman Catholic partner must make
that 'I am resolved, as God's law demands, to preserve my Catholic
faith, and to avoid all dangers of falling away from it. Moreover, I

sincerely undertake and I will, as God's law also requires, do every-
thing possible, so far as in me lies, to have all the children of our
marriage baptised and brought up in the Catholic Church', must be
taken to imply the eventuality that the children may not, in fact, be
brought up in this way. Nevertheless, the Directory later states that if
it is clear in the course of preparation for the marriage that there is 'a
serious conflict of conscientious convictions, the only acceptable
solution may be that the proposed marriage should not take place'.
How these clauses are interpreted, and how much emphasis will be
placed on them, can vary from bishop to bishop.

Vatican II's Declaration on Religious Freedom holds to the supremacy of *parental* choice in the religious education of their children:
'Parents, moreover, have the right to determine, in accordance with
their own religious beliefs, the kind of religious education that their
children are to receive.'.[40] This has often been quoted by Protestants
to show that there is an element of inconsistency between the Declaration on Religious Freedom and the mixed marriage regulations of
the Roman Catholic Church. Although it should be noted that the
above quotation from the Declaration is in the context of schooling
(and indeed, as Professor McDonagh has indicated, was introduced
into the text of the Declaration 'at the suggestion of Cardinal Conway
of Armagh amongst others'[41]), the principle is surely also applicable
to the mixed marriage situation if equal rights – equal human rights
– between the partners in the marriage are to be recognized.

Despite Cardinal Cahal Daly's insistence that 'the Catholic Church's
attitude (to mixed marriages) can never be understood if it is interpreted in political or demographical or sociological terms. It is a question of doctrine, of ecclesiology, of how the Church understands herself',[42] Protestants feel that this Roman Catholic self-understanding
suggests a degree of spiritual superiority that is unwarranted and seems
to imply a contradiction of Vatican II's wider vision of the nature of the
Church.

These remain grounds of dissatisfaction for Protestants. There has,
however, been some progress made in Ireland in very recent years.
The human dimension and the rights of the non-Roman Catholic
were emphasized by Bishop Cassidy (now Archbishop) in the Public
Session of the New Ireland Forum in February 1984, when the Irish
Hierarchy sent a delegation to the Forum:

> The promise required of the Catholic is to do all that is possible, and
> to do all in his or her power, no more and no less, to ensure the
> Catholic baptism and up-bringing of the children. In giving the

promise to do all that is possible two things have to be kept firmly in
mind – the rights of the other person, the conscientious rights and
convictions of the other person and the total context of the marriage, the unity of the relationship.[43]

Moreover, there has been progress in the area of joint pastoral care;
this clearly depends upon the personalities involved, but there is a
growing number of diocesan specialist consultants for mixed marriages. A particular advance was achieved in the Diocese of Ferns
where, in January 1985 at an ecumenical service in St. Peter's Church
of Ireland church, Kilscoran, Bishop Willoughby and Bishop
Comiskey (the Church of Ireland and Roman Catholic bishops)
made the following joint declaration:

> We recognize that as long as the Churches remain divided, Mixed
> Marriage will involve difficulties which cannot be completely re-
> solved by legislation or pastoral care. For this reason, as a general
> policy, we do not encourage Mixed Marriages. At the same time, a
> Mixed Marriage where partners have a genuine commitment to their
> own Church, can be a sign of the unity we all seek in Jesus Christ.
>
> We feel it is our duty . . . to ensure the fullest pastoral care of
> Mixed Marriage couples and their families, before and after the
> wedding, in this Diocese of Ferns. Accordingly we have appointed
> the Very Reverend David Earl, The Deanery, Ferns and the Rever-
> end Aiden Jones, Riverchapel, Courtown Harbour, to specialise in
> Mixed Marriage counselling. Together with these two specialists we
> are forming a Committee of Priests from both our Churches to
> advise on how best to implement the recommendations for joint
> pastoral care contained in our respective documents. We acknowl-
> edge and encourage the good work done by the Association of Inter-
> Church Families.
>
> We make this declaration in an endeavour to remove misunder-
> standing that has arisen, to encourage ecumenical discussion about
> Christian understanding of marriage and to further co-operation
> between our Churches.[44]

The committee reporting on this Ferns initiative emphasized that
'the religious education of the children is a joint and equal responsibility of the couple', and welcomed the 'increased frequency' with
which dispensations from canonical form were being granted in
Ireland.[45] This initiative has been a positive development, and it is to
be hoped that as this work continues and as other diocesan special-

ists in inter-Church marriages continue their work, procedures and approaches may be developed which will lead to a progressive improvement in this area of Church relations throughout Ireland. In the meantime, the work of the Ballymascanlon Joint Standing Committee continues; an important contribution which this national body could make would be in encouraging and assisting such local initiatives as that in Ferns.[46]

4. Integrated Education

In a situation of social alienation, division and violence such as Ireland has experienced unrelentingly for the past twenty years and more, it is natural for individuals to reflect on what the future holds; this naturally turns attention to young people. While there have been advances in ecumenical youth work, there is a particular concern for all Irish people in what happens in the school. In the formative years of life, what values are being inculcated, what norms are being presented, what prejudices may be being reinforced? Irish society faces the task of promoting those things that make for real peace. There are various dimensions to this contemporary Irish education question: What is the place of religion in school? What kind of history is taught in a society where memories need to be reconciled? What are the implications of segregated education, the *de facto* situation for so many Protestant and Roman Catholic young people in Ireland? To this last question in particular we now turn.

Integrated Education: Philosophies and Stances

In his research into denominational and integrated education in Ireland, J. Fulton indicates that while for both Protestant and Roman Catholic supporters of denominational schooling the school is seen as having to support the values of the home environment, the Roman Catholic Church's policy of no change in the school system is often defended by a 'pre-ecumenical' theology.[47] The Roman Catholic school system is seen as 'a matter of faith and moral conscience for Roman Catholics and is directly connected to their obligation to bring up their children as Roman Catholics'.[48] Yet, while Vatican II's Declaration on Christian Education reminded Roman Catholic parents of their 'duty to entrust their children to Catholic schools, when and where this is possible . . .',[49] it also spoke of the 'Catholic school' as an 'ideal', affirming that such schools 'can take on forms which vary according to local circumstances'.[50] Further, Vatican II's Declaration on Religious Freedom – as we have seen in our consideraton of mixed marriages – affirmed the right of parents to determine the kind of their children's religious education. The prevailing situation in Northern Ireland presents a special circumstance in which the Roman Catholic Church could be more supportive of those parents who choose an integrated pattern of education. The Executive of the Irish Theological Association, in its submission to the New Ireland Forum in 1983, highlighted this issue of developing integrated education as a contribution to improved community relations.[51] However, in the Irish Episcopal Conference's submission to the Forum the Roman Catholic bishops, disputing 'the charge of divisiveness levelled against the existence of Catholic schools', stated:

> More positively, we would wish to claim that the values which are the inspiration of the Catholic school system are incompatible with violence, hatred or intolerance. These central Christian values include the sacredness of human life; love of all people irrespective of religious, political or other difference; reverence for truth and justice. The inherent weakness of man will, undoubtedly, make it difficult for us all, whether or not in Catholic education, to realise these values consistently in our lives. But a major task of Catholic education is to transmit these values and to seek to encourage and to promote their practice in Ireland today. Without being unaware of weakness in our educational system, and being committed to its constant improvement, we think it not unreasonable to claim that, had it not been for the exemplary dedication of the vast majority of Catholic teachers in Northern Ireland, many more of our young people might, in recent years, have been caught up in the appalling web of terrorist violence.[52]

In responding to a question on the subject of integrated education from the then Senator Mary Robinson (now President), Bishop Cahal Daly (now Cardinal) replied:

> The Church does nothing to oppose or obstruct the efforts of people whose sincerity we respect and who feel that this is the way forward. However, even those who believe in the value of integrated education must recognize that their solution would attract very few. It could not, for long established historical and geographical reasons, be realised between, say, the Falls Road and the Shankill Road other than by some process of bussing which would expose young children to real physical danger, intimidation, threat to which no

parent would would subject their children. We feel it is much better to try to reach the greatest number of people and expose the greatest number of our pupils to ecumenical and inter-denominational contacts. We feel this is best done through contact between the schools . . .[53]

The proponents of integrated education firmly maintain that the segregated system is divisive; it is precisely this charge that defenders of Roman Catholic schools have called into question. Fr. Denis Faul could write in 1977 that 'the Catholic school system is the real, genuine peace movement, day by day, week by week, year by year, preaching truth, justice, freedom and charity . . . Our syllabus, our curriculum is Holiness, Love and Charity.'.[54] Cardinal Conway, three years earlier, published the booklet *Catholic Schools* in an attempt to explain his Church's position to 'honest enquirers'. Conway declared:

In addition to Great Britain, there are many European countries with a mixed Catholic-Protestant population where Catholics have their own schools. In none of them, Great Britain, Germany or Holland for example (where the proportion of Protestants to Catholics is roughly the same as in Northern Ireland) has the existence of separate schools created a divided community. The same is true of the United States.[55]

Consistently, defenders of Roman Catholic schools in Northern Ireland have emphasized the high moral standards which are taught and the fact that in other countries separate schooling has not had an adverse effect on community relations. Drawing parallels between Northern Ireland and other countries, however, can be methodologically questionable. M. McKeown has aptly commented:

There has, undoubtedly, been an attempt on the part of many commentators to universalize the Northern Ireland conflict by placing it within a global context. To reject the divisive effect of the dual systems (of education) in Northern Ireland by invoking the non-divisive models to be found elsewhere is to be guilty of this fallacy of universalism. The Northern Ireland situation is peculiar to itself and systems effective elsewhere might not be justifiable within that particular context.[56]

Both the researches of Fulton and the submission of the Irish Episcopal Conference to the New Ireland Forum indicate that there is a division of opinion among educationalists as to the precise effects of segregated education. The Churches, both Roman Catholic and Protestant, have been only too aware of the difficulties of implementing an integrated pattern of education in such a divided society as Northern Ireland – divided both culturally and in many areas geographically – and have not been able to commit themselves fully to such a policy. The integrated education movement has gained its impetus from outside official Church structures, but it could now be opportune for the Churches' educationalists to consider possibilities for 'ecumenical schooling', particularly in view of the Northern Ireland Department of Education's commitment to furthering community relations through the educational system,[57] and given the recent success of the four major Churches in drawing up a common religious education course for the same Department.

5. The Irish School of Ecumenics

The ecumenical opportunities following Vatican II's Decree on Ecumenism were clearly seen by one Irish Jesuit in particular, the Rev. Michael Hurley. He was the driving force behind the establishing of the Irish School of Ecumenics, a unique venture in ecumenical scholarship in Ireland. The School was founded in 1970 with distinguished patrons drawn from the four main Churches. The world ecumenical movement was represented at the inauguration of the ISE by the Rev. Dr. Eugene Carson Blake, then General Secretary of the World Council of Churches.

Although a Church-related institution, the ISE's independence from Church control has been jealously guarded, but has meant that from the beginning the School has depended upon voluntary financial support. This has come indirectly from the Irish Churches (e.g. through Roman Catholic religious orders, the Church of Ireland Priorities Fund, voluntary contributions of parishes), from individuals, from firms and industry, from foundations in Great Britain, and from the Churches in Holland, West Germany, the United States and Australia. Approximately seventy-five per cent of funding comes from within Ireland; since 1984 there has been a grant from the Department of Foreign Affairs in Dublin in view of the School's contribution towards reconciliation, and since 1985 from the Northern Ireland Office in view of its work in Northern Ireland (see further below). The Jesuit Community at Milltown Park in Dublin has provided classroom, library and administrative facilities, while the purchase of Bea House

(20 Pembroke Park) allowed the provision of some residential accommodation for ISE students as well as a valuable library.

Soon after its foundation the ISE was affiliated to the University of Hull in England. This association, which meant that the ISE could offer M.A. degree and Diploma in Ecumenics courses, was brought about through official negotiations helped by the personal interest of the Rev. Professor A.T. Hanson of Hull (whose brother, the Rt. Rev. R.P.C. Hanson was the then Church of Ireland Bishop of Clogher). In addition to the M.A. and Diploma courses, the ISE's Northern Ireland Programme has, since 1979, offered a Certificate in Ecumenics from NUU/UU; in the first year it was awarded by the University of Hull.[58]

During 1980-81 negotiations between the ISE and the University of Dublin led to an institutional agreement whereby, as from October 1982, the ISE would be affiliated to the University of Dublin for the M. Phil. (Ecum.) degree and for a Diploma in Ecumenics; thus the link with Hull was gradually severed. The ISE has also been associated with UCD through a 20-lecture adult education course on 'World Religions and Christianity', and 'The Church and the Churches' (alternate years), and with the People's College (Adult Education Association) through two evening courses in the early 1980s.

The ISE defines itself as an institution for research and teaching.[59] The four main areas of study in the School today are: Inter-Church Dialogue, Inter-Faith Dialogue, Religion and Society, and Peace Studies. There is thus a broad approach to ecumenics, faithful to the full meaning of *oikumene*. The style of theology promoted by the School is based on what might be described as a concept of God's Church and God's world; there is no rigid distinction here, no setting of Church and world, sacred and secular, in separation. The unity which the School aims to promote is Christian unity, but also the unity of the 'whole inhabited earth'. The ISE has also related its work to the situation in which the Churches find themselves in contemporary Ireland; inter-Church and inter-faith dialogue – international concerns – are complemented by studies in Church, society and peace, all with direct relevance to the Irish experience today. The model of Church with which the School has operated is thus that of God's people prefiguring the perfect unity of the Kingdom in their historical context; the Church's life in a way is to prefigure the destiny of humanity, of the whole created order. The Church here is, to use the terminology of Vatican II, the 'sacrament of salvation' for God's created.

The ISE, born of the Irish situation, has thus challenged the Irish Churches with a thoroughly modern ecumenical outlook. J.P.

Rajashekar, Secretary for Church and People of Other Faiths at the Lutheran World Federation in Geneva, has written:

> . . . have we not reached a point in our ecumenical pilgrimage where ecumenical theology could now begin to broaden the scope and contents of its discussion? Can Christian self-identity be defined in isolation from vital theological issues and concerns that impinge upon Christian existence in the world, such as the challenges of poverty and oppression, of justice and peace, of other faiths and ideologies? Is not our ecumenical theology likely to run the risk of becoming so introverted, ecclesio-centred and self-celebrating that its own ecumenical vision of seeking to reach the whole oikumene is undermined?[60]

These issues which Rajashekar has identified as those which belong to any truly ecumenical theology, are all part of the study agenda of the ISE. The School has thus provided the Irish Churches and Irish Christians with an ecumenical vision which challenges them to a critical reflection on their relations with one another, their role in society, and their witness to the fulness of the Gospel.

Despite these ambitious programmes, however, the ISE's impact on Irish life in general, and Irish Church life in particular, has been of a limited nature; in its M. Phil. and Diploma courses, half of the students are usually from outside Ireland, and in its Certificate and Northern Ireland courses there are only a few students each year. Nonetheless, under successive Directors – Michael Hurley, Robin Boyd, John May and Alan Falconer – the Irish School of Ecumenics has brought an independent and truly critical dimension to Irish ecumenical thought and has, through its consistent attempts to keep in touch with the local Church, performed a service of engendering ecumenism, the fruits of which service have yet to be fully reaped.

6.   The Council of Churches for Britain and Ireland

The British Inter-Church Process, 'Not Strangers But Pilgrims', was launched at a meeting held in Friends Meeting House, Euston Road, London on 18th September 1984 and was programmed as a three-year process of 'prayer, reflection and debate' on the nature and mission of the Church.[61] This process would take place at three geographical levels – locally, regionally and nationally. It was a joint initiative of the British Council of Churches and the English and Welsh Roman

Catholic Hierarchy and the purpose was to discover what the Churches – from the person in the pew to Church leadership – really wanted in terms of ecumenical structures. The story of the Irish involvement in this exercise and in its fruit, the Council of Churches for Britain and Ireland, is illustrative of the state of Irish Church relations in very recent years.

The ecumenical experience of the British Churches in the 1960s and 1970s had left many people disappointed, if not disillusioned. During those years various schemes and proposals for Christian unity were under discussion in England, Scotland and Wales – as indeed also in Ireland. The English experience was perhaps the one most clearly characterized by failure. Church of England – Methodist proposals for Church union reached the brink of success, only to fall in 1972. Proposals for a Churches' Covenant for Unity in England foundered ten years later. These national failures, however, were not the whole story of ecumenical life in England. There was a steadily growing number of 'local ecumenical projects' which involved officially structured ecumenical collaboration at parish level.

By the early 1980s it seemed that the local Church was finding far more ecumenical success than the national Church. Then, in 1982, came the Papal visit to Britain which, unlike the 1979 Irish visit, had a very high-profile ecumenical dimension. Pope John Paul II encouraged Roman Catholics in Britain to participate fully in the search for Christian unity. At Bellahouston Park in Glasgow he told a gathering of Christians from many traditions: 'We are only pilgrims on this earth, making our way towards that heavenly Kingdom promised to us as God's children. Beloved brethren in Christ, for the future, can we not make that pilgrimage together, hand in hand?'[62] Then again, between 1982 and 1984 there appeared several reports from international dialogues between theologians of different Church traditions, showing much greater convergence in Christian faith than had previously been thought possible: the W.C.C.'s Lima Report, *Baptism, Eucharist and Ministry* (1982); the *Final Report* of ARCIC-I (also 1982); the report of the Anglican-Lutheran European Dialogue (1983); the Anglican-Orthodox *Dublin Agreed Statement* (1984); and the Anglican-Reformed International Commission's report, *God's Reign and Our Unity* (also 1984).[63] Finally, by the mid-1980s, partnerships had been formed in places between the more established British Churches and the ethnic minority 'Black-led' Churches, and more and more people were aware of the need for these positive relationships to be the rule rather than the exception.

As a result of these happier experiences, four features were at the heart of the Inter-Church Process. First, there was an emphasis on prayer, reflection and debate at local level – leading to regional and national conferences; second, there was an emphasis on ecclesiology, the nature of the Church and its mission; third, the Roman Catholic Church in England and Wales and in Scotland was fully involved; and fourth, the smaller, Black-led Churches were also fully involved.

The Irish Churches, it must be admitted, felt rather on the fringe of these events in 1984-85, particularly as the Irish Inter-Church Meeting had not been consulted before plans were set in motion. The three Irish B.C.C. member-Churches (the Church of Ireland and the Presbyterian and Methodist Churches) opted for 'Observer' membership in the Process, and the Irish Inter-Church Meeting joined in this capacity in the final Swanwick Conference in 1987. That Swanwick Conference recommended the winding up of the British Council of Churches and the formation of a new Council which would have full Roman Catholic and ethnic-minority participation. Certain structural changes would be required if the Roman Catholic Church were to join. For example, the Roman Catholics were not satisfied with the way in which the six-monthly B.C.C. Assemblies seemed to pronounce on any and many current affairs. The new Council would have a new *modus operandi*, enabling the Churches actually to work together rather than being more detached from the Churches as had been the B.C.C. As a result, the Council of Churches for Britain and Ireland was born in 1990, but with the Irish representation limited to the Church of Ireland and the Methodist Church as full members and the Roman Catholic Church in Ireland as an Observer Church. At the Inaugural Assembly in Liverpool, on 8th September 1990, the Church of Ireland Bishop of Tuam, the Rt. Rev. John Neill, was elected as one of the C.C.B.I.'s four Presidents. The architects of C.C.B.I., and the Inaugural Assembly, clearly wanted the Council to be for Britain *and Ireland*, and we may note briefly some of the factors that undoubtedly influenced the rather muted response in Ireland.

The Presbyterian and Roman Catholic Churches in Ireland both declined full membership of C.C.B.I. While the Hierarchy did apply for observer status, the General Assembly – despite an eloquent case for membership being put by the Rev. David Nesbitt, Inter-Church Board Convener – did not go even that far. For the General Assembly, the sticking point appears to have been the C.C.B.I.'s commitment to closer communion between the Churches and to Church unity.[64] But the Presbyterian Church had already for some time been moving to the theological right, with a strong body of opinion wanting withdrawal from all ecumenical councils. It had been widely feared that the

General Assembly would take precisely the stance that it did regarding C.C.B.I. membership.

The Roman Catholic Hierarchy did not wish to adopt any position that might upset ecumenical relations within Ireland, or prejudice relations with the Presbyterian Church. Nonetheless, the Hierarchy saw the value in the C.C.B.I. and therefore did accept observer status. Beyond the British Isles, just as the three major Protestant Churches are members of the Conference of European Churches, the Irish Hierarchy is also closely involved in the work of the Council of European Episcopal Conferences, and indeed the CEC and CCEE are currently developing closer relations.

The Church of Ireland was strongly in favour of membership of C.C.B.I., the membership resolution being unanimously endorsed by the General Synod. There had been no major debate about this issue within the Church of Ireland; the view tended to be that this was simply a continuation of the Church of Ireland's ecumenical commitment in the former B.C.C., only now in a much more representative ecumenical structure. The Bishop of Connor, Dr. Poyntz, had played a prominent role over many years in the B.C.C. and was a leading advocate of the new structures as they were being negotiated.

The Methodist Conference was also strongly in favour of full C.C.B.I. membership. The Methodists had of course also been very involved in the B.C.C., and the Rev. Charles Eyre, General Secretary to the Methodist Conference at the time, was supportive of the new moves. The Methodist Church in Ireland has strong links with British Methodism and no doubt this also was an influential factor in the Conference's decision to maintain ecumenical contacts.

The C.C.B.I. has been in existence for an extremely short period; it is clearly in its infancy. It is certainly true that the British Churches want the Council to be more fully representative of the Irish Churches. But it cannot be said to be seriously unrepresentative of Ireland as it stands, for while only the Church of Ireland and the Methodist Church are full member-Churches, the Irish Hierarchy is officially represented at C.C.B.I. Assemblies by observers, and the General Secretary of the Irish Council of Churches is an ex-officio member of the main committees of the Council. David Bleakley, I.C.C. General Secretary from 1980 until 1992, when Dr. David Stevens took over this post, played a full role in the Inter-Church Process and in the formation of the C.C.B.I., and the Roman Catholic Bishop Anthony Farquhar and Fr. P. Devine – both noted ecumenists – attended the 1992 C.C.B.I. Assembly; Bishop Gerard Clifford, before his appointment as Auxiliary Bishop of Armagh, had been an official observer at the 1987

Swanwick Conference, and – along with Bishop Farquhar – at the 1990 Inaugural Assembly of the C.C.B.I..

In many quarters hopes are nurtured that the Presbyterian General Assembly may think again about its membership of the C.C.B.I., particularly after the successful Coleraine Assembly which affirmed 'biblical ecumenism' and seemed to mark the beginning of a process of reconciliation between the major divisions within Irish Presbyterianism. The then Moderator, Dr. Finlay Holmes, affirmed in his foreword to the 'Coleraine Declaration' that 'a sense of unity was evident as we were bound together in our common faith in Christ and search for His will for the way ahead for our Church.'[65] There are also hopes that the Irish Hierarchy might eventually upgrade its membership; Roman Catholics in Britain certainly would welcome such a move, as indeed would all the member-Churches in C.C.B.I.

A strengthening of the Irish link in C.C.B.I. is certainly required, but the Inter-Church Process and the emergence of the C.C.B.I. as a new-style ecumenical instrument have been important factors contributing to current serious discussion about the reform of Irish ecumenical structures; the most obvious way forward would be for the Churches to move towards a merging of the I.C.C. and the Irish Inter-Church Meeting.

CHAPTER 7

Past, Present and Future: Concluding Reflections

Our survey of Irish Church relations in the twentieth century has suggested different ways in which the ecumenical movement gained impetus in Ireland: from the Irish Churches' awareness of the ecumenical movement outside Ireland – as in the Protestant Churches' moves in the earlier years of this century to form a United Council, in later reunion discussions and in the Irish response to the Second Vatican Council; from individuals who themselves were ecumenically committed, as in the student movement in the 1920s and 1930s and in Roman Catholic figures like J.G. McGarry who saw the need for renewal already before the Vatican Council, and who by their writings prepared Roman Catholics in Ireland for the new approaches which the Council affirmed; and from the Churches' recognition, in more recent years, of the need for co-operation and contact as a witness against sectarianism and as a contribution to reconciliation. All of these factors have helped the Irish Churches to experience ecumenical life.

Historically, Irish religion and Irish politics and culture have been so closely inter-related that the latter, 'non-theological factors' have had a profoundly adverse effect on inter-Church relations. The education debates of the 1920s through to the 1940s have been supremely illustrative of the way in which the Protestant Churches and the Roman Catholic Church not only had different outlooks on education, but inhabited very different cultural worlds. Again, the experience of World War II served to emphasize the fundamentally different national identities of Roman Catholics and Protestants in Northern Ireland, and the issue of the Roman Catholic Church's mixed marriage regulations proved to be a stumbling-block between both communities in both parts of Ireland.

Nationally and politically, the Irish experience in the twentieth century has been one of frustrated ambitions. Nationalists have not seen the emergence of a 'unitary' republican state and unionists have seen their vision of Britishness marred by violence and radical dissent within Northern Ireland. Unionists, also, were to be particularly wary of London after the signing of the Anglo-Irish Agreement in 1985;

Archbishop Eames has written of the 'traumatic effect' which the Agreement had on them, and Cardinal Daly has declared unionists as 'justifiably aggrieved'.[1] In terms of the Churches there has been division reinforced by the traditional, cultural and political associations of religion in Ireland. Frustrated ambition and division are the legacy of attempts to realize Irish dreams of all kinds. These have been attempts at self-affirmation through the domination or destruction of opposing traditions. This conflict, historically, has not only been in the heart and mind but also on the streets. The past has dominated the imagination, giving each tradition hopes of final victory and triumph.

The polarisation between Protestants and Roman Catholics in Ireland has hindered the one Church in its effective proclamation of the Gospel of reconciliation. The ground of this polarity, which F.S.L. Lyons describes as a lack of 'coherence' in the Irish experience,[2] lies in folk memory, with its powerful sway over both communities. The challenge facing the Irish Churches in their ministry of reconciliation lies in the 'reconciling of memories'.[3] The symptoms of unreconciled memories are constantly with us: violence, intransigence, bigotry, ignorance, suspicion. These are the factors which impede ecumenical growth in Ireland and they can be overcome only through a very fundamental process of reconciliation.

Opposing cultures and traditions in Ireland, with their consequences in the political arena, will not disappear; they are given data in the contemporary Irish experience. In terms of Heidegger's existentialist philosophy they are part of the givenness of our being, and we are necessarily part of this world. The question for us is how to deal with these data and what role the Churches can have in the process of reconciliation. This brings us to the essentially hermeneutical task which has particular relevance in the context of contradictory Irish traditions.

The Irish experience today is one in which the past, with its symbols and myths, dominates; the present is confused, and the future unclear. This leads to what existentialist philosophy terms 'inauthentic' being. When one aspect of time and experience dominates, there is a distorted existence. J. Macquarrie has written:

What constitutes existence or personal being is a peculiar and complex temporal nexus in which the three dimensions of past, present, and future are brought into a unity. Man differs from a thing or even from an animal in so far as he is not only aware of the present but remembers the past and anticipates the future . . . In an existence that is scattered and disrupted, the existent has cut himself off from one or other of the temporal dimensions of existence, and his existence declines toward the kind of being that belongs to things or animals, though of course he can never lose himself, as it were, in an entirely dehumanized way of being. On the other hand, in an existence that is fulfilling its potentialities, the three dimsensions are held together in unity. Their balance and tension are maintained.[4]

In the Irish mind there is a need for a process of the balancing out of past, present and future in order to gain wholeness of perspective. Maurice Bond has shown how Hans-Georg Gadamer draws out the implications of Heidegger's philosophy of 'Dasein' (Being) for tradition. Gadamer's concern is with the 'rehabilitation of tradition': the dangers of tradition lie not in the traditions themselves but in the way in which they are interpreted. There must be 'progressive' rather than 'static' interpretation. Without a dynamic interpretation of traditions they cannot be preserved in ways which are relevant to successive generations. So for Bond, Gadamer 'would insist that interpretation as opposed to mere repetition is the one way in which man may have a real sense of belonging in his historically constituted world'.[5] Gadamer's 'fusion of horizons' affirms the givenness of traditions in their historical context and with their historical horizon, but calls for a re-interpretation of the past to meet the requirements of the contemporary situation.[6] In this way, past and present horizons are fused into a new and relevant unity. This demands the 'analogical imagination' of David Tracey, who affirms that unless past events are re-interpreted for each generation they will be relegated to the 'dustbin of history'.[7] Furthermore, R. Kearney draws attention to the dangers inherent in trying simply to forget the past: 'To attempt to erase historical remembrance can result in enslavement to the ephemeral immediacies of the present.'[8]

In terms of a praxis for Ireland this will mean asking fundamental questions about the meaning today of 1690, 1916, 1922, 1968 or whatever year or date, and interpreting past events in new ways. This is the 'retrieval' of meaning and is the basis for progressive interpretative method as opposed to static repetition. Traditions thus become dynamic and relevant; in the end, this is also the only way of preserving tradition in a meaningful, helpful and creative way. For example, Orangeism might be seen as a celebration of the freedom of the individual, his or her individual rights and responsibilities in conscience, the revelation of God in Scripture, affiliation to British institutions and values (present horizon), rather than as a static celebration of a Protestant victory over Roman Catholics in battle (past horizon). Similarly, 1916 might be interpreted as an affirmation of distinctively Irish life and Gaelic culture, hope for an independent future, a national identity with a contribution to the global experience (present horizon), as opposed simply to a military victory over the British (past horizon).

In the context of our study of Church relations in Ireland, we must recognize that the Churches have not been able to distance themselves sufficiently from their past in order to make a consistently prophetic contribution in the midst of the relative turmoil of the twentieth century Irish experience. Divided Church and divided nation were themes which the students and young graduates of the 1920s and 1930s could consider, but the obstacles to truly Christian witness in Ireland, posed by the ecclesiastical-political associations, have never been adequately confronted by the Churches themselves. Just as there has to be a distancing of oneself from the past in order to make a radical critique of history, so there must be a distancing of oneself from the present to enable a similar, radical critique of the contemporary situation.

Can we find any new direction for the Irish Churches? In attempting to do so, we shall consider the life of the Churches in the context of four fundamental ecclesiological themes: renewal, diversity, universality and the pilgrim people.

Renewal

The Gospel imperative of one Church and one mission can be forwarded only through renewal in the Churches. Such renewal comes most effectively through concrete example. This has been experienced in Latin America where 'basic church communities' represent a new form of Church life, not in opposition to the institutional Church but as a response to pastoral needs and in the service of wider ecclesial renewal. The liberation theologian, Leonardo Boff, writes: '. . . basic church communities, while signifying the communitarian aspect of Christianity, and signifying it within the church, cannot pretend to constitute a global alternative to the church as institution. They can only be its ferment for renewal.'.[9] In terms of renewing the Irish Churches for a greater realization of the one Church with the one mission, examples will similarly provide a real way forward. As in the basic Church communities of Latin America, and now also in parts of Europe, ecumenical community provides the basis for ecumenical example in Ireland. Such ecumenical communities as Corrymeela, Columbanus, Cornerstone, Glencree, or the Renewal Centre in Rostrevor, provide instances of ecumenical action, convey hope, and encourage other ecumenical attempts: they have a renewing influence. Corrymeela provides opportunities for cross-community encounter and ecumenical formation; the Columbanus Community, on Belfast's Antrim Road, engages in 'prayer, reflection and work for unity in the Church, justice in society and peace on earth so that the world may believe'; Cornerstone aims to encourage cross-community 'living, working and praying' in the Shankill-Falls area of West Belfast; Glencree promotes cross-community relations through meeting, encounter and experience; the Rostrevor community aims to be 'a place of prayer, renewal and reconciliation'.[10] These are concrete examples of ecumenical praxis and are salutory reminders that Church life is intended to be, at its heart, 'communitarian'.

The Latin American sociologist, Pedro Demo, could observe that, 'A large organization can be renewed by a community, but it cannot be transformed into a community';[11] so the institutional Churches in Ireland can find ecumenical renewal through the life of ecumenical communities, but they cannot themselves become such communities 'writ large'. They are institutions and will remain institutions; if they form a union or unions of Churches, they will remain institutional. Institutionalism is, however, a necessary part of human life and need not have negative connotations. The W.C.C. study, *Institutionalism*, placed this subject in its sociological context:

> Cultural history indicates that man has always lived in some form or structure of institutional arrangements which aided him in fulfilling basic social needs and gave meaning, authority, and stability to the cultural order in which he lived. These structures or institutional arrangements have not been merely instrumental, however; they have often expressed his very nature. All cultures thus exhibit types of institutional life as parts of the permanent social existence. Such things as economic order, government, family, communication, art and religion are so basic as to be called by some anthropologists the functional prerequisites of culture.[12]

Institutionalism is thus not a negative concept *per se*; rather, it is a fundamental social phenomenon. In terms of ecclesiastical institutionalism, there remains an inherent paradox: the Church is the community of faith, but is also a social institution. It can never be de-institutionalized but it can be renewed, and if *koinonia* is one of its essential concerns, it will best be renewed by communitarian examples.

In the contemporary Irish context this renewal comes in the form of challenge. As ecumenical communities and groups go about demonstrating a reconciled way of living, they challenge the Churches as institutions to a similar style of relationships. Boff writes: 'Christianity, with its values rooted in love, forgiveness, solidarity, the renunciation of oppressive power, the acceptance of others, and so on, is essentially oriented to creation, within societal structures, of the communitarian spirit'.[13] A vital channel of renewal for the Irish Churches will come through the one Church's life and mission being lived out in exemplary and challenging ways by ecumenical communities. This renewal must, however, be allowed to challenge – and to change – wider Church relationships.

Diversity

Diversity is a characteristic both of creation and Creator. The world which we inhabit is rich in its diversity – physically, culturally and in religious experience – and within the Godhead there is the 'society' of the Trinity. Diversity is at the heart of reality itself and is fundamental to our being, as it is to the being of God.

Hans Küng, during his visit to Ireland in 1985, elaborated on his view of history as a succession of 'paradigm-shifts', from the Jewish-Christian apocalyptic paradigm, to the Hellenistic-Byzantine, the Roman Catholic medieval, the Reformation, and the Modern/Enlightenment paradigm. History, for Küng, was now experiencing a further paradigm-shift, from the Modern/Enlightenment one to a post-Modern paradigm. The post-Modern world, for Küng, will be characterized, amongst other things, by an affirmation of pluralism. It is certainly true that as the world grows smaller through ever greater ease of communication and travel, helped by the new technology, humanity will increasingly be aware of itself as inhabiting a truly global village. The Swiss experience, Küng declared in his lecture, had been one of internal conflict, but there was now a recognition 'that people, despite their different languages, cultures and religions, can live together, that dogmatic all-or-nothing programmes can never help, that compromise is not surrender, that the only realistic way out entails the effort of mutual understanding, moderation, accommodation and co-operation . . . and last, but not least, that the most elementary presupposition for such a solution is to build up trust, one small step at a time.'[14]

There are various models of Church unity current in the contemporary ecumenical discussion: organic union, conciliar fellowship, reconciled diversity, communion of communions, unity as solidarity.[15] All of these recognize the rightness of diversity. Organic union, which was affirmed as the goal of the ecumenical movement at the 1961 New Delhi WCC Assembly, allows for diversity in life and worship, but unlike the other models does not consider the preservation of separate ecclesiastical, denominational identities as desirable in a truly reconciled Church. Ecumenical growth can only come, however, by steps. The 1981 Anglican document *Unity by Stages* set forth various progressive objectives for Churches in dialogue: Fellowship in Faith and Mission, Limited Eucharistic Sharing, Full Communion, Organic Union.[16]

Writing in the American ecumenical journal, *Mid-Stream*, the British ecumenist, Martin Conway, has considered five 'stages of the pilgrimage into unity', marking a growth in ecumenical understanding within the Churches: from competition to co-existence, to co-operation, to commitment, to communion.[17] The Irish Churches, as national institutions, have moved from a spirit of competition through co-existence to a position of co-operation. Within Northern Ireland, however, there still obtain situations at local level where Protestants and Roman Catholics are at the stage of co-existence, if not competition. Duncan Morrow, in the 1991 University of Ulster's Centre for the Study of Conflict report, *The Churches and Inter-community Relationships*, draws the sad conclusion that the Churches have a tendency 'to become protective fortresses for threatened people rather than places of open and profound discussion',[18] although in the previous year Professor John Whyte took a rather less negative view of the Churches' contribution to sectarianism and conflict in Northern Ireland.[19] Nevertheless, even at best, there still is a serious lack in the fourth stage discussed by Conway: commitment. An Irish praxis of diversity will demand of the Churches that they move from co-operation to commitment, not only recognizing one another as Churches, not only doing things together, but entering into a commitment to be the one people of God in Ireland in life, faith, worship and witness. This will mean a fundamental sharing of concerns and an entering into one another's life as an integral part of all ecclesial experience – the ideal at the heart of the British Inter-Church Process, 'Not Strangers But Pilgrims' which led to the formation of the Council of Churches for Britain and Ireland in 1990 (See further Ch. VI, Section 6). As Professor McDonagh writes: 'The present concern is not some radical transformation of the Irish Churches into some great Church but a more profound conversion to one another that will release them from their quasi-political Babylonian captivity.'.[20] Thus the development of an ecumenical praxis of diversity will require commitment through such a 'conversion to one another'.

Universality

The Irish Churches do not exist in ecclesiastical isolation, but share their ecclesial life with the whole Church of God universal; this universal Church can bring new perspectives and new life to the local Church in Ireland. There are vast horizons here for Irish Christians to appropriate – horizons which can have a profound influence on their own outlook, appreciation and contribiution to the contemporary Irish experience. The local and universal aspects of ecclesial reality form a creative symbiosis in the life of the whole Church: the local Church contributes its distinctive features and traditions to the life of the whole Church; the universal Church challenges the local community to reflect on its life with wider perspectives than it alone can provide. The universal Church experience acts as a means of raising the life of the local Church from the narrower context of local concerns to a life which looks towards wider horizons. In challenging the local Church, the universal Church experience also exercises a critique of local life, asks fundamental questions, and calls the local Church to a more profound reflection on its life and witness in the local scene. This universal Church experience can stimulate the local Church to a wider and more balanced appreciation of its own life and role in society. The rich diversity of the universal Church enables it to speak in many and direct ways to local situations.

In this context the Irish Churches might ask what they have to learn from the experience of Churches in other situations. How can the Churches in Ireland grow towards a greater common concern for justice and social issues, such as is manifested in many other national Church experiences? What do the Churches of Ireland, and indeed of other countries, have to learn from the experience of the Church in China where denominationalism is unknown among Protestants? What implications does the Chinese Christian experience have for Churches and communions which have been trying for decades to reach doctrinal agreement? What have we to learn from the suffering of the Church in many foreign lands? In terms of the mixed marriages issue, what can we learn from the ecumenical experience in Holland or Germany or Switzerland, for example?

These questions are all vital ones and speak directly to the Irish experience. There are, no doubt, countless similar questions which we could pose by way of example of the potential for challenge in the ecumenical praxis of universality. This theme is closely related to those of renewal and diversity. All of these themes are further brought together in what is essentially the eschatological context.

Pilgrim People

The constant process of renewal, which is vital if the Church is to relate positively to each succeeding generation, is part of its eschatological journey; as the Church experiences renewal, it shapes its life for mission and its experience is clearly seen as growth in Kingdom-life. The Church is on a pilgrimage into the fulness of the Kingdom and as it renews itself for mission in successive ages, its life as journey is clearly illustrated. The history of salvation, under the sovereignty of the God who sustains the created order, tends towards the Kingdom and as the Church participates in this unfolding experience it journeys towards the Kingdom: renewal is for the sake of the Kingdom.

This Kingdom, which the Church announces to the world, is inclusive in its life; it brings creation, with its rich diversity, to new and fuller life. The Church therefore, as agent of the Kingdom and as 'sacrament of salvation', is called to an affirmation of diversity and to a ministry of integration – bringing together, under the rule of Christ, the plural and universal life of humankind and all creation. This is fundamental to the mission of God's pilgrim people.

The concept of the pilgrim people was introduced to the contemporary ecumenical context by Edmund Schlink at the Lund Faith and Order Conference in 1952.[21] With its eschatological implications, which Schlink had stressed, the pilgrim people concept was subsequently reflected in the official documents of Vatican II. Prior to the Council, the Roman Catholic Church had been reluctant to embrace this style of ecclesiology for it was felt that it tended to suggest the imperfection of the Church, its limitations and inadequacies. This ran counter to the Roman Catholic Church's pre-Conciliar ecclesiology, shaped by Vatican I with its apologetic and juridical characteristics.

It was in Chapter VII of *Lumen Gentium* that Vatican II expounded the pilgrim Church most fully. Here the Constitution declares that the Church 'will receive its perfection only in the glory of heaven . . .'. Further, 'until there be realized new heavens and a new earth in which justice dwells (cf 2 Pet. 3:13) the pilgrim Church, in its sacraments and institutions, which belong to this present age, carries the mark of this world which will pass, and she herself takes her place among the creatures which groan and travail yet and await the revelation of the sons of God (cf. Rom. 8:19-22).'[22]

The image of the pilgrim people is particularly evocative in the Irish context, for in Ireland we are very familiar with the pilgrimage. The pilgrim makes his or her religious journey in a marginalized situation: there is dislocation, as well as devotion, penitence and the joy of the Spirit. The purpose of the pilgrimage is to grow in spirit and to be more authentically Christian. There must always be what V. and E. Turner have described as the 'liminoid' experience for the pilgrim people, a moving out from the familiar, the routine, into the unfamiliar, even the dangerous.[23] This is necessary if the Church is to fulfil its calling to prefigure and to promote the Kingdom. For Irish Christians there is an abiding challenge in the call to be a pilgrim people: it is the challenge to stand back and truly to recognize the need to transcend the cultural and societal moulds and to choose another pilgrimage. The Irish Churches can indeed find a way forward, by pursuing the way of renewal, by recognizing the rightness of diversity, by entering into that creative exchange between the local and the universal Church, and by standing back together from both past and present to gain a new vision of that future which is God's alone.

NOTES

(Abbreviation: JGS = Journal of the General Synod of the Church of Ireland)

Chapter 1

1. The latter two are now known as the World Alliance of Reformed Churches and the World Methodist Council.
2. The Secession arose in the mid-18th century, mainly over the issue of patronage. Cf. R. G. Crawford, *The Second Subscription Controversy and the Personalities of the Non-Subscribers*; R. F. G. Holmes, *Controversy and Schism in the Synod of Ulster in the 1820s*; and J. Thompson, *The Formation of the General Assembly* – all in *Challenge and Conflict: Essays in Irish Presbyterian History and Doctrine*, Antrim, W. & G. Baird Ltd, 1981, pp 96-115, 116-133 and 134-148 respectively.
3. Primitive Wesleyan Methodism was founded by Adam Averell, who resisted the authorising of Methodist ministers to administer the sacraments (Irish Methodists received the sacraments in the Church of Ireland until 1878); cf. ed. R. Rouse and S. Neill, *A History of the Ecumenical Movement: 1517-1948*, SPCK 1954, p 301.
4. The former descended from the 17th century Secession and the 19th century Disruption, at the root of both of which lay the issues of establishment and patronage; both united in 1929 to form the present Church of Scotland, with a small United Free Church remnant. The 'Wee Frees', mainly of the Highlands, refused to recognize the Union in 1900 of the Free Church and the United Presbyterian Church, and have remained separate to this day.
5. First meeting: 10th October, 1905.
6. The Presbyterian and Methodist Churches' Inter-Church Relations Committees were formed in 1946 and 1955 respectively, from committees which had already been dealing with reunion matters.
7. General Assembly Minutes 1873, pp 481f.
8. As in ed. R. Rouse and S. Neill, *A History of the Ecumenical Movement 1517-1948*, SPCK 1954, p 251.
9. Although the Quadrilateral remains a fundamental document, modern ecumenical dialogue involving Anglicans is more broadly-based. The report of the sixth meeting of the Anglican Consultative Council, Badagry, Nigeria 1984, entitled *Bonds of Affection* (ACC 1984, p 76) commented on the Quadrilateral as follows: 'The issues it outlines remain critical and central, but the agenda is now our ecumenical documents. This is where Anglicanism is growing in its relationship to other churches and in its self-understanding.'. Cf. also S. G. Poyntz, *The 1888 Chicago-Lambeth Quadrilateral: A Contemporary Review*, in *Search* Vol. 11 No. 1 Spring 1988, pp 53-60; and J. F. Woolverton, *The Quadrilateral and the Lambeth Conferences*, together with *Comments* by S. Neill, J. Gibbs and J. C. Maraschin, in *Historical Magazine of the Protestant Episcopal Church* (USA) Vol. LIII No. 2 June 1984 – *Anglican Self-Understanding and Ecumenism: Papers for the Anglican Consultative Council, Nigeria 1984* (Woolverton article pp 95-109; Neill, pp 111-121; Gibbs pp 123-125; Maraschin pp 127f).
10. JGS 1910, p 305.
11. *ibid.*, pp 305f.
12. Bishop of Clogher, 1908-1923.

163

Chapter 1—continued

13. J. A. F. Gregg, *The 'Ne Temere' Decree*, Dublin, APCK, revised ed. 1943, pp 9f.
14. *Anglican-Presbyterian Relations*, in *Irish Anglicanism 1869-1969*, Allen Figgis Ltd, Dublin 1970, p 67.
15. F. S. L. Lyons, *Ireland Since the Famine*, Weidenfeld & Nicolson 1971, p 12.
16. *World Missionary Conference, 1910*, IX, p 331.
17. R. Rouse & S. Neill, *A History of the Ecumenical Movement 1517-1948, op. cit.*, p 416 (for a detailed account of the various delegations, cf. pp 407ff).
18. Cf M. Blondel, *Les premier écrits de Maurice Blondel*, Paris 1956 (ET *The Letter on Apologetics and History and Dogma*, London 1964); A. Loisy, *L'Évangle et l'Église*, 1902; G. Tyrrell, *Christianity at the Crossroads*, London 1963 (reprinted). On Blondel cf. J. Lacroix, *Maurice Blondel: sa vie, son oeuvre*, Paris 1963 (ET *Maurice Blondel: An Introduction to the Man and his Philosophy*, New York 1968); on Loisy, cf. E. Poulat, *Histoire, dogme et critique dans la crise moderniste*, Casterman 1962; on Tyrrell, cf F. M. O'Connor's article in *New Catholic Encyclopaedia*, XIV.
19. M. Schoof, *Breakthrough: Beginnings of the New Catholic Theology*, Gill and Macmillan 1970, pp 46 & 48.
20. Cf J. H. Newman's *Essay on the Development of Christian Doctrine* and *Grammar of Assent*. On Newman, cf J. H. Walgrave, *Newman the Theologian*, London 1960, and C. Biemer, *Newman on Tradition*, London & New York 1967.
21. G. Daly, *Catholicism and Modernity*, in *Journal of the American Academy of Religion*, LIII/3, p 778; cf also G. Daly, *Transcendence and Immanence: A Study in Catholic Modernism and Integralism*, Oxford, Clarendon Press, 1980
22. Cf A. Gardeil, *Le donné révélé et la théologie*, Paris 1932; on Rousselot, cf special issues of Fourviere journal *Recherches de science religieuse* (53) 1965.
23. JGS 1912. p 355.
24. *ibid.* 1913, p 366.
25. *Anglican-Presbyterian Relations, op. cit.*, p 68.
26. Cf ed Moody, Martin and Byrne, *A New History of Ireland*, VIII/I (Chronology), Oxford 1982, p 384.
27. Cf *ibid*, p 385.
28. *ibid.*
29. Cf *ibid.*, pp 385ff.
30. The Archbishop of Armagh (Crozier), the Rev. James Bingham (Presbyterian Moderator), the Rev. W R Budd (Methodist Vice-President) and Cardinal Logue.
31. Cf *A New History of Ireland, op. cit.*, pp 377 & 384.
32. JGS 1920, p 316.
33. *The Spectator*, 17 February 1917, p 200; cf. Report of UCCCRCI in JGS 1923, p 317.
34. The Archbishop of Armagh (D'Arcy) (who had succeeded to Armagh in 1920), the Bishops of Meath (Plunkett), Clogher (Day), Derry (Peacocke), Down (Grierson), Kilmore (Moore), Tuam (Ross), Cashel (Miller), Cork (Dowse) and Ossory (Gregg).
35. *The Report of Lambeth Conference 1920*, SPCK 1920, p 26.
36. JGS 1920, p 314.
37. L. Vischer, *Christian Councils – Their Future as Instruments of the Ecumenical Movement*, in *Study Encounter*, WCC Vol. IV No. 2 1968, pp 97-108; cf also on Councils of Churches, *Mid-Stream* (USA) Vol. XXII No. 2 April 1983.
38. Cf JGS 1924, p 315.
39. Cf *ibid.*, p 318.
40. ed. R Rouse and S Neill, *A History of the Ecumenical Movement 1517-1948, op. cit.*, p 298.
41. '. . . it is clear that the Apostolic See can by no means take part in these assemblies (inter-Church conferences on Reunion), nor is it in any way lawful for Catholics to give to such enterprises their encouragement or support. If they did so, they

Chapter 1—continued

would be giving countenance to a false Christianity quite alien to the one Church of Christ. Shall we commit the iniquity of suffering the truth, the truth revealed by God, to be made a subject for compromise? For it is indeed a question of defending revealed truth.' *Mortalium Animos*, as in ed. G. K. A. Bell, *Documents on Christian Unity 1920-1930*, 2nd edition, Oxford 1930, p 57.

42. JGS 1926, pp 310f.
43. P. Corish, *The Irish Catholic Experience – a historical survey*, Gill & Macmillan 1985, p 224.
44. ed. R. Rouse and S. Neill, *A History of the Ecumenical Movement 1517-1948, op. cit.*, p 540.
45. JGS 1925, p 288.
46. JGS 1924, p 316.
47. JGS 1928, p 343.
48. JGS 1929. p 346
49. *Irish Anglicanism, op. cit.*, p 72.
50. Irish bishops present: Armagh (D'Arcy), Meath (Orr), Clogher (Macmanaway), Derry (Peacocke), Down (Grierson), Kilmore (Barton), Tuam (Harden), Dublin (Gregg), Cashel (Miller), Cork (Dowse), Killaloe (Patton), Limerick (White) and Ossory (Day).
51. F. S. L. Lyons, *op. cit.*, p 13.
52. J. M. Barkley, *Anglican-Presbyterian Relations, op.cit.*, p65.
53. Cf D. Keogh, *The Vatican, the Bishops and Irish Politics: 1919-1939*, CUP 1986, pp 7ff.

Chapter 2

1. For the beginnings of the SCM in the British Isles one must look to the 1870s and 1880s and what Bishop Stephen Neill described as 'a great renewal of interest in the Christian faith (which) had been sweeping through Britain, and in particular was touching the ancient Universities of Oxford and Cambridge.' (*Men of Unity*, SCM 1960, p 16). In Ireland, the Dublin University Christian Association was founded in 1889, in which year it sent two representatives to the Oxford Inter-Collegiate Conference. Inter-University Christian Groups – the precursors of the SCM – were formed in the University of Dublin several years later in 1893, in Queen's in 1894, in Galway and Londonderry in 1896, in the Royal College of Surgeons in 1898 and in other higher education establishments in Ireland in subsequent years. In some cases there were separate groups for men and women. In Dublin, the University Christian Association affiliated to the Inter-University Christian Union in 1894. The year 1910 saw the formation of the Irish Inter-Collegiate Christian Union as an integral part of the Student Christian Movement of Great Britain and Ireland.
2. F. C. Baur, 1792-1860; D. F. Strauss, 1808-1874.
3. S. Neill, *The Interpretation of the New Testament: 1861-1961*, OUP 1964, pp 30f.
4. The rooms were those of Professor William Kennedy, the father of Bishop Donald Kennedy.
5. Alan R. Cole and T.H. Lyle were former members of both the EU and the Trinity SCM (the No. 40 group became the Trinity EU). Alan Cole subsequently taught theology in Singapore and Australia.
6. Herbert Carson, formerly of the Church of Ireland, is now a Baptist pastor; Ernest Strathdee was a member of the SCM committee in Queen's in the early 1940s, but later became President of the Queen's Bible Union.
7. The Federation was formed in Sweden, at Castle Vadstena, beside Lake Vettern, at the beginning of a world tour of universities and colleges by Mott.

Chapter 2—continued

8. Interview.
9. A. I. C. Heron, *A Century of Protestant Theology*, Lutterworth 1980, p 69.
10. C. H. Hopkins, *John R Mott*, Eerdmans/WCC 1979, p 384.
11. *ibid.*, p 385.
12. 'The War and Our Faith' was the title of a conference held at the Rev J S Rutherford's manse in Dun Laoghaire in 1939; 'Believing in God and Living in Ireland' was an ICF conference held in 1944.
13. *Ireland's Hope: A Call to Service*, SCM 1913, p 1.
14. *ibid.*, p 3.
15. *ibid.*, p 163; cf also p 174.
16. *ibid.*, p 175.
17. *Towards a Better Ireland: The Report of a Conference on Applied Christianity Held in Dublin, January 1926*, Talbot Press, Dublin and Cork 1926, p 34.
18. 'Copec': Conference on Christian Politics, Economics and Citizenship – held in Birmingham in 1924; it was a preparation for the 1925 Stockholm Conference. (See also Ch. I, *ad loc.*)
19. *Report, op. cit.*, Intro., p 5.
20. On the Social Gospel, cf G. W. Forrell, *Christian Social Teachings*, Augsburg Publishing House, Minneapolis, 1971.
21. See Ch. I, *ad loc.*
22. *Ireland's Hope, op. cit.*, p 8.
23. F. S. L. Lyons, *Ireland Since the Famine*, Weidenfeld & Nicolson 1971, p 42.
24. *ibid.*, p 46.
25. L. M. Cullen, *The Emergence of Modern Ireland: 1600-1900*, Gill & Macmillan 1981, p 157.
26. *ibid.*, p 164.
27. *ibid.*, p 171; cf. also K. A. Miller, *Emigration, Ideology and Identity in Post-Famine Ireland*, in *Studies* LXXV 1984, pp 300ff.
28. J. C. Beckett, *The Anglo-Irish Tradition*, Faber and Faber 1976, p 71.
29. J. C. Beckett, *The Making of Modern Ireland: 1603-1923*, Faber and Faber 1966, p 183; cf also M. E. Daly, *Dublin the Deposed Capital: A social and economic history*, Cork 1984.
30. J. C. Beckett, *The Anglo-Irish Tradition, op. cit.*, p 71.
31. *ibid.*, p 72.
32. Cf also B. C. Waller, *Hibernia, or The Future of Ireland*, London, Kegan Paul, Trench and Trubner, no date.
33. *Ireland's Hope, op. cit.*, p 4.
34. *ibid.*, p 13.
35. *Looking at Ireland*, by members of the ICF, SCM 1937, pp 64f.
36. *ibid.*, p 61.
37. *ibid.*, pp 56f.
38. *ibid.*, p 61.
39. *ibid.*, p 123.
40. *ibid.*, p 139.
41. T. M. Barker, Irish Secretary from 1911-13 and 1931-32 became a missionary in China (during 1931-2, his second term as Secretary, he was home on leave); J. E. Neill was a Methodist SCM member who went as a missionary to China; K. Huggard played a particularly active role in the life of the ICF as well as in countless other ecumenical efforts; M. A. (Molly) McNeill, a founder member of the Irish Association, was deeply committed to the cause of reconciliation, and her writings included *The Life and Times of Mary Ann McCracken*; B. Waller worked with the League of Nations until his early death; J. S. Rutherford wrote *Christian Reunion in Ireland*; Donald Kennedy, Irish Secretary from 1940-42, subsequently

Chapter 2—continued

became a bishop in the Church of North India (he was ordained as a Presbyterian); Isabel Megaw (now Mrs Kennedy) was Irish Women's Secretary from 1940-43; J. R. Boyd was Belfast Secretary from 1941-44 and Schools Secretary from 1944-49, and later became Professor of Practical Theology at Assembly's College, Belfast; Sinclair Stevenson, a Presbyterian who attended the 1927 Lausanne Faith and Order Conference, served in Gujurat; G. O. Simms was Church of Ireland Primate from 1969-80; Brian Harvey became Dean of Ossory and was joint-author of *The Loom of God* (with R. P. C. Hanson); R. H. S. Boyd was Director of the Irish School of Ecumenics from 1980-87; A. T. and R. P. C. Hanson (Bishop of Clogher, 1970-73) were both closely involved.

Such a short list is not intended to be exhaustive, but as an illustration of the influence which the SCM had on later Irish Church life. For the background to the early SCM see T. Tatlow, *The Story of the Student Christian Movement of Great Britain and Ireland* (SCM, 1933). For a study of the SCM in Ireland in more recent years, see M. Rowan, *The Student Christian Movement in Ireland: 1950-1980*, University of Dublin M. Phil. (Ecum.) dissertation, unpublished, 1985.

42. E.g. Tom Barker, who was influential in planning the early SCM activities in Ireland; Kathleen Huggard, who was widely involved in inter-Church, missionary and charitable activities; Bolton Waller, who gave profound thought to world peace issues; and many others (see previous note).

43. For an appreciation of Kathleen Huggard, see I. M. Ellis, *In Retrospect* article, *Search – A Church of Ireland Journal*, Winter 1985, pp 83-7.

44. In ed M. Hurley, *Irish Anglicanism: 1869-1969*, Figgis, Dublin 1970, pp 214f.

45. This work is unpublished. It is among Rutherford's papers deposited at the Irish School of Ecumenics, Dublin.

46. Amongst papers deposited at the Irish School of Ecumenics, Dublin.

47. *ibid.*, for source.

48. Cf further, ed. W. A. Phillips, *History of the Church of Ireland, Vol III: The Modern Church*, OUP 1933, pp 131-3.

49. J. M. Barkley, *Irish Presbyterianism and Inter-Church Relations*, General Assembly Board of Inter-Church Relations 1975, p 3.

50. *ibid.*, pp 5-7.

51. J. S. Rutherford, *Christian Reunion in Ireland*, Dublin, Friends of Reunion, no date (Foreword: June 1942), pp 30-37.

52. *ibid.*, p 80.

53. P. McKevitt, *The Background of Rerum Novarum*, in *Christus Rex*, Vol. V No. 4 Oct 1951, pp 336-345.

54. J. D. Holmes, *The Papacy in the Modern World*, London, Burns & Oates 1981, p 80.

55. *ibid.*, p 81.

56. Cf J. H. Whyte, *Church and State in Modern Ireland: 1923-1970*, Gill & Macmillan 1971, p 63.

57. *ibid.*, p 66.

58. Cf S. Rynne, *Father John Hayes*, Dublin 1960.

59. E. McDonagh, *Between Chaos and New Creation: Doing theology at the fringe*, Gill & Macmillan 1986, p 168.

60. *Rerum Novarum*, see *Irish Ecclesiastical Record*, June-August 1891 Vol. XII; *Quadragesimo Anno*, see *ibid.*, August-September 1931 Vol. XXXVIII.

61. In *Christus Rex* Vol. II No. 2 April 1948, p 6.

62. New Catholic Encyclopaedia, *ad loc.*

63. *ibid.*

64. C. B. Daly, *Christus Rex Society*, in *Christus Rex*, Vol. I No. 1 1947, p 27.

65. C. Lucey, *The Ethics of Nationalisation*, in *Christus Rex*, Vol. I No. 1 January 1947, p 26.

Chapter 2—continued

66. M. J. Browne (Most Rev., Bishop of Galway), *Why Catholic Priests Should Concern Themselves with Social and Economic Questions*, in *Christus Rex*, Vol. I No. 1 January 1947, pp 3-9; and E. Boyland, *The Priest, Social Studies and Spirituality*, in *ibid.*, Vol. I No. 4 October 1947, pp 46-55.

67. Both quotations, *ibid.*, pp 6 and 53f.

68. Cf. Whyte, *Church and State in Modern Ireland: 1923-1970, op. cit.*, pp 333f.

69. In *The Irish Catholic*, 11th August 1983. Betjeman, the future Poet Laureat, was an active committee member and a frequent speaker at the meetings of the Mercier Society. At the time he was a member of the wartime staff of the British Embassy in Dublin, as Press Attache. He had a particular interest in the Protestant denominations, although he himself was an Anglo-Catholic.

70. T. O'Flynn, *Frank Duff as I Knew Him*, Dublin, Praedicanda Publications 1981, p 35.

71. The Clonard Mission was the result of a successful course which was held in Advent 1947 and which aroused much interest amongst Protestants. In the following year, the Clonard 'Mission to Non-Catholics' commenced with a Lent programme which attracted an estimated audience of 800 people. The nature of the proceedings has been described as follows: 'The preachers emphasized that the purpose of the mission was information. The Catholic teaching on a certain subject was explained, then questions submitted by listeners were answered. After the Service the congregation was invited to inspect the Church and the Sacristy with the sacred vessels, vestments and liturgical books.' (*Clonard Church and Monastery*, privately published, no date, p 39). In the 1960s the Mission was still attracting considerable numbers, although by no means as many as in its early days. The Vatican II years prompted a change of name in 1965 to 'The Mission for our Separated Brethren'; in the following year it was billed as 'Talks for all religious Communions on Vatican II, Constitution on the Church'. In 1967 it was simply entitled, 'Lectures for all Communions'. The following year saw the last Clonard Mission, although contacts with Protestants are still fostered at Clonard today.

72. L. O Broin, *Frank Duff: A Biography*, Gill & Macmillan 1982, pp 63f.

73. See M. O'Carroll, *A Society Ahead of its Time*, in *The Irish Catholic*, 11.8.1983.

74. D. Bowen, *The Protestant Crusade in Ireland: 1800-1870*, Gill & Macmillan/McGill-Queen's University Press, 1978, pp, 259f.

75. After Vatican II, at which he was appointed a *peritus*, Frank Duff founded the Pauline Circle, a small inter-denominational study group which still meets today. He died on 7th November 1980, having attended the Pauline Circle for the last time only three days previously.

Chapter 3

1. Formed in December, 1924; Secretaries—Rev. J. Quinn (Church of Ireland), Rev. W. H. Smyth (Methodist) and Rev. W. Corkey (Presbyterian). Cf W. Corkey, *Glad did I Live: Memoirs of a Long Life*, Belfast News Letter 1962, p 246.

2. This United Committee is, of course, completely distinct from the later Protestant Secondary Education Committee (Church of Ireland – Presbyterian – Methodist – Friends) which was formed in the Republic in 1965-66. Protestant concerns were different in the Republic: first, there had been the issue of the imposition of the Irish language, and then a debate about the provision of free secondary education in the 1960s, which gave rise to the Protestant Secondary Education Committee, as Protestant interests were, again, held in common. The Southern Government used the educational system – without particular concern

Chapter 3—continued

for the educational good of Irish children – for the purposes of furthering the Gaelic Revival. R Fanning writes: 'Hence the so-called gaelicisation of the primary schools where, from 1926, all infant classes were taught through Irish regardless of the educational consequences for children who spoke not a word of Irish in their homes.' (*Independent Ireland*, Helicon History of Ireland, Helicon 1983, p 81).

Regarding Protestant reaction, A. V. O'Connor and S. M. Parkes write: 'There was much resistance to the teaching of Irish among the Anglo-Irish community, partly because of (the) compulsion and partly because it was not seen as part of their culture. Some others felt that the language had little value outside Ireland, and that the teaching of languages such as French and German would suffer as a consequence.' (*Gladly Learn and Gladly Teach: Alexandra College and School 1866-1966*, Blackwater Press, p 149).

A major finding of the Southern Government's 1966 report *Investment in Education* was that the percentage of children not progressing from primary to post-primary education was still too high. The report included many statistical analyses, including one showing the numbers of pupils in full-time education at the three levels (February, 1964): First level: 496,068; Second level: 129,365; Third level: 16,819 (*Investment in Education*, p 4, Table 1.2). As a result of the findings of this study the Government embarked on a series of reforms, which have been summarized by F.S.L. Lyons: 'The list. . .includes a much more determined drive than hitherto to consolidate and amalgamate the small or rural schools; the building of comprehensive schools designed to combine both grammar-school and vocational courses for scattered communities; a massive development of vocational education in general, with particular emphasis upon the establishment of regional Colleges of Technology; the provision of free secondary education, though on terms that make the participation of the Protestant schools difficult, and also of free transportation; the allocation of much larger funds for scholarships, especially to the universities; the revision of the Leaving Certificate syllabus to allow of greater specialisation.' (*Ireland Since the Famine*, Weidenfeld & Nicolson, London 1971, p 642). The Protestant Churches were dissatisfied with the proposals for free secondary education because, while the Government's *per capita* grant of £25 was acceptable to the Roman Catholic authorities (for they made considerable savings through their religious orders), it was wholly inadequate for Protestant schools in which the fees were on average at least double the capitation grant. In addition, a considerable number of Protestant children lived too far from day schools and had to board. The Minister of Education agreed to make a 'block grant' to compensate Protestants, but they remained dissatisfied because the fund was not adequate to meet the costs of Protestant secondary schooling and parents would therefore have to be subjected to a means test.

3. Education Act (N.I.) 1923, 13 & 14 Geo. 5, ch. 21.
4. W. Corkey, *Episode in the History of Protestant Ulster*, (privately published), p 37.
5. See *Codex Iuris Canonici* (1917), in *Acta Apostolicae Sedis*, Annus IX, Vol. IX, Pars II, Rome 1917.
6. W. E. Davison, *A Critical Analysis of the Decisions of the General Assembly of the Presbyterian Church in Ireland on Social Issues, 1921-1970*, doctoral thesis, QUB 1977, Vol. 1, p 158. Cf. Government of Ireland Act 1920, 10 & 11 Geo. 5, ch. 67
7. Education Act (N.I.) 1925, 15 Geo. 5, ch. 1
8. W. Corkey, *Episode, op. cit.*, p 47.
9. D. H. Akenson, *Education and Enmity: The Control of Schooling in Northern Ireland 1920-1950*, David & Charles: Newton Abbot / Barnes & Noble Books: New York 1973, pp 86f.

Chapter 3—continued

10. Bishop Mageean; see *ibid.*, pp 113f.
11. Report on Primary Education, General Assembly Reports 1930, p 116. Cf. Education Act (N.I.) 1930, 20 & 21 Geo. 5, ch. 14, and Corkey, *Episode, op. cit.*, p 85.
12. *ibid.*, p 86.
13. Akenson, *op. cit.*, p 109.
14. *ibid.*, pp 110f.
15. W. Corkey, *Episode, op. cit.*, p 91.
16. Akenson, *op. cit.*, p 127.
17. W.. S Kerr (Church of Ireland), W. H. Smyth (Methodist) and W. Corkey (Presbyterian).
18. In 1943, Professor Corkey had been appointed as Minister of Education by the Prime Minister (Sir Basil Brooke), who had also appointed another Presbyterian cleric, the Rev. Robert Moore, as Minister of Agriculture.
19. Corkey, *Episode, op. cit.*, p 105.
20. *ibid.*, p 107.
21. General Assembly Minutes 1944, pp 50f; cf W E Davison, *op.cit.*, p 368.
22. W. Corkey, *Government White Paper*, a pamphlet, as in W. E. Davison, *op. cit.*, p 368.
23. Akenson, *op. cit.*, p 165.
24. W. Corkey, *Episode, op. cit.*, p 116.
25. *ibid.*, pp 114f.
26. W. E. Davison, *op. cit.*, p 382. Cf. Education Act (N.I.) 1947, 10 & 11 Geo. 6, ch. 4.
27. P. Corish, *The Irish Catholic Experience: a historical survey*, Gill & Macmillan, Dublin 1985, p 165.

Chapter 4

1. In ed. R. Rouse and S. Neill, *A History of the Ecumenical Movement: 1517-1948*, SPCK 1954, p 594.
2. B. C. Waller, *The Church and Political Systems*, reprinted from *The Church of Ireland Gazette*, 1936. Cf also, Waller, *Paths to World Peace*, London, George Allen & Unwin 1926.
3. Two quotations: *The Church and Political Systems, op. cit.*, pp 5 & 7.
4. ed. Moody, Martin & Byrne, *A New History of Ireland*, VIII, Part I, Oxford 1982, p 452. Much of the detailed information in this section has been found in this reference work.
5. Cf. statement in *Irish Historical Record*, 5 Series, Vol. LIII No. 6 (June 1939), p 665, as in D. H. Atkinson, *Education and Enmity: the control of schooling in Northern Ireland, 1920-1950*, David & Charles, Newton Abbot; Barnes & Noble Books, New York 1973, pp 147f.
6. J. T. Carroll, *Ireland in the War Years: 1939-45*, David & Charles, Newton Abbot; Crane, Russak & Co Inc, New York 1975, p 24.
7. The new World Council of Churches, established in 1948, was instrumental in organizing a £1m fund to restore the churches of Europe; the Irish Protestant Churches made their contribution.
8. Cf *Full Employment in Ireland*, Brown & Nolan Dublin – the report of the committee.
9. P. Corish, *The Irish Catholic Experience*, Gill & Macmillan 1985, p 251.
10. N. Browne, *Against the Tide*, Gill & Macmillan 1986, p 177.
11. *ibid.*, p 170.
12. P. Corish, *op. cit.*, p 12.

Chapter 4—continued

13. The Joint Church of Ireland-Presbyterian Committee for Reunion, as appointed in 1931, was composed as follows: *Church of Ireland*: The Lord Primate (D'Arcy), the Archbishop of Dublin (Gregg), the Bishop of Cork (Dowse), the Bishop of Down (Grierson), the Bishop of Ossory (Godfrey Day), the Bishop of Limerick (White), the Dean of Christ Church (Kennedy), the Archdeacon of Dromore (W S Kerr), Canon Drury, Canon Hearn, Rev H.W. Rennison, Lord Farnham, Lord Justice Best, Capt. Carden, Messrs. J. Bristow and J.A. Maconchy. *Presbyterian Church*: Very Rev Drs Clarke, Haslett, Morrow, Rev W.M. Cargin, Rev Prof Davey, Rev Principal Paul, Revs J.J. Macaulay, R.L. Marshall, A.F. Moody, J.S. Rutherford, J. Waddell, Prof Macalister, Prof McElderry, Messrs J. McCaughy, S.J. Payne and J.H. Robb KC, MP.

14. JGS 1934, p 407.

15. *ibid.*, p 408.

16. *ibid.*

17. *ibid.*, p 410.

18. JGS 1935, p 363.

19. Geo. Seaver, *John Allen Fitzgerald Gregg*, Faith Press, Dublin 1963, pp 176-179.

20. Cf *ibid.*, p 177.

21. JGS 1936, pp 363f.

22. *Appeal to All Christian People*, Lambeth 1920, Sections VI and VII.

23. JGS 1936, p 364.

24. Seaver, *op. cit.*, p 112.

25. C. F. D'Arcy, *The Adventures of a Bishop*, Hodder & Stoughton 1934, p 220.

26. *ibid.*

27. *ibid.*, p 276.

28. JGS 1974, p 182.

29. J. A. Gurrieri, *Sacramental Validity: The Origins and Use of a Vocabulary*, in *The Jurist*, 41 – 1981, pp 27f.

30. *ibid.*, p 40.

31. R. Hooker, *Laws of Ecclesiastical Polity*, Oxford 1841, *ad loc.*, as in Gurrieri, *op. cit.*, pp 41f.

32. Gurrieri, *op. cit.*, p 32 (cf also p 46). The principle of the *leges irritantes* was that 'the law could render null and void those things which are contrary to it'; Gurrieri continues: 'While medieval canonists taught that *leges irritantes* could be applied to the sacraments, they did not consider it possible that they could have a bearing on the *substantia sacramenti*.' (p 32).

33. *ibid.*, p 58.

34. B. J. Leeming, *Principles of Sacramental Theology*, Longmans, Green & Co, London, New York & Toronto 1956, p 266.

35. *ibid.*

36. ed A. Richardson and J. Bowen, *A New Dictionary of Christian Theology*, SCM 1983, p 175; see also J. G. Davies on *Validity*, p 594.

37. M. Villain, *Can there be Apostolic Succession outside the Continuity of the Laying-on of Hands?*, in *Concilium*, Vol 4 No 4 April 1968, p 52.

38. *The Final Report of ARCIC*, CTS/SPCK 1982, Authority II, para 7, p 84.

39. P. Avis, *Reflections on ARCIC-II*, in *Theology*, November 1987, p 454.

40. Cf R. Hooker, *Laws of Ecclesiastical Polity*, VII, xiv, p 11, as in Gurrieri, *op. cit.*, p 42: '. . . there may be sometimes very just and sufficient reason to allow ordination made without a bishop, (for example) when God doth of himself raise up any, whose labour he useth without requiring that men should authorize them (or) when exigence of necessity doth constrain to leave the usual ways of the Church, which otherwise we would willingly keep: when the Church must needs have some ordained, and neither hath nor can have possibly a bishop to ordain; in any case of such necessity, the ordinary institution of God hath given oftentimes, and

Chapter 4—continued

may give, place . . . These cases of inevitable necessity excepted, none may ordain but only bishops.'

41. Both quotations: E. Schillebeeckx, *The Mission of the Church*, Sheed & Ward 1973, pp 213f.
42. E. Schillebeeckx, *The Catholic Understanding of Office in the Church*, in *Theological Studies* 30 (December 1969), p 573. Cf also F. J. van Beck, *Towards an Ecumenical Understanding of the Sacraments*, in *Journal of Ecumenical Studies* 3 (1966), pp 57-112, and *Sacraments, Church Order and Secular Responsibility*, in *Theological Studies* 30 (December 1969), pp 613-634, as in Gurrieri, *op.cit.* p 43, n 90.
43. Cf M. Villain, *op. cit.*, p 51.
44. Two quotations, H. Küng, *What is the Essence of Apostolic Succession?*, in *Concilium*, Vol. 4 No. 4 April 1968, pp 16 & 17.
45. *ibid.*, p 19.
46. J. Remmers, *Apostolic Succession: an Attribute of the Whole Church*, in *Concilium*, Vol. 4 No. 4 April 1968, p 20.
47. *ibid.*, p 24.
48. JGS 1948.
49. Methodist Conference Minutes 1948, pp 125f.
50. JGS 1952, pp 206f.
51. Cf Anglican – Lutheran 'Interim Eucharistic Sharing' in USA/Europe: Reports of Anglican Consultative Council 6 and 7 (1984 & 1987).
52. Cf S. Neill, *Towards Church Union 1937-1952*, WCC Faith and Order, SCM 1952, p 52.
53. Cf Reports and Minutes of the General Assembly of the Presbyterian Church in Ireland, 1943-1951.
54. Minutes of the General Assembly 1959, *ad loc.*
55. *ibid.*
56. *ibid.*
57. The Church of North India was duly constituted at Nagpur in November 1970, and the Presbyterian Church in Ireland was represented on that occasion by the then Moderator, J. L. M. Haire. Dr A. A. Fulton has noted: 'On Saturday 27 July 1974, the Rev Cyril Young, the Presbyterian Church in Ireland's Convener of The Foreign Mission, was present when the only Bishop not an Indian was appointed. This was an Irish Presbyterian missionary whose character and service had won the recognition and love of all his Indian brethren. This richly deserved and nobly earned honour was accorded to Dr. Donald Kennedy.'. (A.A. Fulton, *Church in Tension – In the Twentieth Century – Mainly*, in *Challenge and Conflict: Essays in Irish Presbyterian History and Doctrine*, W. and G. Baird Ltd, Antrim 1981, p 181.)
58. M. Hollis, *The Significance of South India*, Lutterworth, London 1966, p 54.
59. *ibid.*, p 8.
60. *Partners in Mission*, A.C.C. meeting, Dublin July 1973, *Report* p 5.
61. Lambeth 1930, *Report* p 51.
62. B. Sundkler, *Church of South India: The Movement towards Union 1900/47*, Lutterworth Press, London 1954, p 23.
63. H. G. G. Herklots, *Amsterdam 1948*, SCM 1948, pp 85f.
64. *Irish Amsterdam* (1949), United Council, p 6.
65. *ibid.*, p 17.
66. *Irish Evanston* (1956), United Council, p 21.
67. *ibid.*, p 22.
68. See J. H. Whyte, *Political Life in the South*, in ed. M Hurley, *Irish Anglicanism 1869-1969*, Figgis, Dublin 1970, pp 150f.
69. British Faith and Order Conference, Nottingham 1964.
70. J. M. Barkley, *Anglican-Presbyterian Relations*, in *Irish Anglicanism*, *op. cit.*, p 76.

Chapter 5

1. G. Daly, *Transcendence and Immanence – A Study in Catholic Modernism and Integralism*, Oxford, Clarendon Press, 1980, p 148.
2. C. Stuhlmueller, *Vatican II and Biblical Criticism*, in *The Impact of Vatican II*, Herder 1966, p 31.
3. ed. A. Flannery, *Vatican Council II – The Conciliar and Post Conciliar Documents*, 1981 edition, Dominican Publications, Dublin, pp 757f.
4. ed. W. M. Abbott and J. Gallagher, *The Documents of Vatican II*, G. Chapman, London 1966, pp 107f.
5. *ibid.*, pp 9f.
6. As in *ibid.*, p 10.
7. B. McSweeney, *Roman Catholicism: The Search for Relevance*, Blackwell 1980, p 99.
8. Cf Paul M. Minus, *The Catholic Rediscovery of Protestantism – A History of Roman Catholic Ecumenical Pioneering*, Paulist Press, New York, 1976.
9. ed. A. Flannery, *op.cit.*, p 357, n 8.
10. *ibid.*, p 470, n 24.
11. *ibid.*, p 456, n 4.
12. K. McNamara, *Ecumenism in the Light of Vatican II*, in *Irish Ecclesiastical Record* 1966 Vol. CV, p 152.
13. ed. A. Flannery, *op.cit.*, p 463, n 13.
14. K. McNamara, *The Church: A Theological and Pastoral Commentary on the Constitution on the Church*, Veritas, Dublin 1983, pp 101 and 151.
15. H. Conzelmann, *An Outline of the Theology of the New Testament*, SCM (ET) 1969, p 36.
16. R. Bultmann, *Theology of the New Testament*, Vol I, SCM (ET) 1956, p 133.
17. ed. Abbott and Gallagher, *op. cit.*, p 364, n 22.
18. *ibid.*
19. *New Delhi Report*, p 116.
20. *Baptism, Eucharist and Ministry*, WCC, Geneva 1982, p 3, para 6.
21. G. C. Berkouwer, *The Second Vatican Council and the New Catholicism*, Wm. B. Eerdmans Publishing Co, Grand Rapids, Michigan 1965, pp 203f.
22. In interview.
23. ed. A. Falconer, E. McDonagh, S. MacReamoinn, *Freedom to Hope? – The Catholic Church in Ireland Twenty Years After Vatican II*, Columba Press 1985, p 1.
24. E. McDonagh, *Between Chaos and New Creation: Doing theology at the fringe*, Gill & Macmillan 1986, p 177.
25. *ibid.*, p 182.
26. *The Irish Times*, 5 August 1977.
27. ed R. Rouse & S. Neill, *A History of the Ecumenical Movement: 1517-1948*, SPCK 1954, p 728.
28. *Mystici Corporis Christi*, 1943, Section 13.
29. W. Conway, Comment on the *1949 Instruction*, in *Irish Ecclesiastical Record*, 1950 Vol LXXIII, pp 360-365.
30. *The Furrow*, January 1956.
31. Text of the Pastoral Letter lodged at the Representative Church Body Library, Dublin.
32. J. H. Whyte, *Church and State in Modern Ireland 1923-1970*, Gill & Macmillan 1971, p 356.
33. *ibid.*, p 357.
34. *The Furrow*, January 1963, p 17.
35. M. Hurley, *Towards Christian Unity*, CTS Ireland 1960.
36. F. Clark, *Anglicanism*, in ed.. K McNamara, *Christian Unity: Lectures of Maynooth Union Summer School 1961*, Maynooth, The Furrow Trust 1962, p 73.

Chapter 5—continued

37. J. Höfer, *The Word of God: Towards a Catholic-Lutheran Dialogue*, in *ibid.*, p 74.
38. Cf ed B. Leeming, *Augustin Cardinal Bea – The Unity of Christians*, G Chapman 1963, esp. Chs. 9 & 10 – *Protestants and the Council*, pp 129-153.
39. For details of the dates of different Orthodox Churches joining the WCC, cf ed. H. E. Fey, *The Ecumenical Advance: A History of the Ecumenical Movement, Vol II: 1948-1968*, SPCK 1970, pp 14f.
40. P. J. Hamell, *The Ecumenical Movement*, in ed. K. McNamara, *Christian Unity, op. cit.*, p 29.
41. E. McDonagh, *Roman Catholics and Unity*, London, Mowbray, Star Books on Reunion 1962, pp 23f.
42. *ibid.*, p 74.
43. *The Furrow*, January 1963, pp 33f.
44. The prayer for the Second Vatican Council was approved by the Archbishops of Armagh and Dublin. The full text was published in *The Church of Ireland Gazette*, 24th August 1962; in the introduction, it is noted that three observers from the Anglican Communion would be present at the Council. Cf also Letters to the Editor, 7.9.1962 and 21.9.1962.
45. General Assembly Minutes, 1963.
46. *The Furrow*, January 1963, p 36.
47. *ibid.*, p 51.
48. Cardinal Jan Willebrands, Address to the Greenhills Ecumenical Conference, 21 January 1985, *Twenty Years Since Vatican Two* (Text from the Catholic Press and Information Office, Dublin).
49. Cf J. Turner, *Glenstal Abbey Ecumenical Conferences 1964-1983*, Belfast 1983 (privately published) pp 3f.
50. R.C.: Dom G. McGinty, Dom P. Murray, Dom C. Breen, Rev. Prof. E. McDonagh; C. of I.: Rev. W. G. Proctor, Very Rev. G. Mayes; Pres: Rev. W. D. Bailie; Methodist: Rev. R. A. Nelson.
51. Text supplied by the Catholic Press and Information Office, Dublin.
52. JGS 1966, p 154.
53. As quoted by M Hurley in *Presbyterians in Council*, in *Studies*, Autumn 1964, pp 293f.
54. Ed. A. Falconer, E. McDonagh & S. MacReamoinn, *Freedom to Hope?*, *op. cit.*, pp 37f.
55. Cf Notes 24 & 25, *ibid.*, pp 101f.
56. *An Irish Theological Association*, in *Irish Theological Quarterly*, October 1965 Vol. XXXII No. 4, p 351.
57. *The Catholic Biblical Association of Ireland*, in *ibid.*, April 1966 Vol. XXXIII No. 2, p 165.
58. *ibid.*
59. However, we may note the appearance in 1958 of two articles by E. McDonagh on 'Anglican Ecclesiology', followed by two in 1959 on 'An Anglican View of the Primacy', B. Leeming's 'Protestants and Our Lady' in 1960, M. Hurley's two articles on the WCC's 'New Delhi Assembly' in 1960-61, P. Fannon's 'The Protestant Approach to Mariology' in 1962, M. Hurley's 'Ecumenism and Conversion' in 1964, B. Kelly's 'Ecumenism and the Missions' in 1965, D. Flanagan's 'Marian Theology in the Ecumenical Discussion' in 1966, and – a new Presbyterian contributor – J.L.M. Haire's 'Ecumenical Insights' in 1967.
60. ed. Abbott and Gallagher, *op. cit.*, p 353, n 9.
61. JGS 1972, pp 168f.
62. In its report for the year 1972-3, the Irish Council of Churches recorded an invitation from the Roman Catholic Episcopal Conference 'to discuss the whole field of ecumenism'. This was in response 'to overtures from members of the Council (ICC)'.

Chapter 5—continued

63. Cf ed C. Daly and S.Worrall, *Ballymascanlon*, Christian Journals Ltd/Veritas 1978, pp 9f.
64. Archbishops of Canterbury (Fisher and Ramsey), Church of Scotland Moderator (Craig); Cf JGS 1961, p 163, and ed H. E. Fey, *op. cit.*, p 357. Cf. also W. Purcell, *Fisher of Lambeth – A portrait from life*, Hodder & Stoughton 1969, pp 268ff.
65. See Vatican Secretariat for Promoting Christian Unity, *Information Service*, for regular documentation of all dialogues involving the Roman Catholic Church.

Chapter 6

1. *The Uppsala Report 1968*, WCC Geneva, p 5.
2. Cf T. O'Neill, *The Autobiography of Terence O'Neill – Prime Minister of Northern Ireland 1963-1969*, Rupert Hart-Davis, London 1972.
3. E. Gallagher, *Ecumenism in Northern Ireland* in M. Ledwith and E. Gallagher, *Ecumenism in Ireland*, Irish Catholic Bishops' Conference/Irish Council of Churches 1981, p 32.
4. For historical data, cf Moody, Martin and Byrne, *A New History of Ireland*, VIII, Oxford, Clarendon Press 1982, ad loc.
5. E. Gallagher and S. Worrall, *Christians in Ulster, 1968-1980*, Oxford University Press 1982, p 131.
6. Irish Episcopal Conference, *Irish Directory on Ecumenism*, Veritas Publications, Dublin 1969.
7. E. Gallagher and S. Worrall, *op.cit*, p 132.
8. *ibid*.
9. The following are the reports produced to date: Drug Abuse (1972), Housing in Northern Ireland (1973), Use of Alcohol (1974), The Churches' Response to Underdevelopment in Rural Ireland (1976), Violence in Ireland (1976) (by special delegation), Environment (1980), Leisure (1982), The Church and the Technological Age (1985), Marriage and the Family in Ireland Today (1987), Young People and the Church (1990), The Challenge of the City (1990). A report on Sectarianism is currently being prepared. The Joint Group is now the Department of Social Issues of the Inter-Church Meeting and its terms of reference have been broadened.
10. JGS 1971, p 27. Gallagher & Worrall (see note 5, this chapter) indicate that the Churches' Industrial Council 'was in the fifties and sixties the only inter-church body with Roman Catholic participation. As such, it was under constant pressure to deal with matters not strictly within its brief.' (*op. cit.* p 28).
11. C. B. Daly and S. Worrall, *Ballymascanlon: An Irish Venture in Inter-Church Dialogue*, CJL/Veritas 1978, pp 10f.
12. Seven meetings were held between 1973 and 1984: 26 September 1973, 1 May 1974, 23 April 1975, 17 May 1977, 6 March 1981, 3 March 1984 and 8 November 1984.
13. The latter was formerly the ICC/Roman Catholic Joint Group on Social problems.
14. Text of the *Declaration of Intent*: We, the duly appointed representatives of the Church of Ireland, the Methodist Church in Ireland and the Presbyterian Church in Ireland, acknowledging our several churches as being within the Church of God, and seeking to preserve the truths in our several traditions, affirm our intention to seek together that unity which is both God's will and his gift to his Church. It is our conviction that without this unity the fulfilment of Christ's mission to the world is being hindered. We make no claim to know the exact form which unity should take or whether we shall attain it. We are seeking

Chapter 6—continued

no unity apart from the will of God and we solemnly undertake to submit ourselves to what God will say to us together through His Word and through the witness of our several churches. We recognise in so submitting ourselves that any such unity between our Churches will involve changes for us all.

As we engage in these conversations, we will seek to discover how our churches may do together at all levels those things which conviction does not require us to do separately. We know that our churches will move to a deeper expression of unity only by drawing together. We gladly acknowledge how great is the measure of our agreement on the common faith revealed in our earlier conversations. We recognise the need of mutual trust, involving sincerity on the part of each church and the acceptance of the sincerity of others. We recognise the need of penitence for any prejudiced or uncharitable attitudes displayed by our respective churches in the past. Above all, we acknowledge the need of constant renewal by the Holy Spirit.

As we seek together under the guidance of the Holy Spirit for the unity which Christ wills according to the Scriptures, we are not concerned for ourselves alone. We will welcome an approach to our Churches by any other Christian church or communion which wishes to join in the quest for this unity. We pray God that he will bless and direct our conversations and that he will use them for the enrichment of the whole Church of Christ. (JGS 1968, pp 154f.)

15. *Towards a United Church*, Tripartite Consultation 1973.
16. JGS 1978, p 161.
17. Source for statistics: J. M. Barkley, *Tripartite Consultation 1968-80*, unpublished Tripartite Consultation document.
18. *ibid.*
19. JGS 1974, p 182.
20. *The Full Mutual Recognition of Ministries*, unpublished Tripartite Consultation document, 1979.
21. E.g. at meetings of the Irish Council of Churches and the Tripartite Consultation.
22. In 1983 the Tripartite Consultation embarked on a 'five-point programme': (1) the preparation of a draft common service of confirmation/reception and (2) Holy Communion, (3) a review of the rules 'agreed elsewhere regarding forms of service and other arrangements for inter-Church occasions . . . , (4) the drawing up of proposals for a joint consultative and advisory Board of Mission, and (5) an examination of the Lima Report of the WCC, *Baptism, Eucharist and Ministry*, with particular attention to be given to Ministry.
23. Concern over the activities of the WCC's Programme to Combat Racism was a major factor leading to the Presbyterian Church's withdrawal; there were, however, underlying conservative theological trends in Irish Presbyterianism which were at variance with WCC theological approaches. In 1976 the Presbyterian Church had decided, by a majority of 100 votes, to continue its membership, but the announcement in 1978 of grants to the Patriotic Front in the then Rhodesia came at the same time as reports of the murder of several Northern Ireland missionaries in that country. A special meeting of the Presbyterian General Assembly was called, and membership of the WCC was suspended (for constitutional reasons immediate withdrawal was not possible). In 1980 the Presbyterian Church in Ireland withdrew completely from the WCC.
24. ed. O. S. Tomkins, *The Third World Conference on Faith and Order, Lund 1952*, SCM 1953, p 16.
25. Cf *The Lambeth Conference 1968*, p 41; Resol. 44.
26. Cf *The Furrow*, 9 September 1969, p 498, as in I.J.E. Knox, *The Sharing of Church Resources in Ireland*, dissertation submitted for the degree B. Phil. (Univ. of Hull), 1975, p 26.
27. I. J. E. Knox, *ibid.*, p 20.

Chapter 6—continued

28. Annual report of the Tripartite Consultation, 1986. A different adaptation of the Lima Liturgy was drawn up for consideration at the 1986 Glenstal Conference, and a 'Glenstal' text has resulted.
29. Also known as Inter-Church Marriages, especially when both partners are committed members of their respective Churches. The distinction is, however, difficult to sustain, and the terms are generally used interchangeably.
30. G. Wadding, *The Promise: 'All in my Power'*, in *Reality*, May 1975, p 12.
31. *ibid.*
32. *Directory on Mixed Marriages*, Irish Episcopal Conference, Veritas 1983, p 3.
33. J. A. F. Gregg, *The 'Ne Temere' Decree*, APCK, Dublin, revised edition 1943, pp 9f.
34. *Lambeth 1948*, Resol. 98, p 50.
35. Inter-Church Meeting (Ballymascanlon 1975): Report of Working Party on Social and Community Problems; in *Directory on Ecumenism*, Irish Episcopal Conference 1976, Appendix.
36. ed. M. Hurley, *Beyond Tolerance: The Challenge of Mixed Marriage*, G. Chapman 1975, p ix.
37. Cf. *The Pope in Ireland: Addresses and Homilies*, Veritas, Dublin 1979, p 24.
38. *Submission from the Church of Ireland members of the Irish Council of Churches representatives on the Joint Standing Committee on Mixed Marriages, to Cardinal O Fiaich at his request*, unpublished. (Quoted with permission)
39. Statement as published in *The Church of Ireland Gazette*, 25 November 1983.
40. E. McDonagh, *The Declaration on Religious Freedom of Vatican Council II: The Text and a commentary*, Darton, Longman & Todd, London 1967, p 19.
41. *ibid.*, p 46.
42. C. B. Daly, *Inter-Church Marriages: The Position of the Irish Episcopal Conference*, in *The Furrow*, January 1974.
43. New Ireland Forum, Public Session, Thursday 9th. Feb., 1984, Dublin Castle, *Report of Proceedings*, p 27.
44. Statement as published in *The Church of Ireland Gazette*, 1 February 1985.
45. *Inter-Church Marriages*, Diocese of Ferns, 1986.
46. In addition to the official dialogue and developments which have taken place between the Churches, a considerable amount of expertise in this area of mixed marriages has been gained by the voluntary organizations in Ireland – The Northern Ireland Mixed Marriage Association (NIMMA) and the Association of Interchurch Families (based in the Republic). Quite apart from the influence which these organizations have had as pressure groups, they have played – and continue to play – a vital role as support groups for mixed marriage couples. Both NIMMA and the Association of Interchurch Families have campaigned for a better understanding of the problems facing mixed marriage couples and their families. They have tended to highlight particular aspects of current regulations which they see as unsatisfactory. Without doubt, the whole question of intercommunion is a priority, and more recently there has been considerable discussion on the issues of joint baptisms, baptisms in the home, and dual Church membership. Cf. A. Heron, *Two Churches – One Love*, APCK, Dublin 1977.
47. J. Fulton, *The Debate on Denominational and Integrated Education in Ireland*, in *Research Bulletin*, Department of Theology, University of Birmingham 1981; cf. p 90.
48. *ibid.*; cf. Canon 1374.
49. *Declaration on Christian Education*, in ed. W. M. Abbott, *The Documents of Vatican II*, G. Chapman, London 1966, p 647, n 8. Cf. Canon 798 *The Code of Canon Law* (1983, ET, London, Collins): 'Parents are to send their children to those schools which will provide for their catholic education. If they cannot do this, they are bound to ensure the proper catholic education of their children outside the school.'.

Chapter 6—continued

50. *ibid.*, n 9.
51. *The New Ireland Forum: Submission by the Executive of the Irish Theological Association, November 1983*, in *The Furrow*, Vol. XXXV No. 2, February 1984, pp 123-126.
52. *Submission to the New Ireland Forum from the Irish Episcopal Conference*, January 1984, Veritas, p 28.
53. New Ireland Forum, No. 12, *Report of Proceedings*, 9 February 1984.
54. D. Faul, *Why Catholic Schools in Northern Ireland?* in *The Furrow*, Vol 28, No 1, January 1977
55. W. Conway, Cardinal, *Catholic Schools*, Dublin, Veritas, 1974, pp 13f.
56. M. McKeown, *Integrated Education – The Debate Surveyed*, in *The Furrow*, Vol. 28, No. 1, January 1977, p 12.
57. Cf DENI Circular 1982/21, urging all schools to recognize their role in fostering good community relations. The Christian Education Movement and the ICC/ICJP Peace Education Programme have both contributed in special ways to mutual understanding.
58. The NI Course has been based at the following locations: University of Ulster at Coleraine; the Service Priory, Benburb, Co. Tyrone; St. Anne's Cathedral, Belfast; the Columbanus Community, Belfast; Magee College, Londonderry; and QUB.
59. The research aspect of the School's life has been particularly significant. The first subject which was tackled was the sensitive one of mixed marriages. Following extended research by staff and students, a major international consultation was held in Dublin from 2nd – 6th September 1974 (see ed M. Hurley, *Beyond Tolerance*, G. Chapman 1975 – a record of the consultation). Subsequently, the ISE embarked on a research programme on Human Rights; a similar pattern of research followed by an international consultation was followed. The results of this 1978 Dublin International Consultation were edited by the Rev. A. Falconer and publised by the ISE in 1980: *Understanding Human Rights: An inter-disciplinary and inter-faith study*. Further research programmes have been on denominational and integrated education (see J Fulton, *The Debate on Denominational and Integrated Education in Ireland, op.cit.*), the Compassionate Society – the future of Ireland in a technological and nuclear age (co-ordinated by B. McSweeney), and the Reconciliation of Memories (see ed. A. Falconer, *Reconciling Memories*, Columba Press 1988).
60. J. P. Rajashekar, *Dialogue with People of Other Faiths and Ecumenical Theology* in ed. S. Amirtham and C. H. S. Moon, *The Teaching of Ecumenics*, WCC, Geneva 1987, p 80.
61. For literature related to the Inter-Church Process the reader should consult CCBI Publications, Inter-Church House, 35-41 Lower Marsh, London SE1 7RL.
62. *The Pope in Britain: Collected Homilies and Speeches*, London, St. Paul Publications, 1982, p 79.
63. *Baptism, Eucharist and Ministry*, Faith and Order Paper No. 111, Geneva, W.C.C., 1982; *The Final Report of the Anglican-Roman Catholic International Commission*, London, CTS/SPCK, 1982.; *Anglican-Lutheran Dialogue: The Report of the European Commission*, London, SPCK, 1983; *Anglican-Orthodox Dialogue: The Dublin Agreed Statement 1984*, London, SPCK, 1984; *God's Reign and Our Unity*, London, SPCK/Edinburgh, The Saint Andrew Press, 1984.
64. Cf. The *Swanwick Declaration*, in *Not Strangers But Pilgrims: Report of the Swanwick Conference, 31 August to 4 September 1987*, London, BCC/CTS. Cf. also The Constitution of C.C.B.I. Cardinal Basil Hume's words at the 1987 Swanwick Conference may be noted: '. . . I hope that our Roman Catholic delegates at this Conference will recommend to members of our Church that we move now quite deliberately from a situation of cooperation to one of commitment to each other. By 'commitment to each other' I mean that we commit ourselves to praying and working together for Church unity and to acting together, both nationally and locally, for evangelisation and mission.' (in B. Hume, *Towards a*

Chapter 6—continued

Civilisation of Love: Being Church in Today's World, London, Hodder & Stoughton, 1988, p 145).

65. *The Coleraine Declaration*, issued by the Coleraine Assembly, 10 – 13 September, 1990, marking the 150th anniversary of the formation of the General Assembly.

Chapter 7

1. R. H. A. Eames, *Chains to be Broken*, London, Weidenfeld & Nicolson, 1992, p 50; C. B. Daly, *The Price of Peace*, Belfast, Blackstaff Press, 1991, p 175.
2. F. S. L. Lyons, *Culture and Anarchy in Ireland 1890-1939*, Oxford, Clarendon Press 1979, p 2.
3. Cf. ed. A. D. Falconer, *Reconciling Memories*, Dublin, Columba Press 1988, and M. Santer, *The Reconciliation of Memories* in ed. M Santer, *Their Lord and Ours*, SPCK, 1982.
4. J. Macquarrie, *Principles of Christian Theology*, London, SCM 1966, p 67.
5. Cf. M. Bond, *Reconciliation: an Ecumenical Paradigm*, in ed. A. D. Falconer, *Reconciling Memories, op. cit.*, p 118.
6. Cf. H.- G. Gadamer, *Truth and Method*, London, Sheed & Ward, ET, 1975.
7. Cf. D. Tracey, *The Analogical Imagination: Christian Theology and the Culture of Pluralism*, London, SCM 1981.
8. R. Kearney, *Myth and the Critique of Tradition*, in ed. A. D. Falconer, *Reconciling Memories, op. cit.*, p 9; Cf. also R. Kearney, *Transitions: Narratives in Modern Irish Culture*, Dublin, Wolfhound Press 1988.
9. L. Boff, *Ecclesiogenesis: The base communities reinvent the church*, Collins 1986, p 6.
10 Cf. ed. I. M. Ellis, *Peace and Reconciliation Projects in Ireland: A Directory*, 3rd ed. revised, ICC 1986. Renewal is of course also furthered by non-residential ecumenical groups, such as Protestant and Catholic Encounter (PACE).
11. P. Demo, article in *Communidades: Igreja na base*, Estudos da CNBB no. 3 (Sao Paulo: Paulinas 1975,) p 93, as in L. Boff, *Ecclesiogenesis, op. cit.*, p 6.
12. *Report on Institutionalism*, Fourth World Conference on Faith and Order, Montreal, 12-26 July 1963, WCC Faith and Order Paper No. 37, Geneva 1963, p 6.
13. L. Boff, *Ecclesiogenesis, op. cit.*, p 6.
14. H. Küng, *Church and Change: The Irish Experience*, Dublin, Gill and Macmillan 1986, cf pp 21-72 (quotes here, pp 27 & 50).
15. Cf. P. A. Crow Jr, *Ecumenics as Reflections on Models of Christian Unity*, in ed. S. Amirtham and C. H. S. Moon, *The Teaching of Ecumenics*, Geneva, WCC, 1987, pp 23-28.
16. Cf. *Unity by Stages: The Charney Bassett Statement*, in *Steps Towards Unity: Documents on Ecumenical Relations presented to ACC-6*, Anglican Consultative Council 1984, pp 29-31.
17. M. Conway, *Growing into the Unity Christ Makes Available: The Promise of Pilgrimage in Councils of Churches*, in *Mid-Stream*, Vol. XXII No. 2 April 1983, p 170.
18. D. Morrow, *The Churches and Inter-Community Relationships*, Univ. Ulster, Centre for the Study of Conflict, 1991, p 123. The Belfast-based Churches' Central Committee for Community Work is one inter-Church body which aims to promote Protestant-Roman Catholic co-operation specifically in the area of social and community work.
19. J. Whyte, *Interpreting Northern Ireland*, Clarendon Press, Oxford, 1990, pp 26ff.
20. E. McDonagh, *Between Chaos and New Creation: Doing theology at the fringe*, Dublin, Gill and Macmillan 1986, p 154.
21. Cf. E. H. Robertson, *Lund 1952*, SCM 1952, pp 26f.
22. ed. A. Flannery, *op. cit.*, p 408 (Constitution no. 48).
23. Cf V. and E. Turner, *Image and Pilgrimage in Christian Culture: Anthropological Perspectives*, Basil Blackwell, Oxford 1978, pp 1-39.

INDEX